Disfigurement

Disfigurement: Understanding Visible Difference is a collection of essays which brings together an all-star cast of researchers, clinicians, advocates, and activists around the world, many of whom have lived experience with disfigurement. Seeking to reduce stigma around disfigurement, they explore the experience of looking different, including interventions to help with social integration, social media issues, and prejudice towards physical difference. The collection serves as a call for activism and offers a direction for future research.

This book responds to the three themes prevalent in the literature on disfigurement: (1) the psychosocial aspects of body image and identity, (2) interventions, and (3) representations of disfigurement. In section one, the book explores the psychosocial aspects of body image and identity among people with disfigurement. Section two looks at interventions, including those involving social media. In response to this misrepresentation, section three offers the voices of people who are helping to change public opinions through media and activism.

This book is invaluable reading for all clinicians, researchers, activists, people with disfigurement, and those who care about them. *Disfigurement: Understanding Visible Difference* is a crucial resource for students of disability studies, social work, and health psychology.

Lise Deguire, PsyD, is a clinical psychologist, author, and burn survivor. After being severely burned as a four-year-old, she spent much of her childhood in the hospital, undergoing countless surgical procedures. Dr. Deguire is the author of the multiple award-winning book, *Flashback Girl: Lessons on Resilience from a Burn Survivor*. Dr. Deguire attended Tufts University, graduating summa cum laude, Phi Beta Kappa. She earned her doctorate in clinical psychology from Widener University and is in solo practice in New Jersey. Dr. Deguire has appeared on NPR, NBC, ABC, FOX, and Sirius XM. She is a TEDx speaker, a national keynote speaker and has presented for The American Psychological Association, the World Burn Congress, The Security and Exchange Commission, and The American Burn Association. She writes for *Psychology Today*, and has been featured in *Huffington Post*, *Thrive Global*, and *Tiny Buddha*. Dr. Deguire blogs regularly about psychological resilience.

Miriam Jaffe, PhD (English), LSW, is Associate Teaching Professor in the Writing Program at Rutgers University and the lead editor of five collections on social justice issues (Routledge, 2016–2022). Her publications on narrative activism – from narrative medicine in literature to mental health and racial justice awareness in the social sciences – span 15 years. She's worked as associate editor for the journal *Writing and Pedagogy*. She recently won Rutgers University's Beloved Community award. Miriam is also a psychotherapist specializing in trauma using EMDR and play.

Disfigurement

Understanding Visible Difference

Edited by Lise Deguire and Miriam Jaffe

Routledge
Taylor & Francis Group
NEW YORK AND LONDON

Designed cover image: Statue of liberation (Portrait of Tonya) by Grace Athena Flott.

First published 2026
by Routledge
605 Third Avenue, New York, NY 10158

and by Routledge
4 Park Square, Milton Park, Abingdon, Oxon, OX14 4RN

Routledge is an imprint of the Taylor & Francis Group, an informa business

ISBN: 978-1-032-87959-8 (hbk)
ISBN: 978-1-032-87500-2 (pbk)
ISBN: 978-1-003-53559-1 (ebk)

DOI: 10.4324/9781003535591

Typeset in Times New Roman
by Typesetter Apex CoVantage, LLC

This book is dedicated to the many people around the world (like me) who live in visibly different bodies. May they all find peace, love, acceptance, compassion, and joy. ~ L.D.

This book is dedicated to my life-changing teachers at HYR in Metuchen, NJ, who taught me to reclaim my body and soul, breath by breath. ~ M.J.

Contents

Acknowledgements

We are deeply grateful to the visual artist Grace Athena Flott, who provided the cover image. Grace is an artist and also a burn survivor.

This portrait features Tonya Meisenbach, influencer, social activist, and burn survivor.

We gratefully acknowledge Dr. Kathleen Bogart, who advised us and introduced us to many of the contributors in this book. Similarly, we gratefully acknowledge Dr. J. Michael Murphy, for introducing us to colleagues in Britain, who became contributors to this volume.

Many thanks go to Rachele Puddu, Fulbright Researcher from the University of Udine/University of Trieste, visiting Rutgers University, for her help in preparing this volume.

Contributors

Beenish Ambereen is serving as Visiting Assistant Professor at the Shaheed Zulfiqar Ali Bhutto Institute of Science and Technology (SZABIST) in Islamabad. Her research interests focus on gender and human rights.

Alex Clarke is a Clinical Psychologist and Visiting Professor at the Centre for Appearance Research (CAR) at the University of the West of England in Bristol, UK (UWE Bristol). Her research interests focus on the development and evaluation of evidence-based interventions in visible difference. She is a regular contributor to both the academic and self-help literature.

Lise Deguire, PsyD, is a psychologist, author, childhood burn survivor, and author of the award-winning book, *Flashback Girl: Lessons on Resilience from a Burn Survivor*. She has appeared on NPR, NBC, ABC, and FOX. Dr. Deguire is a TEDx speaker ("SCARRED not Scary"), whose written work on disfigurement has been featured in *Psychology Today*, *Huffington Post*, *The Psychotherapy Networker*, and *Thrive Global*.

Rasheera D. Dopson, MPH, is a digital storyteller and advocate who leverages multimedia platforms to promote reeducation and awareness of the intersections of race, gender, and disability. As a nationally recognized speaker, author, producer, and host of the *Womanhood & Disability* podcast, she amplifies the voices and experiences of women and girls with disabilities.

Grace Athena Flott is an American visual artist and burn survivor fascinated by the myth of normalcy and social constructions of health, beauty, and gender. Influenced by Western art history dynamics of representation, her paintings, printmaking, and public art are exhibited internationally. Her work is held in numerous public collections including with the State of Washington, City of Seattle, and University of Washington Medicine.

Jasmine "Jaz" Gray, PsyD, is a communication professor, advocate, and transformational storyteller from Memphis, Tennessee. She delivers keynotes, moderates panels, and leads workshops on a range of topics including the ethical implications of narratives, the power of stories, media representation, health equity, patient-centered care, well-being, healthy self-image, empowerment, and resilience. Dr. Gray has been featured on affiliate networks for NBC, CBS, ABC, and Fox discussing her advocacy work including her nonprofit Jaz's Jammies and on national and international platforms including NPR and BBC Radio discussing media representation of marginalized communities, like those with craniofacial differences.

Ella Guest is a Senior Research Fellow and Registered Health Psychologist at the Centre for Appearance Research (CAR) at the University of the West of England in Bristol, UK (UWE Bristol). Her research focuses on understanding the experiences of individuals living with visible differences and examining how social media can reduce appearance-related stigma and foster acceptance of appearance diversity. As part of the Vocational Training Charitable Trust (VTCT) Foundation team, she employs mixed-methods research and innovative visual approaches, including photo-elicitation, to explore social media and visible difference.

Diana Harcourt is a Professor of Appearance and Health Psychology at the Centre for Appearance Research (CAR) at the University of the West of England in Bristol, UK (UWE Bristol). Her research focuses on the psychosocial impact of an altered appearance or visible difference of any kind, and the development and evaluation of interventions to support those who are affected. This involves working closely with health professionals and charitable organizations that support people whose lives are affected by visible difference.

Miriam Jaffe, PhD, LSW, is Associate Teaching Professor at Rutgers University, where she is a writing specialist. She works across three fields of Clinical Social Work, American Literature, and Composition to engage in Narrative Activism. She has edited five other collections on topics of health, justice, and empathy.

Sora J. Kasuga (any/all) is an activist, writer, speaker, professional circus artist, and the founder of The FaceOut Project, who has spoken at the United Nations with Face Equality International, been featured on Today.com, and was published in the anthology *Owning It: Tales from Our Disabled Childhoods*. Proudly Japanese-American, disabled/facially different, neurodivergent, and queer, Kasuga's many identities fuel their work to shift individual and collective perceptions in order to create a more inclusive, equitable, and just world.

Abbi Mathews is a PhD student on the Vocational Training Charitable Trust (VTCT) Foundation team at the Centre for Appearance Research. Her research focuses on using social media to increase the acceptance of appearance diversity and reduce appearance-related stigma among the general public. Through her PhD, Abbi is exploring how social media can be effectively used to promote inclusivity and challenge societal norms surrounding appearance.

J. Michael Murphy, PsyD, is a staff psychologist at Massachusetts General Hospital, Associate Professor of Psychology at Harvard Medical School, and Research Associate at Shriners Hospital in Boston where he conducts studies related to appearance concerns in children and adolescents recovering from burns, including a clinical trial of a version of the Face IT program for young people. Dr. Murphy's work also includes seeing patients and teaching psychiatric residents. He is married with three grown children.

Alyson Norman is Associate Professor in health and clinical psychology at the University of Plymouth. Alyson's primary research interest relates to the involvement of service users in healthcare choices and treatment decisions across a range of health conditions. Alyson has specific research experience in the areas of visible difference, including cleft and pituitary care.

Zali O'Dea, PsyD, is the Founding Director and Principal Counsellor/Educator of Karibu Anawim meaning "Welcome to The Way of Victory". Zali regularly presents and is involved nationally and internationally educating relevant parties, raising awareness about issues pertaining to living with facial eye disfigurement (any eye altering appearance condition) and facial disfigurement. Dr Zali is a published researcher in this field and holds insider status. She is a survivor of a car accident as a newborn and lives with third nerve palsy.

Charlene Pell is the founder and executive director of Facing Forward Inc., a nonprofit helping individuals with disfiguring conditions contend with staring and communicating confidently. She is also the award-winning author of *In This Altered Body: A Survivor's Story of Resilience and Love*, and an advocate for people with burns and facial disfigurement. She holds a master's degree in communication studies from The University of North Carolina at Greensboro.

Amy Slater is a Visiting Professor at the Centre for Appearance Research and a leading expert in body image and visible difference, with a focus on the impact of sociocultural factors including social media. She leads a research stream on social media and visible difference, which is funded by the Vocational Training Charitable Trust (VTCT) Foundation.

Jane Southcott is Professor, Faculty of Education, Monash University, Australia. As a phenomenologist, Jane researches cultural identities and hybridity, inclusion and disabilities, and community engagement with the arts focusing on lifelong education. Her writing in inclusion addresses the lived experiences of people with diverse abilities, framed within the disability discourse as actions that are resistant, defiant, and subversive.

Phyllida Swift is an appearance activist, TEDX and United Nations speaker, and the current CEO of Face Equality International. Having volunteered and worked in the face equality space ever since she was in a car accident in 2015, in which she sustained facial scarring, Phyllida's focus is on building an equitable society with and for the facial deformity community. Outside of work you'll find her in the gym, at a gig, or enjoying the outdoors.

Maia Thornton is a Senior Research Fellow at the Centre for Appearance Research (CAR) based at the University of the West of England in Bristol, UK (UWE Bristol). Her work is focused on the experiences and psychosocial impact of living with a visible difference. She has a particular interest in developing and evaluating evidence-based psychosocial interventions.

Pippa Tollow is a Senior Research Fellow and Senior Lecturer in Health Psychology, at the Centre for Appearance Research (CAR), University of the West of England in Bristol, UK (UWE Bristol). Her research primarily focuses on the psychosocial impact of appearance-altering conditions, including cancer and burn injuries.

Faye Linda Wachs is a professor of Sociology at Cal Poly Pomona, with specialties in sport, embodiment, media, and equity in education. She is the author of two books, *Metamorphosis: Who We Become After Facial Paralysis*, and *Body Panic: Gender, Health and the Selling of Fitness* (co-authored with Shari Dworkin). A Los Angeles native, in her spare time she enjoys snowboarding, hiking, and biking with her family.

Farhan Navid Yousaf is working as Professor of Sociology and Director, Institute of Social and Cultural Studies, University of the Punjab, Lahore. His research interests, among others, include gender, human rights, and public policy.

Fabio Zucchelli is a Senior Lecturer in Psychology at the University of the West of England in Bristol, UK (UWE Bristol), and is an active researcher affiliated with the Centre for Appearance Research (CAR). His work focuses on understanding the experiences of individuals with visible differences, and developing and testing novel psychological support tools based on Acceptance and Commitment Therapy. He also explores the influence of masculinities in the experiences of men with visible differences.

Dina Zuckerberg has served as the Director of Family Programs at myFace for 10 years. Born with a unilateral cleft lip, no vision in her left eye and hearing loss in both ears, Dina is the host of *myFace, myStory: Voices from the Craniofacial Community* podcast. She has spoken at over 300 schools for the Wonder Project. In 2021, she was the recipient of the American Cleft Palate-Craniofacial Association Family Services Leadership Award, given to an individual or group who has demonstrated exceptional service and leadership on behalf of individuals with cleft or craniofacial conditions.

The Introduction in Two Parts

Lise Deguire and Miriam Jaffe

Part 1: Lise

I never intended to spearhead this book, or to ever discuss my disfigurement.

As a child, all I wanted was to fit in. I longed for symmetrical lips and smooth cheeks. I wanted an even skin tone and arms I could fully extend above my head. I dreamed of doing cartwheels and pirouettes. I yearned to don a bathing suit and to stand unnoticed among other children, blending in like a white goose in an endless, unvarying flock of other white geese. Instead, I had become the ugly duckling.

When I was four years old, my family drove to Lake Winnipesaukee for a brief vacation. It was our first night there, and time for dinner. My mother rummaged through the borrowed cabin, searching for lighter fluid to start the charcoal grill. Thinking she had found some, she stood on the porch with me, her little four-year-old, by her side. She squirted the fluid (a highly flammable household solvent) on the grill, and it exploded into a ball of flame, enveloping us. Panicked, my mother fled into the lake, leaving me behind in the fiery blast.

My father rescued me from the explosion, but not before the fire eviscerated my bottom lip, chin, neck and two-thirds of my body's skin. Through the miracles of modern medicine, and an exceptionally skilled burn team, I survived. But my journey toward health and wholeness took decades of surgeries and psychotherapy.

I suppose anyone viewing my scarred face and body can vaguely envision this medical and psychological odyssey. Where imagination fails is the social journey. As a child, I endured relentless bullying and exclusion. As a teenager and young woman, I found myself placed tacitly but firmly outside the dating world, not even considered as an option. To this day, when I go out with my scars exposed, strangers stare and frown.

Recovering from these traumas has taken decades of healing and care, which I was privileged to be able to access. Now, well and whole (mostly), I can focus on the journey of others who walk with different faces and bodies. There are many of us. Some are born with cleft palates, birthmarks, eye issues, or cranio-facial differences. Some of us acquire disfigurement through burns, accidents, disease, or cancer treatment.

(Note: the term "disfigurement" itself can be controversial, with many preferring the term "visible difference." I use the term disfigurement, as it is a commonly understood word, and also the phrase "visible difference.")

DOI: 10.4324/9781003535591-1

At least 1% of the world's population is disfigured (Julian & Partridge, 2007). We don't have good statistics. We do know that people with visible differences endure staring, social ostracism, bullying, job discrimination, and social media trolling (Disfigurement in the UK, 2017). Alarmingly, one third of a study of disfigured people reported having been the victim of a hate crime.

Bleak as these numbers sound, things are likely much worse. The study cited earlier comes from a 2017 British survey (Disfigurement in the UK, 2017). Britain is probably the most advanced nation in the world in terms of disfigurement awareness, thanks to the pioneering efforts of James Partridge, a burn survivor and activist, and the Centre for Appearance Research. It is safe to assume that the plight of visibly different people is more dire in most other countries.

* * *

I was a teenager when the movie *Return of the Jedi* was released, the third *Star Wars* film. I went with my friends, and we were spellbound by the spectacle, the music, and the story. However, the movie had an unanticipated lifelong impact on me.

At the end, Darth Vader lies mortally wounded. As he dies, he asks his son Luke to remove his helmet. Darth Vader is the most evil person in the *Star Wars* universe, and no one has seen him without his black helmet, which silently evokes the Nazis' SS, through which he laboriously breathes. The audience leaned forward as one, waiting for the dramatic moment. Slowly, Luke Skywalker raises the helmet, exposing a massive lump of scars. Darth Vader is revealed to be . . . a burn survivor.

The audience gasped at the sight of Darth Vader's disfigured face. I gasped as well, but for an entirely different reason. *This* was Darth Vader's backstory? He was burned and that somehow explains why he is so evil? *This* is the big reveal?

Darth Vader was only the beginning. Year after year, I witnessed burned and disfigured people portrayed on screen as either evil or pathetic. The strange thing was, no one else seemed to notice it. I began writing about the phenomenon, thinking that somehow, I was the only person who perceived the problem.

After my book *Flashback Girl* came out, I was introduced to Face Equality International, one of the organizations that James Partridge founded in Britain. There, I met a community of disfigured people, who had tracked this same issue, and who had already made impressive strides against it. The organization Changing Faces, also founded by James Partridge, had a full public relations campaign, entitled #IAmNotYourVillain. They were successful in educating many people in England. They lobbied the British Film Institute, which agreed to stop funding films that portrayed disfigured villains. However, I had never heard of #IAmNotYourVillain in the US, nor had anyone I knew. Changing Faces had made great strides in public awareness in Britain, but this progress had not traveled across the Atlantic to the USA. Most certainly, Hollywood had not received the message.

In the USA, disfigurement is recognized by the Americans with Disabilities Act as a form of disability, so people with visible difference are theoretically protected from discrimination. Reality is different.

Disfigured people seem to be the one marginalized group left that movies and TV routinely mock. Disfigured people are often portrayed as evil villains in movies (e.g. Voldemort, Freddie Krueger, the two current villains in *House of the Dragon,* Saturday Night Live's sketch "The Anomalous Man"). The pattern is relentless.

Given that many people have never met a disfigured person face-to-face, these screen portrayals are often the only way a person "knows" someone with disfigurement. These screen portrayals teach the general population to be wary of disfigured people. The relentlessly negative portrayals reinforce prejudice against people with visible difference, making our challenging lives even harder. Visibly different people are exhausted, trying to convey that these screen portrayals are stigmatizing and prejudicial. No one seems to be listening. *No one even seems to see it.*

Even more insidiously, children's movies teach kids to be wary of people who look different at the earliest ages. *The Lion King* features a disfigured villain, so identified by his appearance that his name is literally "Scar." In *Beauty and The Beast*, a fairy turns the prince into an ugly monster when the prince is mean, and makes him handsome again when the prince learns to be kind. The Wicked Witch of the West in *The Wizard of Oz* is notable by her glowing green skin. These movies, and many others, teach children to associate beauty with goodness, and disfigurement with evil.

In contrast, the entertainment industry has advanced admirably in its portrayals of other marginalized populations. We have come a long way from *Gone With the Wind* to *Moonligh*t, with far more nuanced and sensitive portrayals of Black people. So too, the portrayals of LGBTQ people have advanced, now with such films as *Call Me By Your Name* and *Brokeback Mountain.*

For people with visible difference, there has been little to no advancement. In 2024 alone, *The Joker II* and *The Penguin* were released, each featuring a villain who is scarred. Disfigured people have had little success so far, trying to stop negative portrayals and advance more positive ones.

Having said all of this, we are so lucky in the USA. Stigma against the visibly different is rampant around the world. In India, Nepal, and Pakistan, as well as other countries, women can be the victims of acid attacks from the rage of a rejected suitor, causing permanent scarring. These scarred women then face prejudice and victim blaming from their community; in some lower and middle income countries, parents abandon their visibly different child when born (Face Equality International). One report from Kenya found that children born with cleft palates are sometimes regarded as inhuman, and therefore may be killed (Kimotho & Macharia, 2020).

Much of this mistreatment rests in belief systems that attribute disfigurement to moral failing. Many lower and middle income countries hold beliefs that a person's disfigurement is best explained by their inherent evil, or by the immoral actions of their parents.

* * *

An editor proposed that I develop this book about disfigurement. However, my story is just my singular (American) tale of trauma, recovery, healing, and resilience. As challenging as my experiences have been, I have had the benefit of excellent medical and psychological care, in the USA, a country rich with resources. My co-editor, Miriam Jaffe, and I knew that the most compelling volume on this topic would draw from voices around the world, from academicians, scholars and clinicians, and also from people with lived experience.

Sprinkled among these chapters, you will find "interludes" written by people with lived experiences of disfigurement. We want the reader to have a profound sense of the experience of looking different in this world. We also know that real-life stories can feel more alive than research findings, and that readers often learn the most from an engaging walk in another person's shoes. The lived experience of marginalized populations requires the platform of storytelling as a qualitative research method (Barone, 1992; Wilkins, 2000; Palacios et al., 2015; Toliver, 2021). Specifically, we adapt the model of Johnson et al. (2017), where stories run counter to dominant narratives, where stories perpetuate justice through empathy and understanding. It is crucial to us that even scientific-research-driven chapters be as accessible as the accompanying interludes, personal reflections, making space for voices that have often been left out of traditional scholarship, often due to discrimination.

Miriam and I connected with each contributor on Zoom prior to writing. Some of the contributors were devoted academicians and scholars. The majority of the contributors came to the call wearing their expertise on their face. These Zoom calls were intense. We asked people to share not only their academic expertise, but also their personal stories of looking different. I found myself connecting emotionally to each writer. My own journey as an activist for the disfigured came about organically. But as I wrote about being burned, I learned more about the experiences of all kinds of people with visible difference. I learned how similar our stories are. Most of us have been teased and taunted. Most of us have been rejected in love. Most of us have pretended to have unblemished faces.

Many of us have developed amazing social skills, able to put a wary stranger at ease like a ninja, deploying a kind word or wry observation. Many of us are hilarious, developing a quirky view of the world from our unusual experiences. Many of us have learned to love ourselves as we are, regardless of society's relentless focus on beauty.

Most of us are traumatized. Most of us are exceptionally kind and sensitive to others, as we understand suffering.

All of us have endured, and in doing so, have deep wells of resilience and grit.

I hope this volume serves to introduce the reader to a remarkable world. You may think you know a disfigured person by gazing at their scars, or misshapen features. You may assume that is the most important thing about them. Actually, walking through life looking different often deepens people. The very people whom strangers shun may be the most compelling and compassionate people they could ever hope to meet.

Let us introduce you to a few.

Part 2: Miriam

This book responds to the three themes prevalent in the psychological, sociological, and scientific scholarly literature on disfigurement: (1) the psychosocial aspects of body image and identity, (2) interventions, and (3) representations of disfigurement. Much of the existing literature comes from the United Kingdom, where appearance research is firmly recognized as a pursuit of social justice. One early voice from the UK's plastic surgeon's community called disfigurement "the last bastion of discrimination" (McGrouther, 1997, p. 91). More recently, a collaboration between Phyllida Swift, the CEO of Face Equality International, a UK-based organization, and Kathleen Bogart, Professor of Psychology and Director of the Disability and Social Interaction Lab at Oregon State University, centrally inspired our work. Their article, "A Hidden Community: Facial Disfigurement as a Globally Neglected Human Rights Issue" (2021), revealed the need for better public education and policy to combat systemic "face-ism" in our communities and health networks, especially considering that "disfigurement doesn't fit neatly into the definition of any form of disability" (p. 652). We aim to broaden the conversation about disfigurement and human experience with this collection of voices from around the world.

In section one, we explore the psychosocial aspects of body image and identity among people with disfigurement. One of the first people to write on this topic was Frances Cook Macgregor, whose groundbreaking sociological study on injured soldiers "Facial Deformities and Plastic Surgery: A Psychosocial Study" (1953) opened the door to understanding disfigurement as a social problem. Early psychological understandings of disfigurement relied on Erving Goffman's *Stigma: Notes on the Management of Spoiled Identity* (1963), which discussed the relationship between disfigurement, acquired stigma, and identity disruption in selves that mirror societal judgements: internalized stigma. Thomas Cash, founder of *Body Image: An International Journal of Research* and Editor-in-Chief of *The Encyclopedia of Body Image and Human Appearance* (2012), was also a major influence on appearance studies during the 1970s and 1980s.

Throughout the 1990s and early 2000s, conversations about how to define disfigurement emerged. It was clear that disfigurement can be caused by congenital malformation, traumatic events, and disease processes (Harris, 1997). These conversations brought attention to the manifold psychosocial impacts of disfigurement, including higher than average levels of depression, anxiety, shame, and low self-esteem (Thompson & Kent, 2001). The seminal work of Nichola Rumsey and Diana Harcourt in "Body Image and Disfigurement: Issues and Interventions" (2004) has helped to define and promote terminology related to disfigurement that reduces negative bias, "replacing [widely understood] 'disfigurement' with 'difference' where appropriate" (p. 84); their review of early literature on disfigurement captured the complexity of social processes, self concept, family environment, and developmental stages throughout the lifespan in people with visible difference.

Later research theorized disfigurement through the lens of identity process theory, also known as the theory of identity threat, where a lack of self-efficacy, belonging, meaning and positive self-regard-such as "feeling flawed" or getting excessive attention for a negative "distinction" lead to interpersonal challenges and loneliness (Jaspal, 2012, p. 332). The newest focus in disfigurement research, prescient in *Saving Face: Disfigurement and the Politics of Appearance* (Talley, 2014), are debates about the impacts of reconstructive and facial transplant surgeries. Sarwer et al. (2022) examined transplantation of vascularized human body parts as a treatment for disfigurement with the psychosocial burden of traumatic injury. The *AMA Journal of Ethics* published a literature review to evaluate the psychosocial consequences of reconstructive and transplant surgery on personal identity (Rifkin et al., 2018). Martindale and Fisher's (2019) phenomenological narrative study of adults with acquired disfigurement built upon questions about surgical reconstruction, highlighting the research indicating that the degree of an individual's identity disruption cannot be predicted by the severity of bodily change (Coulson, 2017). Overall, this research reflects the concurrent growth of Disability Studies, which boomed – in the United States – after the Americans with Disabilities Act (1990) legalized employment protections and public accommodations for populations meeting certain criteria. However, in the United Kingdom and in the European Union, "the parameters of the severe disfigurement provision" are not as well-codified (Saunders, 2020, p. 21). Legal protection, insurance coverage, and public policy are issues requiring more context in Disability Studies, especially in relation to visible difference. We hope our collection helps provide this context and promotes further conversation.

To start this conversation, Faye Linda Wachs, the author of *Metamorphosis: Who We Become after Facial Paralysis* (2023), offers her personal story as the catalyst for a qualitative study of how it feels when acquired changes in facial expression alter communication. Her chapter entitled "Confronting Embodied Ableism: Learning from Synkinesis" (Chapter 1) paints the experience of acquired facial changes against the backdrop of neoliberal able-ism and the emphasis of facial beauty in Western culture. Chapter 2, "Acid Violence and Disfigurement: Lived Experiences of Women Survivors," by Beenish Ambereen and Farhan Navid Youseaf, takes us to Pakistan, which – like other South Asian nations – has a high incidence of revenge acid burn attacks. While the impacts of this gender-based violence are recognized in Women's Studies, Disability Studies has scant research in this area (Habib et al., 2021). Acid attacks, often perpetrated by rejected suitors, force victims to quit education and jobs, making long-term outlooks bleak, including social isolation and fear of retaliation. Ambereen and Youseaf's longitudinal approach tracks the lived experiences of women survivors with more than five-year post-incidence, revealing the invisible severity of this women's rights issue. Then, in Chapter 3, Zali O'Dea and Jane Southcott, present a male perspective on facial eye disfigurement (FED). O'Dea and Southcott, from Australia, are at the forefront of research on FED; their previous work on parenting a child with FED (2023a), intergenerational FED (2024), and living with FED (2023b) was hugely inspirational to the format of the chapters in this book for their expertise in storytelling using the case study method.

These three traditional research chapters pave the way for storytelling in an interlude featuring personal reflections. Jasmine "Jaz" Gray's essay, "Living Louder: Uncovering and Unlearning the Lessons in Rejection Stories," and Rasheera Dopson's "Pretty Disability: A Collection of Essays from a Black Girl who has Contemplated her Beauty and Worth," reach well beyond body image and identity, across chasms of difference, like bridges to humanity. Each writer considers her "worth," exploring the self against societal beauty standards and cruelty, to find beauty and to make meaning.

Gray and Dopson's essays exist in a world where a study of neural responses has proven "an implicit '*disfigured is bad*' bias" (Hartung et al., 2019; Jamrozik et al., 2019):

> People with facial disfigurement are not only perceived as less attractive and less likely to be selected as romantic partners, they are also thought to have unfavorable personality traits (e.g. lack of emotional stability, conscientiousness), internal attributes (e.g. unhappiness, lower intelligence), social qualities (e.g. untrustworthiness, unpopularity) and treated poorly in social interactions.
>
> (Hartung et al., 2019, p. 1)

Often, literature has categorized this phenomenon in of terms of "disgust" (Rumsey et al., 1982; Shanmugarajah et al., 2012; Stone, 2021; Rasset et al., 2024), with staring (Halioua et al., 2011) and behavioral avoidance likened to "evolved predispositions" against individuals with infectious disease (Ryan et al., 2012, p. 639). These predispositions require that we raise public awareness and create models of care that include social skills training and effective coping strategies for the reactions of others (Bradbury, 2012; Kish & Lansdown, 2000). Early interventions incorporated "self-help" treatments (Muftin & Thompson, 2013), while novel examples include the use of psychoeducational documentary film (Mathews et al., 2023); and cognitive behavioral therapy, acceptance and commitment therapy, and competitive memory training in group sessions (Siemann et al., 2023).

Section two, on intervention, begins with a contribution from Diana Harcourt, Maia Thornton, Pippa Tollow, Fabio Zucchelli, and Alex Clarke, "Psychosocial Interventions to Support People Affected by Visible Differences" (Chapter 4), which provides an introduction to a variety of evidence-based psychosocial interventions. We are grateful to feature the work of Professor Harcourt and her team at the Centre for Appearance Research at the University of the West of England, Bristol. Her leadership in appearance research is foundational to the development of best practices in intervention, which are taken up in the rest of this section. In "Visible Difference and Social Media: Harnessing a Unique Tool to Increase Support and Reduce Stigma" (Chapter 5), Ella Guest, Abbi Mathews, and Amy Slater discuss the advantages and disadvantages of social media intervention as an effective tool to target the attitudes and perceptions of the general population in relation to visible differences. Chapter 6, "FaceIT@home: An Online Support Tool for Adults with Visible Difference," by Alyson Norman, also discusses the journey to develop an intervention online. FaceIT@Home, a tool freely available internationally through the author or by visiting the website: https://faceitonline.info/, is designed to support adults with visible differences to feel more confident in social situations and better able to manage their appearance-related distress. Norman narrativizes the logistical steps of creating the seven-session program, making her research process accessible to others who may be interested in developing future interventions.

Section two delivers another interlude, featuring Dina Zuckerberg, the director of myFace, and Sora J. Kasuga, a professional circus artist and narrative activist. In "Finding My Voice," Zuckerberg details her experiences as a member of the craniofacial difference community, with an emphasis on creating an educational program based on the book *Wonder*, which has now reached over 100,000 students. In "The Swan Fallacy," Kasuga weaves a story of her many threads: Japanese-American, neurodivergent, facially different (FD), activist, writer, model, and performing artist. She reflects on her family history of imprisonment in a Japanese-American concentration camp, and her transformation of "outsider" to activist. Kasuga uses her presence in the spotlight as a step toward improving representation of people with visible difference across many forms of media.

Much disfigurement scholarship has evolved from the study of textual and visual media. Particularly interesting, *The Disfigured Face in American Literature, Film, and Television* (Klecker & Grabher, 2021) presents an overview of the media's responsibility to dismantle the connection between disfigurement and immorality that the media created. This long standing misrepresentation is currently one of the most important issues among disfigurement activists.

In response to this misrepresentation, section three offers the voices of poeple who are helping to change public opinions through media and activism. In Chapter 7, Charlene Pell, founder and director of Facing Forward, writes about how the depiction of individuals with Down syndrome in film and television is shifting from a focus on medical and biological aspects of disability to more authentic, nuanced, and positive portrayals. These include social and environmental contexts, suggesting that positive media can reduce prejudice. The father of this movement and founder of Face Equality International was James Partridge, who passed away in 2020. We were lucky to have J. Michael Murphy, a clinical and research psychologist at Shriners Hospital for Burned Children in Boston for more than 30 years, who had collaborated with James Partridge, reflect on Partridge's legacy of positive representation and prejudice reduction in Chapter 8, "Facing Up to *IT* is Worth It: James Partridge Revisited." Partridge passed the torch of Face Equality International to Phyllida Swift. Chapter 9 closes out the volume with Swift's narrative on the integral work of Face Equality International in "The Stories that Need to be Told." Swift's tenor of hope for the future, and the example of her activism shows the promise of this field, an inspiration for future work.

I started to understand the promise of Lise's work as soon as we first met. She was writing her memoir, *Flashback Girl: Lessons in Resilience from a Burn Survivor*. This book touched me and changed me. Then, Lise and I began this project together, and each one of the contributors I had the privilege to meet did the same. One reason I learned so much is that, before meeting Lise, I knew essentially nothing about disfigurement. Here I am, a trained social worker and psychotherapist, a social science researcher, and a professor who trafficks in stories of the human experience – yet I knew nothing. The authors in this volume educated me through their stories and their research with such grace. I am honored to help spread their wisdom.

References

Barone, T. E. (1992). Beyond theory and method: A case of critical storytelling. *Theory into Practice*, *31*(2), 142–146.

Bradbury, E. (2012). Meeting the psychological needs of patients with facial disfigurement. *British Journal of Oral and Maxillofacial Surgery*, *50*(3), 193–196.

Cash, T. F. (Ed.). (2012). *Encyclopedia of body image and human appearance*. Academic Press (Elsevier).

Coulson, S. (2017). *Perceived face value: The cost of facial nerve paralysis*. Presentation, International Facial Nerve Symposium. Hollywood, CA.

Disfigurement in the UK. (2017, May). *Changing faces*. https://www.changingfaces.org.uk/wp-content/uploads/2021/05/disfigurement-in-the-uk-report-2017.pdf

Face Equality International. https://faceequalityinternational.org/exposing-human-rights-violations

Goffman, E. (1963). *Stigma: Notes on the management of spoiled identity*. Prentice-Hall.

Habib, Z., Saddul, R., & Kamran, F. (2021). Perceptions and experiences of female burn survivors with facial disfigurement. *Chinese Journal of Traumatology*, *24*(1), 53–56.

Halioua, R. L., Williams, R. S., Murray, N. P., Skalko, T. K., & Vogelsong, H. G. (2011). Staring and perceptions of people with facial disfigurement. *Therapeutic Recreation Journal*, *45*(4), 341–356.

Harris, D. (1997). Types, causes and physical treatments of visible differences. In R. Landstown, N. Rumsey, E. Bradbury, T. Carr, & J. Partridge (Eds.), *Visibly different: Coping with disfigurement* (pp. 79–90). Butterworth-Heinemann.

Hartung, F., Jamrozik, A., Rosen, M. E., Aguirre, G., Sarwer, D. B., & Chatterjee, A. (2019). Behavioural and neural responses to facial disfigurement. *Scientific Reports*, *9*(1), 8021.

Jamrozik, A., Oraa Ali, M., Sarwer, D. B., & Chatterjee, A. (2019). More than skin deep: Judgments of individuals with facial disfigurement. *Psychology of Aesthetics, Creativity, and the Arts*, *13*(1), 117.

Jaspal, R. (2012). Disfigurement: The challenges for identity and the strategies for coping. *Psychological Studies*, *57*, 331–335.

Johnson, L. L., Gibbs Grey, T. D., & Baker-Bell, A. (2017). Changing the dominant narrative: A call for using storytelling as language and literacy theory, research methodology, and practice. *Journal of Literacy Research*, *49*(4), 467–475.

Julian, D., & Partridge, J. (2007). *The incidence and prevalence of disfigurement*. Changing Faces.

Kimotho, S. G., & Macharia, F. N. (2020). Social stigma and cultural beliefs associated with cleft lip and/or palate: Parental perceptions of their experience in Kenya. *Humanities and Social Sciences Communications*, *7*(181), 1–9. https://doi.org/10.1057/s41599-020-00677-7

Kish, V., & Lansdown, R. (2000). Meeting the psychosocial impact of facial disfigurement: Developing a clinical service for children and families. *Clinical Child Psychology and Psychiatry*, *5*(4), 497–512.

Klecker, C., & Grabher, G. M. (Eds.). (2021). *The disfigured face in American literature, film, and television*. Routledge.

Macgregor, F. C. (1953). *Facial deformities and plastic surgery: A psychosocial study*. United States: Thomas.

Martindale, A. M., & Fisher, P. (2019). Disrupted faces, disrupted identities? Embodiment, life stories and acquired facial "disfigurement". *Sociology of Health & Illness*, *41*(8), 1503–1519.

Mathews, A., Costa, B., Mikkola, A., & Harcourt, D. (2023). "Scars: How our wounds make us who we are": Improving appearance-based stigma, conceptualisation of beauty and body esteem through a documentary. *Scars, Burns & Healing*, *9*. https://doi.org/10.1177/20595131231205398

McGrouther, D. A. (1997). Facial disfigurement: The last bastion of discrimination. *British Medical Journal*, *314*(7086), 991.

Muftin, Z., & Thompson, A. R. (2013). A systematic review of self-help for disfigurement: Effectiveness, usability, and acceptability. *Body Image*, *10*(4), 442–450.
O'Dea, Z., & Southcott, J. (2023a). "I'm his mum and it is my job to keep him safe": Mothering a child living with facial eye disfigurement. *Applied Research in Quality of Life*, *18*(5), 2579–2604.
O'Dea, Z., & Southcott, J. (2023b). "My mummy has a hole in her face": Living with facial eye disfigurement. *The Qualitative Report*, *28*(11), 2995–3115.
O'Dea, Z. M., & Southcott, J. (2024). "Everything seems to be the right eye in our family": Intergenerational family living with facial eye disfigurement: An interpretative phenomenological analysis. *The Qualitative Report*, *29*(1), 162–182.
Palacios, J. F., Salem, B., Hodge, F. S., Albarrán, C. R., Anaebere, A., & Hayes-Bautista, T. M. (2015). Storytelling: A qualitative tool to promote health among vulnerable populations. *Journal of Transcultural Nursing*, *26*(4), 346–353.
Rasset, P., Mange, J., & Montalan, B. (2024). (Un)veiling distinct feelings: A typology of affective reactions while meeting people with facial disfigurement for the first time. *Stigma and Health*, *9*(2), 124.
Rifkin, W. J., Kantar, R. S., Ali-Khan, S., Plana, N. M., Diaz-Siso, J. R., Tsakiris, M., & Rodriguez, E. D. (2018). Facial disfigurement and identity: A review of the literature and implications for facial transplantation. *AMA Journal of Ethics*, *20*(4), 309–323.
Rumsey, N., Bull, R., & Gahagan, D. (1982). The effect of facial disfigurement on the proxemic behavior of the general public 1. *Journal of Applied Social Psychology*, *12*(2), 137–150.
Rumsey, N., & Harcourt, D. (2004). Body image and disfigurement: Issues and interventions. *Body Image*, *1*(1), 83–97.
Ryan, S., Oaten, M., Stevenson, R. J., & Case, T. I. (2012). Facial disfigurement is treated like an infectious disease. *Evolution and Human Behavior*, *33*(6), 639–646.
Sarwer, D. B., Siminoff, L. A., Gardiner, H. M., & Spitzer, J. C. (2022). The psychosocial burden of visible disfigurement following traumatic injury. *Frontiers in Psychology*, *13*, 979574.
Saunders, H. (2020). Difficult distinctions in anti-discrimination law: Disfigurement, appearance and disability. *International Journal of Discrimination and the Law*, *20*(1), 21–44.
Shanmugarajah, K., Gaind, S., Clarke, A., & Butler, P. E. (2012). The role of disgust emotions in the observer response to facial disfigurement. *Body Image*, *9*(4), 455–461.
Siemann, I., Custers, J., van den Heuvel-Djulic, S., Pouwels, S., Kwakkenbos, L., & Spillekom-van Koulil, S. (2023). A novel psychological group intervention targeting appearance-related distress among people with a visible disfigurement (inside out): A case study. *Cognitive and Behavioral Practice*, *30*(4), 657–668.
Stone, A. (2021). Facial disfigurement, categorical perception, and the influence of disgust sensitivity. *Visual Cognition*, *29*(2), 73–90.
Swift, P., & Bogart, K. (2021). A hidden community: Facial disfigurement as a globally neglected human rights issue. *Journal of Oral Biology and Craniofacial Research*, *11*(4), 652–657.
Talley, H. L. (2014). *Saving face: Disfigurement and the politics of appearance*. NYU Press.
Thompson, A., & Kent, G. (2001). Adjusting to disfigurement: Processes involved in dealing with being visibly different. *Clinical Psychology Review*, *21*(5), 663–682.
Toliver, S. R. (2021). *Recovering black storytelling in qualitative research: Endarkened storywork*. Routledge.
Wachs, F. (2023). *Metamorphosis: Who we become after facial paralysis*. Rutgers University Press.
Wilkins, P. (2000). Storytelling as research. In *Research in social care and social welfare: Issues and debates for practice* (pp. 144–153). Jessica Kingsley Publishers.

Section 1

The Psychosocial Aspects of Body Image and Identity

1 Confronting Embodied Ableism

Learning from Synkinesis

Faye Linda Wachs

So What Happened?

Life was stressful. I was being furloughed at work, meaning I would be paid 10% less but was not truly receiving any reduction in workload, and I was finalizing a divorce. After years of careful saving, my future seemed uncertain in a city with a high cost of living. I woke up one day not feeling quite right. After the initial terror of realizing something was wrong, I reached out to friends and was advised to head immediately to the ER. The ER confirmed what friends intimated: I had Bell's Palsy. Like almost everyone I interviewed, I was given medication, told not to worry about it, and that I would heal. I, like most, was unaware that 20% of people do not heal and the most common side effect is synkinesis (Slattery & Azizzadeh, 2014). Despite there being no clear reason why some develop synkinesis,[1] as with most of the people I interviewed, I was filled with internalized shame, wondering what I had or hadn't done to end up in this group. I wasn't offered mental health support and follow-up care was left to me. It was 2009, before the Zoom revolution in education, and it was the last week of the quarter. As a professor, I was concerned my illness would negatively impact my students. I tend to teach project-based courses and students were desperately trying to finish several big assignments so they could graduate, I was chairing several committees, I already felt pretty low and somehow believed maintaining productivity would validate my sense of self. But I also didn't want to hide. I wanted my students to know that if their appearance changed radically, I wouldn't value their presence any less. So, I went to work, I lectured, using my hand to hold up my face. In some ways, it was cathartic. My students were amazing, compassionate, and supportive, a few told me about relatives who had Bell's Palsy, and one noted she had it the year before and was now mostly healed. But from a physical health perspective, it was probably too much. I had to call my parents to pick me up, too dizzy to drive home safely after a late-night class.

I was very lucky and got my blink back slowly over time, but my ability to communicate and my physical comfort were deeply impacted. When I talk it's obvious. When it first occurred, it was far more extreme. During the winter break I went on a long-planned trip to Costa Rica. It was hard. I went from being considered reasonably attractive to looking very different. I tried to smile at a child and was

DOI: 10.4324/9781003535591-3

met with cries about "la monstrua." My Spanish isn't amazing, but even I didn't need assistance to translate. I continued to hold onto what doctors had told me, that I would heal. But I didn't. I have the most common complication, synkinesis, a movement disorder in which the nerves regrow to too many places, creating unwanted movement. Many mistake synkinesis for ongoing paralysis because if everything tries to move simultaneously, nothing does. Synkinesis can be painful, and there can be miswiring of salivary glands and tear ducts. One further experiences "wrongfeel," as one's facial tightness creates negative internal experiences impacting self-perception (Wachs, 2023). But I also have relative privilege: supportive family and friends, the luxury of travel, a medical doctor spouse, and a career that allows one to explore and process trauma in a book chapter.

This all sounds too sterile; it's a raw, painful experience. There is a deep and profound sense of loss of self and sociability. There's a very difficult period of adjustment. Araceli B., a Latina in her early 30s, shares how difficult it initially was:

> If you don't have it you can't understand what it feels like. It feels like your world is crashing. It was the lowest I had ever felt. Even when my husband left us years ago, I didn't feel that bad. In those first couple of months, suicide was often on my mind, but I knew I couldn't do that to my kids. . . . This is just something that destroys people's lives.

I would say I had moderate to severe synkinesis, but I also had savings and was in one of the few areas that had people initiating research on treatment for synkinesis at a time when the vast majority of medical practitioners hadn't yet heard of it. I have had three major surgeries (two for synkinesis several years apart and both following an open septo-rhinoplasty to allow me to breathe through my nose). All three were challenging, but in each case the reduction in pain and return of function left me more than satisfied with the physical and literal cost. As I went through this process and reflected on the challenges in finding and paying for treatment, I wondered about the experience of other people facing a rare side effect of a somewhat uncommon condition. When I decided to attempt in-depth qualitative interviews, my friends from graduate school suggested it was inevitable. But I also had fortuitous timing, as a combination of expanding communication technologies, medical advances, and advocacy opportunities allowed for access most lack.

I conducted what are called semi-structured interviews (Corbin & Strauss, 2022; Galletta, 2013) with 113 people with facial paralysis, most with synkinesis, some treatment providers (4), and loved ones of those with facial paralysis (6). Interviews generally lasted between 45 minutes and 3 hours, generally most were around 90 minutes. Interviews took place between 2015 and 2021. A few participants shared personal notes, artwork, and creative writing. Some I spent considerable time with at support events. All participants have been given pseudonyms and details are altered to protect their identity. Interviews were open-coded for themes and analyzed. Initial ideas were presented to academic writing groups for feedback and shared with others with synkinesis.

The interviews themselves were challenging. Synkinesis is more noticeable on camera than in person, and, realizing that synkinetic faces send disquieting messages in communication, was a significant but deeply personal and painful revelation. When people communicate, we mirror others' affects. It's an essential part of the communication process and allows us to share emotion as we communicate (Blairy et al., 1999; Hess & Bourgeois, 2010; Riehle et al., 2017; Ruusuvuori & Peräkylä, 2009). As we discussed synkinesis it was impossible not to notice how much we struggled with this process of mimicry. How our disparate facial movements made one feel uncomfortable, never quite sure if one was adequately communicating, and sometimes receiving jolts of "wrongfeel" initiated by both my own unwanted involuntary movements and unconscious mimicry of the others' synkinetic wrong movements. The general feeling of disquiet, of wondering if I had done something to offend, the uncertainty of positive connection, was a revelation. Is this what others experience in speaking with me? For my participants, they often were having the same epiphany, and our shared frustration, grief, and hopelessness created a deeply personal raw space. Struggling with this became part of the interviewing process. Participants were always offered the opportunity to stop when things became emotionally charged, but no one ever did. We frequently wept together. Many expressed a desire, really a need, to work through it with someone else living with it. Having my experience, my anxieties, fears, failures, and pains mirrored in so many revealed much about how our social world normalizes ableism and encourages self-reliance very much to our own personal detriment. But it was also an amazing experience through which I connected with phenomenally resilient people, many of whom were reconsidering who they wanted to be and how they wanted our social worlds to evolve.

What is Living with Synkinesis?

> I hate that it's just a constant reminder. . . . of what happened. . . . I think a lot of people, if they have issues, can distract themselves. But, you're doing a basic thing like smiling at somebody or talking to somebody, or laughing, or kissing your wife. I kiss my wife for example, and I remember. . . . I have a reminder 100 times a day that you have this. So, I think that's the biggest problem, is the constant reminders all the time. Like, you go to drink something, there goes your eye. You laugh, the side of your neck pulls and your eye goes. So, it's the constant reminders that you have it that kind of wears you down. After a while, you start to try to find reasons and ways not to have that happen.

Brad A., a white male entertainer in his mid 30s, captures the frustration of living with synkinesis from an internal perspective. People living with synkinesis find it exhausting to continually manage misexpression, "wrongfeel" and reminders of loss. People with synkinesis face shared social interaction that is challenging and triggering. As a result, some self-isolate, socialize less than before, and find interacting with new people fraught (Wachs, 2023). Synkinesis changes the experience of identity, both in terms of one's internal experience and also in terms of how one is perceived.

It's important to acknowledge the importance of faces in Western culture. Faces are how we present ourselves to and experience the social world. As previously noted, our faces are critical to communication and sharing experiences. They are crucial to the processing of identity (Wachs, 2023). Those who appear to be different experience social exclusion and face stigma (Garland-Thomson, 2009, 2005). Classist Victorian ideologies that link morality and appearance remain embedded in Western conflations and presumptions (Wachs, 2023). Codified in "ugly laws," people who appear different have been barred from appearing in public in a multitude of places over the last hundred years (Schweik, 2009). Even when not facing legal exclusion, those who appear different encounter norms of social exclusion (Garland-Thomson, 2009), and people with facial difference suffer professional and social isolation (Talley, 2014; Wachs, 2023). As a result, those with acquired facial difference report higher rates of depression while adjusting (Daker-White et al., 2012; VanSwearington et al., 1999). What my participants and I experienced is not so much a challenge adjusting to our new physical reality, but adjusting to our new social reality.

Communicating The New Reality

People acquired a highly stigmatized identity overnight and the loss in social status was communicated in a variety of ways. People faced overt discrimination, on occasion faced violence, bullying, and abject cruelty. A middle aged white woman who now worked in IT shared stories of being bullied as a tween and teen after an accident left her with synkinesis, being forced out of a career in the beauty industry because "no one would want to look at that face," and was currently struggling with a new manager who complained about her attitude and refused to hear her explanations that she wasn't physically capable of a different affect. Another shared being assaulted because the person "didn't like his face." Even as adults, some were bullied by co-workers: one woman reported being mocked by those she thought were her friends in the work lunchroom, another reported ongoing teasing, and several others reported friend groups evaporating overnight.

In my previous work, I discuss microaggressions against those with synkinesis and facial difference at length. Microaggressions refer to the manifestation of inequity in communication. In practice, microaggressions are intended or unintended snubs or discounting of a person because of their identity (Sue, 2010a, 2010b). Microaggressions perpetuate existing inequities and transmit problematic ideologies, stereotypes, and beliefs (Solórzano et al., 2000). Documented micro-aggressions for marginalized people include race (Levchak, 2018; Sue, 2010a, 2010b), disability (Conover et al., 2017; Keller & Galgay, 2010), hidden disabilities (Kattari et al., 2018), gender (Nadal, 2013), sexuality (Haines et al., 2018; Nadal, 2013), facial difference (Wachs, 2023), and various intersections (Lewis et al., 2016). When one is identified as being disabled or having a disability, microaggressions tend to involve into a denial of personal identity, denial that one has a disability, denial of privacy for the individual, assumptions of helplessness and infantilization, assumptions of secondary gain or unearned entitlements, spread effects, patronization, second-class citizenship status, and de-sexualization (Keller & Galgay, 2010). Traditionally, microaggressions fall into three broader categories: microassaults (conscious and intentional actions), microinsults (subtle rudeness or insensitivity in verbal interaction), or microinvalidations (negating the views of the other) (Sue, 2010a, 2010b).

Participants reported a range of microassaults, microinsults, and microinvalidations. One's intersecting identity categories influence the ways microaggressions are experienced. Microassaults tended to ascribe negative identity categories based on facial difference. People were accused of being bad tempered, inebriated, or as exhibiting shameful behavior. One example that stuck with me was a lovely retired white woman, Beverly, who after being diagnosed with Ramsay Hunt syndrome, had developed synkinesis and vertigo. After working up the courage to attempt her own shopping, something she had previously enjoyed, she found other shoppers using a stage whisper to shame her for her "intoxication." Devastated, she wondered if everyone saw her that way. Similarly, Elaine E. recounted that others make assumptions about her mood because of her altered appearance. While waiting in a long line, a stranger chided her: *"You don't have to be so angry, you don't have to be so upset."* Elaine asserted *"I was happy to be there. And I'm sure he didn't even think twice, I mean like, about his comment. . . . But I remember it."* Left to carry the weight of his assumptions, she worried that others now perceived her as an unpleasant person.

Similarly, while many reported microinsults, especially the invisibility of disability (Keller & Galgay, 2010; Garland-Thomson, 2005), others were offered faint praise. Amanda G. found herself presumed to be a "disabled sister" rather than a fiancé on a pre-wedding trip as others praised her betrothed for his kindness. Others reported being told how brave they/we are for "leaving the house like that." I remember well-meaning friends commenting on my resilience for being able to allow myself to be seen like this. As Vi V., a mid 30s Asian American woman, noted, we don't have a choice about getting on with things. In contrast, the potential hyper visibility of appearing different is encapsulated in the microinsult, "What's wrong with your face?" Al L., a late-20s Latino, shared the difference between a microinsult and someone demonstrating interest or care. He noted, "Last year somebody just said, '*What's wrong with your face?' Like very bluntly you know? And that made me very, very uncomfortable because I was around people*." He contrasts this to a different interaction in which an older woman gently took him aside and asked, *"Hey, I noticed something, well not at first, but as I look at you more I realize that something's up, what is it?"* He reports not finding that problematic, noting, *"And I wasn't offended by it because the way that she asked me was more of with care and interest, not as like, 'Hey what's wrong with your face?'"* At the same time, comments like this reveal the loss of privacy that comes with visible stigma (Campbell, 2009).

Finally, we all experienced microinvalidations. Sarah H. was crushed when the place she had been a longtime volunteer for suggested she take time off until she fully recovered, afraid her appearance would frighten others. Retired, living alone, she had valued the ability to contribute to her local community. I interviewed another professor, who adopted many of the same strategies I used to prevent synkinesis from becoming a barrier, from inviting narrative impositions. We both self-disclosed and reminded students that our affects were not indicative of our friendliness throughout the semester. While this helps me communicate more impactfully, it also takes a toll. However, in my classroom, I control the environment. Too often, when people sought to share the frustrations and impacts, they found others generally shut them down with a quick assurance that one looks "normal," framed as one looking "fine." This was incredibly frustrating as people often sought support for loss of function, pain management, or communication challenges. Matty L., a white woman in her mid 50s, shared an example of invalidation:

> I was at a thing for my brother recently, and this has happened before. . . . I don't know, people were just acting a little off to me., "Oh you're his sister? Are you visiting? From out of town?" And it's a bigger question, there's something implied. I don't know why but recently I felt like, I wonder if these people think that I'm not well, like I'm not a fully functional person. Like I'm Jason's broken sister just because of my facial problems. So I thought I would just say something, explain what it is. So I actually tried to explain about my facial paralysis and they cut me off. They flat out wouldn't let me talk about it. Everyone said no, no, no, no, no, no, no of course not, we all have our stuff you know. People like to . . . to sort of trivialize, like, I'm talking to one of my brother's friends and why is she was showing me discoloration of her hand and saying we all have our things. You know, I get it's a big deal for her but for me, it's like your hand it's not your face.

Microaggressions communicate systemic assumptions about people like you. When one microaggresses, one is often oblivious, invoking shared knowledge that validates some at the expense of others. People tend to internalize these messages and find coping strategies to avoid future encounters.

Internalization results in negative psychological outcomes for individuals (Meyer, 2007; Sue, 2010a; Sue, 2010b). Scholars have studied the impact of internalized racism and the impact on self-perception of living in a dominant culture that has negative racial stereotypes (Williams & Williams-Morris, 2000). Scholars have studied internalizations related to chronic illness (Charmaz, 1983), gender (Bearman & Amrhein, 2013), ableism (Campbell, 2009; Kattari et al., 2018), heterosexism (Nadal & Mendoza, 2013; Szymanski & Henrichs-Beck, 2014; Watermeyer & Görgens, 2013), and intersecting subject positions among categories (Szymanski & Henrichs-Beck, 2014; Nadal & Mendoza, 2013). Passing highlights the high value placed on not being identified in a larger culture of "compulsory ableness" in which signs of difference are highly devalued (Campbell, 2009). Matt H., a middle-aged Ashkenazi Jewish man, was enjoying his life, with a satisfying career and children with fulfilling lives. Synkinesis made it harder for this gregarious man to enjoy his active social life. He coped with self-deprecating humor that covered deeper feelings:

> Basically, I apologize to people for how I look. I just apologized up front. But I went on with it. It didn't stop me from doing stuff socially and I attended a wedding. I was actually part of the wedding. It was a big deal. It was okay. It was on my mind but it didn't stop me.

Matt L. demonstrates the compulsory ableness of the larger culture by feeling that he needs to "apologize" for his appearance. Many spoke of having to make significant adjustments in how one approaches the social world.

Shifting Identities

What people are fundamentally adjusting to is a new identity, and how this identity may alter other intersecting or overlapping identities. With identities come presumptions and role expectations that shape our experience of the social world and our views. In sociology, it is commonly understood that some roles and status are ascribed, meaning determined by imposed categories that are socially meaningful in your place and time. Today, things like race, gender, and physical appearance are current examples. Achieved status are those you initiate or work for yourself but, like ascribed roles, these have meaning within a specific historical context and social milieu. Profession, level of education, or being a skilled practitioner are examples of roles one may achieve. It is important to note that your perceived ascribed roles may facilitate, hinder, or render impossible some achieved roles. Disability is an ascribed status that is often assumed precludes other socially valued roles, statuses, and experiences (Darling, 2019). Kattari et al. (2018) found that people perceived to be disabled are granted "second class citizen status." One key example is exclusion from having partners or adult romantic and sexual relations. One participant, Denise, a West Asian woman, noted she didn't know which was worse, the ongoing familial pressure to marry or its immediate cessation when she developed synkinesis.

People with facial difference are often perceived as disabled, but whether the medical community or the people with facial difference considered it a disability was more nebulous. I asked all participants if they considered themselves to have acquired a disability. The majority distanced from disability but acknowledged a shift in status that made them disability adjacent. This meant either noting it may be a disability for others, but not them personally, or that it was disabling, but not a disability (Wachs, 2023). A few rejected the idea of disability altogether. This group tended to invoke neoliberal notions of productivity (Mitchell & Snyder, 2018) to disavow disability status highlighting returns to work, caregiving of others, and contrasting with other types of injuries. Another group adopted disability status, but tended to invoke disability identity models, rather than medical models of disability. Medical models refer to a person with a disability as physically or mentally impaired in ways that limit major life activities or perceptions of these activities. Medical models presume individual deficiency and ongoing needs. Medical models generally fail to consider the social impact of disability or how the social world may be creating barriers (Mauldin & Brown, 2021). One interview stood out as the person shared struggles with chronic pain, found her teeth were moving and creating serious dental challenges, and her loss of her blink and miswiring of tear ducts was putting her vision in jeopardy. She spent considerable time and resources managing her condition and creating her own accommodations. Yet she was also adamant that she wasn't disabled. She could still work, it wasn't like "losing an arm or leg . . ." From a medical perspective, it's hard to not see synkinesis as requiring ongoing treatment and negatively impacting people's lives. Long term impacts of living with synkinesis can be problems with vision, dental problems, chronic pain, challenges eating, and difficulty communicating with people, all of which are very much in line with the Center for Disease Control definition: "a disability is any condition of the body or mind (impairment) that makes it more difficult for the person with the condition to do certain activities (activity limitation) and interact with the world around them (participation restrictions)." Given that the most efficacious treatments were generally too expensive, not covered by insurance, or limited to a few clinics, most people did not receive optimal treatment. Being recognized by the medical model comes with the benefits of insurance coverage, disability insurance coverage, and policy inclusion. Advocates continue to work to change this, and that doesn't mean those advocates subscribe to medical models of disability. Rather, it may be a necessary tool to gain access to services and treatments. It is worth noting that those most likely to subscribe to existing medical models were least willing to put themselves in this category.

Those who asserted it was a disability were far more likely to embrace a disability identity perspective. Disability studies avow societies and cultures as problematic or deficient, not people. In this view, the lived experience from the position of the subject is central (Siebers, 2008). Beliefs and ideologies about disability, rather than physical difference, are problematized. Siebers (2008) complex theory of embodiment considers the social and cultural meanings of disability in conjunction with other aspects of identity. Understanding of the self and what it means to be a person with a disability or a disabled person or a person living with a disability, and how this identity intermixes with other key identities, is complicated. Scholars have noted that for marginalized groups, the necessity to overcome existing negative ideologies makes disability something hidden as it threatened the ability to manage other stigmas (Shalk, 2022, 2018; Vernon, 1999).

It's also not surprising that some simply weren't sure. For people living with synkinesis, larger cultural depictions of disability often failed to resonate. Synkinesis presents an embodied challenge in functioning, but not in ways that people typically contemplate. George Herbert Mead uses the term somatic perception to refer to our making of sense through embodied physical perception (Howson, 2013; Mead, 1934). Through this process, we are the subject perceiving, the object being perceived, and the self, having feelings about perceptions. The mis-feel of synkinesis can exacerbate and complicate this process as individuals may receive incorrect messages and miscommunicate nonverbally, and as a result face social challenges that are anxiety inducing. Having synkinesis means having to recognize somatic misperception and do otherwise. Even if one is aware of miscommunication, that doesn't necessarily mean one can overcome it. One needs to be aware of and willing to interrogate our somatic messages and to question a visceral response.

Synkinesis fundamentally presents a social challenge. This is consistent with research that finds regardless of cause or degree of impaction, for those with facial paralysis, the ability to function socially becomes *the* central challenge (Coulson, 2017; Coulson et al., 2004; Hughes, 1998). Hence, it's not surprising that the concept of a social disability resonated deeply with participants (Wachs, 2023). Social disabilities are embodied challenges that impact an individual's ability to communicate with self and others. Social disabilities are not limited to those with facial differences and could be applied to other conditions.[2] Regardless of whether one rejected, embraced, or distanced oneself from a disability identity, the concept of a social disability could be considered.

As a person ensconced in the disability studies model, I do consider it to be a disability, and I will require lifelong pain management that is available in limited places. I may need more surgeries to maintain or improve function. Sometimes I feel a devastating sense of loss when I catch sight of my reflection, or am caught off guard by an unregulated smile. Having the management of synkinesis taking up this much space in my life leads me to believe it's a disability. But that doesn't mean other views are less accurate or invalid. It's just a different way of coping.

What's Wrong with Your Face?

Previously, I mentioned a common microaggression: "what's wrong with your face."

Most people with synkinesis know "the look." The quizzical expression as others notice the difference in how our faces emote. People also unconsciously mimic, creating more miscommunication. Sometimes one can literally see people thinking, "Is it just the face? What is it? Are they 'normal' otherwise?" or forming a negative impression of our sociability. As noted, people experienced a range of aggressions, microaggressions, and exclusions. Being the other, and very explicitly bearing the medical model label of disability, carries with it a lessening of one's humanity.

In the *Order of Things*, Foucault (1970) discusses how what is considered knowledge is shaped by the categorical difference as a methodological necessity, and contrasts to earlier systems that categorized on similarity. How the presumption of difference and ranking pervades our already presumed world view implies learned categorization with implicit bias of objective ranking. Because, when I first understood the tendency to categorize me as having a disability, my desire for it to not be so, and the depth of that fear that it be seen as cognitive, revealed things about me I didn't want to be true. It is something I continue to confront. Too often as I struggled to write this piece, I could feel the weighty judgement of my own "compassion." Even in compassion, we still impose systems of power.

Gender, race, class, sexuality, the categories of different, abnormal, and other exist to exclude, marginalize, disempower, and dehumanize.

As noted, people tended to reassert social value through neoliberal ideologies of productivity (Mitchell & Snyder, 2018). The assumption that people are inherently more valuable when meeting specific standards of productivity is embedded in how we view disability and treatment (Mitchell & Snyder, 2018). Entangled with neoliberal ideologies of individuality and productivity are concepts like rights and inclusion, which makes advocacy complicated. This is not to say that we don't want rights and inclusion, but rather that a specific type of disabled person is defined, seen, and made part of the public discourse, while other experiences are excluded or rendered unfathomable. Finding policy and budgets that prioritize our needs when we are at our most vulnerable is necessary. We are all vulnerable to varying degrees at different points in our life. The fear of stigma is what befalls those with different arrays of vulnerabilities and resources. Systems of privilege and oppression give an advantage to some identities at the others' expense.

Social Structure is Embodied

As I struggle to sort through the "wrongfeel" of synkinesis, I became so much more aware of every visceral reaction to other people's identities. The assumptions I made about who they were and what that meant are an embodied response at the level of the unthought. It forced me to contemplate the nature of Ideology as an embodied experience. Scholars like Bourdieu (1984) and Du Bois (1906/2006) discuss how social locations are embodied through practice, and how taste reproduces existing relations of privilege and oppression. When it comes to stigma, the reaction is visceral. Becoming someone identified as disabled, struggling with being disabled, and being forced to analyze my visceral response, to sort through the miscommunication that is the nature of synkinesis, and what was being communicated to me, by myself, about myself, mirrored back in conversations with others going through the same experience, was a brutal awakening to my own internalized ableism. It's easy to be furious about the microaggressions; it's more complicated to recognize our own complicity. Despite our best intentions, our bodies betrayal in fear, loathing, disgust, pity, and even compassion are produced in complicated systems of meaning.

People's tendency to blame themselves further revealed existing entrenchments in neoliberal models. This individualized responsibility displaces responsibility for communal care onto individuals, whose own moral failings disqualify. Teri B. is white woman approaching 60 and is now an educator. She has synkinesis after having Bell's Palsy as a teenager. Her complicated set of reactions reveal shame, blame, and pain:

> I felt like I deserved it . . . Because my friends and I had been laughing at people with palsy . . . People who were retarded. So there was part of me that thought it was kind of just, so oddly amusing in a certain kind of way. I don't think I was really overly religious or anything. It was just like, wow okay.

> This is what happens when you are mean to folks then it happens to you. But it was hard. I was part of a little social group at the time. I remember that there was a boy I liked and it was winter time in Wisconsin and we had to go ice skating in one of the parks near my house. My friend was teasing me. She's like, "I don't think Bryan or Tony is going to want to kiss you right now because of your face." I was like, "Yeah, you're probably right about that."

Others highlighted failures in self-care, failing to care enough for others, and musings about what one had done to deserve their condition. People also wondered what one could do differently, or if investment in a new treatment would improve pain, function, and appearance.

Concluding Thoughts

I was blissfully unaware of how deeply ableist I was prior to November 2009. I liked to believe I was better than most, supporting progressive causes, trusting in accommodations, believing tolerance is commensurate with inclusion. The awakening was brutal and traumatic, but I learned enough from it to like who I am becoming more than who I was. I know I still don't have it right. It sounds too self-congratulatory. As if I have achieved something. Instead, I struggle to question what achievement entails. There's a Cat and Girl cartoon entitled *Cat and Girl and the Search for the Total Abnegation of the Self*.[3] The total abnegation of the self refers to embracing selflessness, to have freedom from envy, desire, and comparison. Girl believes she has found it, and full of pride declares she has. It ends with her dejected, giving a homage-filled "rats." Though I may believe I am confronting ableism, these confrontations are a never-ending project with layers of intermingled networks of relations of privilege. I will always be a product of a deeply ableist world and will always have to actively work against a network of beliefs and tendencies, that feel safe and underlie so much of my sense of self-worth and security, literal and ontological. What facial paralysis gave me is the experience of living not "quite right." The internal experience of self and external messages of who one is seen as are permanently impacted. That discomfort with identity is necessary to challenge assumptions, beliefs, and principles that grant privilege, and this process is essential for making a better world and my own personal growth.

It still hurts. Even after doing all this research and writing a book and speaking at events. Even after analysis, and finding gifts within the experience, unexpected revelations, things to like about my resilience, even after all that. It still hurts. I wish I could just smile and laugh and not be forced to think about it. And that's hard enough. No one wants to carry devalued identities. But I also now know the very specific sting of what disability means and that I am no less than I was before. Privilege is having your accommodations pass unnoticed, while being rewarded for those you provide others. Edwardo Bonilla-Silva's (2017) concept of "sincere fictions" comes to mind. In studying race, he argues people create myths about overcoming the past, that racism is no longer a barrier (Bonilla-Silva, 2017). The term "minimalization of race" is used to highlight the belief that race is no longer impacting people's lives. He argues that racism emerges embedded in a host of other arguments that appear to be "color blind" and focus on cultural deficits or markets to explain disparities. Similarly, people mistake awareness for addressing social failures relating to disability. It is too often assumed that ableism is being vanquished by legal demands for accessibility and inclusion. While these are important, they fail to address all the dehumanizing aspects of needing to demand.

Just like Girl in the initial cartoon, even as I work to undermine ableist tendencies, I reify others. What synkinesis gave me was the necessity of ignoring a specific sort of noise in my head. The visceral enmeshments that we don't question forced me to deeply interrogate my embodied responses. When forced to do this, I became more aware of how my embodied responses were entangled with relations of power and privilege. Questioning systemic tendencies that use difference to dispossess, devalue, and dehumanize is imperative. Setting aside neoliberal capitalist values of accumulation and prioritizing the needs of the most vulnerable, looking past our visceral responses for ill or good and toward more humane policy, is essential to achieve a future in which we can all thrive.

Notes

1 Age and severity increase one's risk of developing synkinesis (Slattery & Azizzadeh, 2014). Some suggest e-stim may contribute to developing synkinesis, but that has not been confirmed.

2 For example, several people asked if Gretta Thunberg, the climate activist, had facial difference, but rather her autism would also fall into this category.

3 Cat and Girl is available online and is created by Dorothy. https://catandgirl.com

References

Bearman, S., & Amrhein, M. (2013). Girls, women, and internalized sexism. In E. J. R. David (Ed.), *Internalized oppression: The psychology of marginalized groups*. Springer.

Blairy, S., Herrera, P., & Hess, U. (1999). Mimicry and the judgment of emotional facial expressions. *Journal of Nonverbal Behavior*, *23*(1), 5–41. https://doi.org/10.1023/A:1021370825283

Bonilla-Silva, E. (2017). *Racism without racists color-blind racism and the persistence of racial inequality in America*. Rowman & Littlefield.

Bourdieu, P. (1984). *Distinction: A social critique of the judgment of taste*. Harvard University Press.

Campbell, F. (2009). *Contours of ableism: The production of disability and abledness*. Palgrave Macmillan.

Charmaz, K. (1983). Loss of self: A fundamental form of suffering in the chronically ill. *Sociology of Health & Illness*, *5*(2), 168–197.

Conover, K. J., Israel, T., & Nylund-Gibson, K. (2017). Development and validation of the ableist microaggressions scale. *The Counseling Psychologist*, *45*(4), 570–599. https://doi.org/10.1177/0011000017715317

Corbin, J., & Strauss, A. (2022). *Basics of qualitative research: Techniques and procedures for developing grounded theory*. Sage Publications. ISBN: 978-1-4129-0643-2

Coulson, S. (2017). *Perceived face value: The cost of facial nerve paralysis*. Presentation, International Facial Nerve Symposium. Hollywood, CA.

Coulson, S., O'Dwyer, N. J., Adams, R., & Croxson, G. R. (2004). Expression of emotion and quality of life after facial nerve paralysis. *Otology and Neurotology*, *25*(6), 1014–1019. https://doi.org/10.1097/00129492-200411000-00026. PMID: 15547436.

Daker-White, G., Kingston, H., Payne, K., Greenfield, J., Ealing, J., & Sanders, C. (2012). You don't get told anything, they don't do anything and nothing changes': Medicine as a resource and constraint in progressive ataxia. *Health Expectations*, *18*(2), 177–187. https://doi.org/10.1111/hex.12016

Darling, R. B. (2019). *Disability and identity: Negotiating self in a changing society*. Lynne Rienner Publishers. https://doi.org/10.1515/9781626370951

Du Bois, W. E. B. (2006). The Negro question in the United States. *The New Centennial Review*, *6*(3, 1906), 241–290.

Foucault, M. (1970). *The order of things* (2nd ed.). Routledge. https://doi.org/10.4324/9781315660301

Galletta, A. (2013). *Mastering the semi-structured interview and beyond*. New York University Press. ISBN: 978-0-8147-3294-6

Garland-Thomson, R. (2005, Winter). Feminist disability studies. *Signs*, *30*(2), 1557–1587.

Garland-Thomson, R. (2009). *Staring: How we look*. Oxford University Press.

Haines, K. M., Boyer, C. R., Giovanazzi, C., & Galupo, M. P. (2018). "Not a real family": Microaggressions directed toward LGBTQ families. *Journal of Homosexuality*, *65*(9), 1138–1151. https://doi.org/10.1080/00918369.2017.1406217

Hess, U., & Bourgeois, P. (2010). You smile – I smile: Emotion expression in social interaction. *Biological Psychology*, *84*(3), 514–520. https://doi.org/10.1016/j.biopsycho.2009.11.001. Epub November 11, 2009. PMID: 19913071.

Howson, A. (2013). *The body in society*. Polity Press.

Hughes, M. J. (1998). *The social consequence of facial disfigurement*. Ashgate Publishing.

Kattari, S. K., Olzman, M., & Hanna, M. D. (2018). "You look fine!" Ableist experiences by people with invisible disabilities. *Affilia*, *33*(4), 477–492. https://doi.org/10.1177/0886109918778073

Keller, R. M., & Galgay, C. E. (2010). Microaggressive experiences of people with disabilities. In D. W. Sue (Ed.), *Microaggressions and marginality: Manifestation, dynamics, and impact*. John H. Wiley & Sons.

Levchak, C. C. (2018). *Microaggressions and modern racism: Endurance and evolution*. Palgrave Macmillan.

Lewis, J. A, Mendenhall, R., Harwood, S. A., & Browne Huntt, M. (2016). 'Ain't I a Woman?' Perceived gendered racial microaggressions experienced by black women. *The Counseling Psychologist, 44*(5), 758–80. https://doi.org/10.1177/0011000016641193

Mauldin, L., & Brown, R. L. (2021). Missing pieces: Engaging sociology of disability in medical sociology. *Journal of Health and Social Behavior, 62*(4): 477–492 http://doi.org/10.1177/0022146521109358

Meyer, I. H. (2007). Prejudice and discrimination as social stressors. In I. H. Meyer & E. Northridge (Eds.), *The health of sexual minorities* (pp. 242–267). Washington D.C. APA.

Mitchell, D. T., & Snyder, S. L. (2018). *The biopolitics of disability*. University of Michigan Press.

Nadal, K. L. (2013). *That's so gay! Microaggressions and the lesbian, gay, bisexual, and transgender community, perspectives on sexual orientation and gender diversity series*. American Psychological Association.

Nadal, K. L., & Mendoza, R. J. (2013). Internalized oppression and the lesbian, gay, bisexual, and transgender community. In E. J. R. David (Ed.), *Internalized oppression: The psychology of marginalized groups*. Springer.

Riehle, M., Kempkensteffen, J., & Lincoln, T. M. (2017). Quantifying facial expression synchrony in face to face dyadic interactions: Temporal dynamics of simultaneously recorded facial EMG signals. *Journal of Nonverbal Behavior*, *41*(2), 85–102. https://doi.org/10.1007/s10919-016-0246-8

Ruusuvuori, J., & Peräkylä, A. (2009). Facial and verbal expressions in assessing stories and topics. *Research on Language & Social Interaction*, *42*(4), 377–394. https://doi.org/10.1080/08351810903296499

Schalk, S. (2018). *Bodyminds reimagined: Disability, race, and gender in black women's speculative fiction*. Duke University Press.

Schweik, S. M. (2009). *The ugly laws: Disability in public*. New York University Press.

Shalk, S. (2022). *Black disability politics*. Duke University Press. ISBN: 978-1-4780-92681

Siebers, T. (2008). *Disability theory*. University of Michigan Press.

Slattery, W., & Azizzadeh, B. (2014). *The facial nerve*. Thieme. ISBN: 9781604060508

Solórzano, D., Ceja, M., & Yosso, T. (2000). Critical race theory, racial microaggresions, and campus racial climate: The experiences of African American college students. *Journal of Negro Education*, *69*, 60–73.

Sue, D. W. (2010a). *Microaggressions in everyday life: Race, gender, and sexual orientation*. Wiley.

Sue, D. W. (Ed.). (2010b). *Microaggressions and marginality: Manifestation, dynamics, and impact*. Wiley.

Szymanski, D. M., & Henrichs-Beck, C. (2014). Exploring sexual minority women's experiences of external and internalized heterosexism and sexism and their links to coping and distress. *Sex Roles*, *70*(1), 28–42.

Talley, H. L. (2014). *Saving face: Disfigurement & the politics of appearance*. New York University Press.

VanSwearingen, J., Cohn, J., & Bajaj-Luthra, A. (1999). Specific impairment of smiling increases the severity of depressive symptoms in patients with facial neuromuscular disorders. *Aesthetic Plastic Surgery*, *23*, 416–423. https://doi.org/10.1007/s002669900312

Vernon, A. (1999). The dialectics of multiple identities and the disabled people's movement. *Disability & Society*, *14*(3), 385–398. https://doi.org/10.1080/09687599926217

Wachs, F. L. (2023). *Metamorphosis: Who we become after facial difference*. Rutgers University Press.

Watermeyer, B., & Görgens, T. (2013). Disability and internalized oppression. In E. J. R. David (Ed.), *Internalized oppression: The psychology of marginalized groups*. Springer.

Williams, C. L., Dellinger, C., & Dellinger, K. (2010). *Gender and sexuality in the workplace: 20 (Research in the sociology of work)*. Emerald.

Williams, D. R., & Williams-Morris, R. (2000). Racism and mental health: The African American experience. *Ethnicity & Health*, *5*(3–4), 243–268. https://doi.org/10.1080/713667453

2 Acid Violence and Disfigurement

Lived Experiences of Women Survivors

Beenish Ambereen and Farhan Navid Yousaf

Acid violence, also known as 'vitriolage' refers to an attack in which acid or any corrosive substance is used as a weapon to disfigure a person's physical appearance. This torturing violence, often referred to as *intimate terrorism*, is a life-changing trauma that haunts the victim's life till death (Morrison, 2005, as cited in Mujeeb & Kamal, 2018). Sulphuric and hydrochloric acids are the most frequent weapons of choice, even though the use of the phosphoric has also been recognized alongside the hydrofluoric (Ahmed, 2011). In the premeditated attack, a culprit generally throws acid on the victim's face or body with an intention of permanent disfigurement. When such substances come into contact with skin, they can rapidly dissolve tissues, leading to extensive damage; the severity of the effects depends on the type of acid and the duration of contact (Cambodian League for the Promotion of Human Rights, 2003; Nair, 2014). Long-term effects of these attacks can include blindness, physical deformities, limited functionality (such as reduced mouth or eye movement), psychological distress, and potential social isolation (Song et al., 2019).

Acid violence is considered a gendered phenomenon as a significant majority of the victims tend to be women. For example, Acid Trust International Statistics show that 80% of the victims worldwide are women (ASTI, 2016). Acid Survivors Foundation's (2017) database shows that 68% of the victims in Pakistan are women. The gender disparity is evident in Pakistan's ranking of 145 out of 146 countries for economic, educational, health, and political support for women in the World Economic Forum, Global Gender Report (2022). Additionally, in 2017, the United Nation Development Program (UNDP) rated Pakistan 146th in gender equality with a score of 0.562. Human Rights Commission of Pakistan (2022) reported a worrying increase in acid crimes in Punjab, Pakistan, with cases rising from 34 in 2021 to 59 in 2022. Women in the country continued to suffer from persistent threats such as murder, rape, and other forms of gender-based violence. Additionally, over 400 acid attack victims are recorded annually in Pakistan. The Depilex Smile Again Foundation (2022) also noted a rise in acid attacks against women, with the likelihood of underreporting suggesting the actual numbers are far higher.

The victims of 'vitriolage' are mostly women who are attacked by perpetrators with the brutal intention of disfigurement and lifetime physical and mental ailment

DOI: 10.4324/9781003535591-4

(Hadi, 2017). Chowdhury (2005) argued that chemical attacks are deep-rooted in the belief that a woman's utmost valued asset is her appearance, with rejected male suitors often targeting women to ruin their marriage prospects. The emphasis on beauty and aversion to ugliness has deep historical roots (Eco & McEwen, 2004). Unequal power structures and the low support from society make women feel under privileged (Battered Women's Support Services, 2015). Women are defaced by acid attacks and abused in a Pakistani patriarchal society where they are objectified by men. Furthermore, women are default victims of the fabricated pseudo-power of male figures.

Pakistan, along with other South Asian countries, has a high incidence of acid burn cases, making it a critical area for research. The number of victims, often described as "living corpses," is estimated to be increasing in the country (ASFP, 2017). This violence has a severe impact, forcing victims to abandon education and jobs while suffering from social isolation and low self-esteem. Challenges are exacerbated by illiteracy, financial issues, fear of retaliation, and limited legal awareness.

There is a lack of research on acid violence against women in Pakistan, especially their long-term experiences. Therefore, this study explores the lived experiences of women survivors with more than five years post-incidence to showcase the challenges and factors that make it difficult to regain life normalcy.

Literature Review

Acid violence, reported in many countries of the world, is the worst and most brutal form of human rights violation (Haque & Ahsan, 2014). As a global phenomenon, the United Kingdom and the United States started witnessing it in the 1800s, with a number of reported incidents in Southeast Asia and Africa, and a rapid rise in developing countries, e.g., 20% of burns in Cambodia, 9% in Bangladesh, and 11.5% in Iran (Khoshnami et al., 2017). Recent statistical data from the Health and Social Care Information Centre (HSCIC) from the last ten years depicted a 50% increase in hospital admissions caused by an assault from corrosive substances (Song et al., 2020; The state of human rights, 2013).

Acid Attacks: The Global Context

Table 2.1 clearly indicates the gendered vulnerability to acid violence, with around 1,500 acid attacks reported every year (ASTI, 2018). In 2018, 228 cases were reported in India; 720 attacks were reported in Bangladesh from 2010 to 2018; around 100 cases are reported in Colombia every year; more than 35 are reported in Uganda each year; and 1,485 cases have been reported in Pakistan between 2007 and 2018. However, the actual number of cases might be far more as many victims and the families do not want to file the complaints because of sociocultural barriers and complicated legal issues.

Atiyeh et al. (2009) noted that around 90% of the acid attacks are reported from countries including Bangladesh, India, Nepal, Colombia, Uganda and Pakistan

Table 2.1 Context and data of acid attack victims (ASTI, 2018)

Context of Acid Attacks	*Year*	*No. of Cases*	*Gender of the Victim*
Worldwide	Every Year	1,500	80% victims are female
India	2018	228	ASTI indicates that most of the victims are women and girls
Bangladesh	2010–2018	720	70% victims are female
Colombia	Every year	100	Most of the victims are women and girls
Uganda	Every year	35 plus	Most of the victims are women and girls
Pakistan	2007–2018	1485	ASFP database shows that that 68% of the females are victimized

(Atiyeh et al., 2009). In Bangladesh, Executive Director of the Acid Survivors Foundation (ASF) reported that acid is used by men not to kill women but to disfigure them (Bandyopadhyay, 2003). Pakistan has no exception to acid violence where gender-based violence is normal in the daily lives of women (Social Policy Development Center, 2012, p. 5). Although Pakistan shows a significant acid assault rate, no approved statistical data has been released by the government. Despite the prevalence of such attacks in the country, accurate statistical data is difficult to obtain due to the remoteness of some areas (Zia, 2013) and the underreporting and misreporting of these incidents (Solberg, 2010). The existing literature and data related to acid attacks include reports published by different NGOs because, in Pakistan, NGOs are a significant source of information on the subject (Zia, 2013). Considering the complications of data collection from rural and remote areas, the actual number of acid attacks in Pakistan is likely much higher than reported (Zia, 2013; Solberg, 2010).

ASF has confirmed the continuation of these patterns of acid assaults in more recent years (ASFP, 2015). A woman's face is deformed and her body is disfigured to demolish her identity. Owing to the social importance of the face, facially disfigured individuals are stigmatized. Kuriakose et al., 2017; Swanson, 2002).

The Inter-American Conference on the Punishment, Prevention, and Eradication of Violence against Women defines 'violence against women' as gender-based, with the propensity to include physical disfigurement and mental torture: "Gender-based violence is across the board and is considered as so normal in Pakistani women's lives" (Social Policy Development Center, 2012, p. 5). The physical and long-lasting impacts of 'vitriolage' are more evident after the attack, including pain, possible sightlessness, and facial deformity (Khoshnami et al., 2017). Facial deformity is yet the most gut-wrenching consequence of an acid attack and is directly related to the changes in the body after the act of victimization (Mujeeb & Kamal, 2018). When attacked, victims abruptly cover their faces to stop the substance coming towards their face, which often causes hand injuries (Patel, 2014), mutilating the skin and tissues and often deep into the bones (Haque & Ahsan, 2014). The extent of skin damage is so severe that the victim is unable to tolerate sunlight exposure (Cambodian League for the Promotion and

Defense of Human Rights, 2003). In addition to acid-burned body parts, victims breathe in deadly acid vapors, which typically lead to poisoning of victim's lungs and throat swelling, elevating both the risk of asphyxiation and death (Law Commission of India, 2009).

Acid attacks cause both immediate disfigurement and long-term physical deformity. It results in torturing pain and the victim suffers from a lifetime of defacement (Bandyopadhyay & Khan, 2003). The victims suffer from agonizing lifetime physical and psychological disabilities which make them impaired, disfigured, and disabled (Mannan, 1995 as cited by Islam et al., 2014). Acid leaves severe repercussions even after the wounds are healed. Because of the disfigurement, victims may not be able to close eyelids, and their vision may be partially impaired. They may be unable to open or close their mouth, leading to tooth decay and difficulty in eating. There can be the destruction of ear cartilage and the consequent inability to move it, making the victim more susceptible to further deformity, infections, and difficulties in hearing (Acid attacks expose the victim's life to continuous physical, financial, social, and medical stigma. This stigmatized trauma brings about ongoing physical surgeries to recover from deformity, and psychological therapeutic sessions, particularly from their close family (Anand, 2016).

Methodology

Using a phenomenological approach (Smith, 2017), this research focuses on the lived experiences of disfigured acid attack survivors within the paradigm of an interpretive qualitative research design. Phenomenological interpretation raises the unheard voices of the disfigured female bodies with the sagas of acid attack, both in terms of what was experienced and how. It documents in detail a phenomenon through the participant's personal experiences and unique perception of objects and events.

For this research, 25 participants were recruited. Since the main objective was to explore the long-term experiences of women surviving acid attacks, only women who had experienced acid violence within the last five years were recruited. The participants were approached with the help of two leading non-governmental organizations (Acid Survivor Foundation and Depilex Smile Again Foundation) that work on the issue of acid violence against women in Pakistan. Most of the acid attack victims were from Punjab, particularly southern Punjab, which was the setting of this study. The victims described their long-term experiences and challenges as acid attack survivors with disfigured facial and bodily appearance. Considering the sensitivity of the subject matter, we fulfilled the ethical standards and ensured trustworthiness, took measures to preserve the privacy of victims' information, and maintained confidentiality.

In-depth interviews were conducted with selected participants in their local language. Later on, the interviews were translated, transcribed, and manually coded to extract themes for data analysis. As an inductive and bottom-up approach, phenomenology provides room to read and re-read the raw data (interviews) so that the coding process can help identify important aspects. Contextualization of the acquired data was done by systematic identification of themes and sub-themes (Braun & Clarke, 2006). Considering the sensitiveness of the research, all participants have been given pseudonyms to preserve their privacy.

Findings

Unfolding the experiences of acid attack survivors reveals sagas of anxiety, depression, social isolation, poverty, and a series of traumatic health issues. The lived experiences of acid victims fill the canvas of this research with never-ending suffering. Male dominance as a social dogma has been seen as a prevailing factor in Pakistani society. Men are considered to be the masters and women their subordinates, bound to obey them. Men's superficial power structures are difficult to challenge, and those who voice for their rights or subjective opinion are burnt alive, leaving their bodies disfigured and souls deprived forever.

Combating Health and Treatment Impediments

Health and medical treatment is the foremost concern of acid attack victims. A perpetrator attacks the face of a woman with an intention of deformation and disfigurement. The damage is not only done physically, but it also causes psychological detriment.

Uzma, one of the survivors, was acid-attacked by her lover for rejecting him as a marriage suitor. After this attack, she suffered from major health issues with no proper medical treatments. She had to leave the government hospital due to its lack of medical facilities and she was unable to pay for high-cost treatment in private hospitals. She was left with no option, discontinuing her medical treatment and enduring life-long pain. She said:

> I have lost vision of both eyes due to the acid attack. Doctors say that the cornea has been burnt. Cornea grafting has to be done and right now I am completely blind and cannot learn any skill. I am dependent on others. There have been so many medicines, injections, and painful repeated surgeries; I have to bear and live with it.

Further, she revealed her permanent blindness with no hope of recovery:

> In the beginning my surgeries were planned in government hospitals, like grafting etc., but the government hospitals are not properly equipped with the latest technologies and sometimes the operation would fail. Secondly, in those hospitals the surgeries are free but most of the medicines are always out of stock and we have to buy such expensive medicines on our own, that's why I quit the government hospital and stop [sic] taking the treatment for my eyes and vision. I am unable to take treatments from private hospitals because they are expensive and I cannot afford [sic]. I have to bear; what else can I do?

What emerges from the interviews is that the majority of the acid survivors belong to a lower economic status and could not afford expensive advanced medical treatment. While probing through the acquired data, we found that courage and hope played a pivotal role in acid victims' survival. Nazish, a participant from southern Punjab, was victimized by her husband who suspected an illicit affair. The acid burnt her face thoroughly and stretched her skin so stiffly that her neck was frozen. Nazish stated:

> I have undergone four to five surgeries. Now I need some advanced surgeries on my own expenses. Still, I am in a lot of pain. In winters, I cannot wear a sweater nor can I take a blanket because my skin develops a burning sensation which is intolerable. Whereas in hot summers, the skin sweats and develops intense itching and ultimately starts bleeding. It becomes unbearable to stand the thinnest of fabric on my skin. I am unable to afford long-term medication due to my economic conditions. Neither any NGO nor government has any long-term plan for us. But I am bearing all this with courage and hope that one day I'll be fine.

A legitimate hope of improvement lies somewhere in the survivors' hearts, yet they point out the lack of long-term medical plans, which encompass medication, surgeries, and rehabilitation. The lived experiences with physical impairment and treatment obstacles are harsh realities of their society.

Physical appearance and facial beauty holds great significance, and that is demolished as a consequence of acid attacks. A young participant, Asima, practices different strategies to dodge the trauma by avoiding people or talking back to the bully. In her interview, Asima revealed that she used to react when bullied by someone. She said:

> You know that for a girl, [the] face is highly important as it is the first thing everybody, including men and women, looks at. People make comments at my face and often I feel they don't want to see me. Like some say that when I go in front of them, their children get scared. When I used to pass through the street, people would ask me to frighten their children. At first, I tried to stay calm and did not react to such behaviors. I used to cry when I was alone or I would tell only my mother about it. But later, I started reacting. I said to them that I am not some monster or a joker type thing to whom they are demanding to frighten their children. Why should I frighten their kids?

Maria, another survivor, was victimized by her neighbor out of revenge. She said that she used to hide her mutilated face with a veil, sunglasses, and with her hair. Maria stated, "The face is incredibly important, especially for women. Due to the burns, my eye was permanently damaged, leaving a hollow that noticeably changes how I look. When I go out, people's lingering stares make me feel like I don't belong to this world, constantly reminding me of being an outsider". Naheed, who was burnt by her brother-in-law, stated, "My face is more than 60%

burnt. Only my ears were left un-burnt. Otherwise, my nose, lips, cheeks and forehead were burnt. I usually wear big sunglasses with a covered scarf so no one can see my face." The same kind of statement came from Asia, who was attacked out of jealousy by her husband's first wife. She stated, "By looking at my face or touching my body, I feel traumatized by the skeletal structure. The sockets where my eyes used to be are now like deep ditches, making me feel incredibly ugly and unable to accept this profound change in my appearance".

These claims reinforce the idea of facial beauty as a defining asset for a woman. Acid attacks turn a beautiful face into a deformed entity – depriving the woman of all perks of living as a normal human being for the rest of her life.

Acid Victims' Social Fallout

Social stigma is so much attached to disfigurement that people do not let victims with a deformed appearance live a normal life. This situation is worsened by the lack of empathy from other people.

Acid attacks leave indelible marks on victims' body, mind and soul. The psychological impact of an acid attack leaves the disfigured victim with never-ending feelings of loss, anxiety, depression, and despair. Low self-esteem, sadness, feelings of loneliness and hopelessness prevail over the victims' psyche due to their deformed appearance and crippled life. Lack of interest in life, difficulty in coping with the attack's aftermath, and ongoing sadness lead to chronic depression and anxiety. A sense of worthlessness often leads to thoughts of suicide or self-harm.

Furthermore, disfigurement as a consequence of an acid attack brings another trauma. Along with physical and psychological suffering, a variety of social challenges enter the survivors' life, depriving them of security, and legal and moral support.

Physical impairment not only opens up to a life-long destitution and disability, but also social exclusion. This 'stigma' creates situations where acid victims are subject to social disintegration, judgment, and marginalization. In our indigenous social setup, acid survivors' association with this traumatic event leads to stereotypical labeling and discrimination. Social alienation, based on their physical appearance, is a major 'stigma' that generates a feeling of being 'other.' Its detrimental effects further lead to permanent disconnection from society.

Shahjahan, a survivor who was attacked by her husband, revealed her struggle to reintegrate into society as an acid attack survivor. She stated:

> When I attend family gatherings, marriage functions, most of the time people laugh at me. One day a lady came to me at a marriage function and said, "is it necessary for you to wear such a bright color, look at your face, you look like a joker and you need to stay in [sic] home, our kids are scared because of you." People usually do this, but if someone makes fun of me, it is depressing. That's why I quit to appear [sic] in such gatherings.

Zarmina, another survivor, has been living with one blind eye and severe facial deformity for the past 12 years. To this day, her instinct to hide herself is profound.

Zarmina says, "After so many years have passed, I still avoid facing people . . . at least I cannot hear their pinching words, this is enough for me." Likewise, Maria discussed the social stigmatization and lack of social support as acid attack survivor:

> I rarely attend family functions and social gatherings. If I go there, I have to answer everyone about the things I have gone through and about how I am leading my life, so I believe it's better not to go. The general reaction shown by people is very hurtful, such as they laugh seeing my condition and it shatters my confidence.

Disfigurement not only brings social stigmatization but also social rejection, especially in a world where the beauty or physical appearance of a woman is the most significant criterion of being desirable. An unfortunate fact is that acid survivors' stigmatization forces them to choose isolation. Their deteriorated state of mind and disfigured appearances cut them off from society and contributed to them becoming withdrawn. Samina was attacked by her lover for refusing his marriage proposal: "I started my own little beauty parlor, but unfortunately it didn't work. People don't want to come to get services because of my ugly looks. This is a dilemma: people can't accept me as a normal human being so I stopped working and limited myself to staying at home."

Like other forms of violence, victim blaming is associated with acid violence against women. This occurs when people, media, or others respond to the tragedy of an acid attack with negativity toward and disapproval of the victim. Based on many misinterpretations, the victim is considered to be the one to blame. Amber, a respondent who refused the love proposal of her cousin, stated:

> Now no one wants to see me, neither my family nor relatives nor my fiancé who claimed to love me. Everyone thinks that it was my own fault because they assume that day I invited my cousin inside my home to have some illicit, forbidden relationship with him. It's an accusation on me. I never invited him nor did I ever have any bad intentions of such sort. After this allegation, I cut myself from my whole family because I can't bear their accused words for me.

In the case of acid violence, victim blaming originates at home and spreads its negative outcomes through various segments of life. Victims not only lose their bodily integrity, but also the trust of their family and society. Further, this suffering is attributed to their own wrongdoings. Such unfair accusations lead to far more challenging circumstances. Uzma, who was also attacked by her lover, reflected on the society that failed to discern the plight of the victims, saying, "On the one hand, you have faced a tragedy and on the other hand people of your area and others start blaming the victim, saying that she must have done something to deserve this.

In the rural and under-developed regions of Punjab, victim blaming is more common. Humera, another victim, revealed the relationship between power structures and acid attacks, according to which a husband feels authorized to punish his wife and the gender norms place women at the lowest point of the social hierarchical structures. Acid attacks are particularly a gender-based victimization, thus creating a dual form of marginalization for women. She told us, "Actually, in our society, it is very hard for people to believe that the woman was not at fault and that she is an innocent victim. Our society always blames women. They think she must be doing something wrong because her husband or in-laws have done this to her."

Rehabilitation Challenges

Rehabilitation is an intricate process which intends to empower acid attack victims and move them towards normalcy. It is a multifaceted process of restoration that incorporates vocational training, education, mental well-being, autonomy, employability, entrepreneurship, and reintegration into society. Rehabilitation aims to provide survivors the tools to regain control over their lives and to facilitate their transition to self-sufficiency. However, the data of this research shows that even after many years, the rehabilitation and reintegration of victims remains a serious challenge.

Victims' economic dependence hinders the assertion of their personal identity. They are not allowed to go out or earn money, therefore, their underprivileged financial status is an obstacle towards independence. One of the participants, Zarmina, stated:

> I do not have any education or skill that could provide employment. My economic crises have made me incapable of taking any action against those who have made my life miserable. I want to be independent. But [a] job and income are crucial for reclaiming a sense of normalcy in life. Unfortunately, a lot of women who suffer from this trauma have no empowerment opportunities and jobs. The feeling of being a burden remains constant which deteriorates our efforts to move to life normalcy.

Likewise, another participant Naheed stated that, "When I went to apply for jobs, people asked me how I will survive with this problem. They said that the environment of their office will be affected because of my burnt face. They just don't realize how [sic] their thinking hurts other people; we were not born like this."

In traditional societies like Pakistan, marriage is considered a strong social path to ensure security and support for women. However, women with disfigured faces and bodies do not reach the qualifying beauty standards of society and it becomes really hard for them to find a match for marriage. Thus, such young women are forced to face the challenges of their lives without a life partner. Uzma, a young participant, shared:

> I had some dreams about marriage, children, and happy marital life but my life is finished as nobody wants to marry me because of my injuries. This makes me more upset that I am worthless and have to live all my live [sic]

> alone. Sometimes my mother shows a desire of my marriage but I know this would never happen because people want beautiful faces not beautiful souls.

In Pakistan, women are left unmarried for many reasons, like not having fair skin complexion, less education, dowry, etc. In such a judgmental scenario, there is no safe space for vulnerable and physically deformed women.

Education and skills, apart from medical treatment, are crucial factors for a comprehensive rehabilitation of acid attack survivors. Women are set back on the socioeconomic ladder due to illiteracy. The trauma from an acid attack further hinders victim's access to education, creating a significant barrier to independence. Disability, disfigurement, and negative behaviors make them unable to attend any conventional educational setup. Rubina shared about her health condition, which directly impedes her ability to pursue education:

> My problem is that one of my eyes stays open. It cannot be closed. Even when I sleep, it remains open and water keeps coming out of it. When I try to read something, there comes a lot of stress on my eyes and more water starts pouring out. So, I left my study. I wish I could study and become a lawyer to work free for all acid survivors.

The narratives of the study participants show that some of them had been receiving an education before the acid attack, but due to negative behaviors towards them, they left education. This persistent trend challenges the rehabilitation process for such victims. Noreen shared a similar issue:

> I tried to continue studying and rejoined school. But I did not feel comfortable there. People used to pass comments and looked at me with weird expressions, though I used to keep my face covered throughout the day, but all went in vain. Nobody wanted to even sit with me.

Education and skills can be powerful tools to aid acid attack survivors to regain their independence, sense of self-worth, and confidence. It can guide them to acquire essential skills and resources for their personal and professional growth. However, as shared by many participants, prejudice—reflected in reduced understanding, concern, or sensitivity—takes a toll on the victims, resulting in social withdrawal, making their rehabilitation and reintegration nearly impossible.

Discussion

The overarching themes of health and treatment obstacles, social fallout, and rehabilitation challenges are deeply interwoven with the role of patriarchy, underprivileged socioeconomic status of women, and limited access to basic resources. These themes are a constant murmur in the background of acid victims' life stories.

A report by ASF highlighted Punjab as showing the highest ratio of acid attack cases, particularly in southern Punjab, which demands notice of law enforcement agencies and other stakeholders or policymakers (ASFP, 2017). Higher number of acid attack cases in southern Punjab can be associated with a patriarchal context where men are considered dominant figures of the family and females as a dependent gender. This patriarchal setup has consequently made women more vulnerable to acid attacks (Singh et al., 2018).

In patriarchal family structures, victimizing women has appeared as a learned behavior. In the walls of patriarchy, men exercise their dominance to control women (Khan & Hussain, 2008) and to keep them in subordinate positions. Such undue authority and desire to oppress them. If women assert their decision or opinion, it is considered as disobedience towards their men, which leads to retaliation. Deforming a woman's body appearance satisfies their revenge. Rejected suitors are frequently the perpetrators of acid attacks, where women are victimized by their ex-fiancés and rejected love proposals. In a patriarchal setup, men being rejected by a woman is viewed as a matter of great disrespect. Out of the suffocating walls of patriarchy, women cannot express their preferences for their lives. Men's desire to assert manhood is a prominent motive of acid attacks (Anwary, 2003).

Patriarchal power structures perpetuate violence against women, leading women to a spiraling identity crisis. Women in Pakistan are commonly recognized only as wives, mothers, daughters, and sisters, with little or no self-identity (Mumtaz & Shaheed, 1987). Men use acid as a tool to control women who retaliate against the set patterns of patriarchal norms; thus, the patriarchy is immensely interwoven with women's identity crisis and victimization.

Men are privileged as they are the breadwinners of the family, whereas women are financially dependent. This financial dependence excludes women from the dominant social class and places them in a lower socioeconomic status (Weissman, 2007). The findings show that some victims desired to be financially independent, but their dependence on male family members for decision making hindered their efforts. Conflict dynamics of acid violence highlight that the root cause of this issue lies in the patriarchy and hegemonic masculinity, which create a societal structure where women are dependent on men by default (Chowdhury, 2014). The underprivileged socioeconomic state of the victims, as a significant factor, contributes to the occurrence of acid attacks (Jabeen et al., 2020). Acid victims mostly belong to lower-income families who couldn't bear the expenses of prolonged medication and surgeries. Thus, the low socioeconomic status of acid attack victims hinders their way towards well-being and normalcy in life.

Conclusion

This qualitative research study has a limitation in that it delineates a thorough saga of the lived experiences of acid attack survivors who had experienced acid attacks within the last five years. Participants met the particular criteria to be included in the research. Moreover, this study was limited to those acid survivors who acquired services from Acid Survivors Foundation (ASF) and Depilex Smileagain Foundation, hence all other reported and unreported acid attack cases were excluded.

Acid survivors not only struggle with physical scars, but also damage inflicted on their psyches. Social stigmatization and victim blaming leads to isolation and alienation. Disfigurement not only brings a variety of health concerns, but also opens up a painful saga of rehabilitation challenges. Acid attack survivors mostly belong to a lower socioeconomic status and cannot afford expensive medical treatments after an acid attack. Moreover, the pain of losing facial beauty with no chance of regaining it is a constant challenge. Acid attacks cause life-lasting social and physical disfigurement "for survivors to endure."

References

Acid Survivors Foundation, Pakistan. (2015, September). *Acid violence in Pakistan: A situational analysis*. https://asfpakistan.org/wp-content/uploads/2017/02/SAAV-report-2015.pdf

Acid Survivors Foundation, Pakistan. (2017). *Report: "Countering acid burn violence in Pakistan: A success story*. https://asfpakistan.org/wp-content/uploads/2018/04/Countering-ABV-in-Pakistan-2017.pdf

Acid Survivors Trust International. (2016). *Survivor stories: Naieema, Pakistan*. http://www.acidviolence.org/index.php/survivors/stories/naieema/pakistan

Acid Survivors Trust International. (2018). *Acid attack statistics Pakistan*. https://www.asti.org.uk/a-worldwide-problem.html

Ahmed, N. (2011). Acid attacks on women: An appraisal of the Indian legal response. *Asia-Pacific Journal on Human Rights and the Law*, *12*(2), 55–72.

Anand, J. (2016, April 7). New guidelines to tackle acid attacks. *The Hindu*. https://www.thehindu.com/news/cities/Delhi/new-guidelines-to-tackle-acidattacks/article6724502.ece

Anwary, A. (2003). Acid violence and medical care in Bangladesh: Women's activism as care work. *Gender & Society*, *17*(2), 305–313. https://doi.org/10.1177/0891243202250851

Atiyeh, B. S., Costagliola, M., & Hayek, S. N. (2009). Burn prevention mechanisms and outcomes: Pitfalls, failures and successes. *Burns*, *35*(2), 181–193. https://www.sciencedirect.com/science/article/abs/pii/S030541790800199X

Bandyopadhyay, M., & Khan, M. R. (2003). Loss of face: Violence against women in South Asia. In L. Manderson & L. R. Bennett (Eds.), *Violence against women in Asian societies* (pp. 61–75). Routledge.

Battered Women's Support Services. (2015). *Facts on violence against women and children*. https://www.bwss.org/resources/information-on-abuse/numbersare-people-%20too/#_ftnref33

Braun, V., & Clarke, V. (2006). Using thematic analysis in psychology. *Qualitative Research in Psychology*, *3*(2), 77–101. https://doi.org/10.1191/1478088706qp063oa

Cambodian League for the Promotion and Defense of Human Rights. (2003). *Living in the shadows: Acid attacks in Cambodia*. Project Against Torture. https://www.licadhocambodia.org/reports/files/41acid%20report%20English.pdf

Chowdhury, E. H. (2005). Feminist negotiations: Contesting narratives of the campaign against acid violence in Bangladesh. *Meridians: Feminism, Race, Transnationalism*, *6*(1), 163–192. https://doi.org/10.1353/mer.2005.0018

Chowdhury, E. H. (2014). Rethinking patriarchy, culture and masculinity: Transnational narratives of gender violence and human rights advocacy. *Hawwa*, *12*(1), 79–100. https://doi.org/10.1163/15692086-12341253

Depilex Smile Again Foundation. (2022). *Annual report 2022*. https://staging.depilexsmileagain.com/wp-content/uploads/2023/03/Depilex-Smileagain-Annual-Report-2022.pdf

Eco, U., & McEwen, A. (2004). *History of beauty*. Rizzoli International Publications. https://www.biblio.com/book/history-beauty-eco-umberto-alastairmcewen/d/1396635666

Hadi, A. (2017). Patriarchy and gender-based violence in Pakistan. *European Journal of Social Sciences Education and Research*, *4*(2), 297–304. https://doi.org/10.26417/ejser.v10i2.p297-304

Haque, S. E., & Ahsan, H. (2014). Human rights violations against women: Acid violence in Bangladesh. *American Journal of Preventive Medicine*, *46*(2), 216–217. https://doi.org/10.1016/j.amepre.2013.10.013

Human Rights Commission of Pakistan. (2022). *State of human rights in 2022*. HRCP. https://hrcp-web.org/hrcpweb/wp-content/uploads/2020/09/2023-State-ofhuman-rights-in-2022.pdf

Islam, M. J., Uddin, M. J., Hossain, M. S., Amin, M. R., Khandaker, M. N., Rahman, A. M., & Taher, A. (2014). Characterization of acid burn victims in two selected health facilities in Dhaka City. *Bangladesh Medical Journal*, *43*(2), 94–99. https://doi.org/10.3329/bmj.v43i2.21391

Jabeen, S., Riaz, M., & Omer, S. (2020). Applying socioecological framework to acid attack violence: An exploration of inhabitant factors. *Journal of Interpersonal Violence*, *36*(23–24).

Khan, A., & Hussain, R. (2008). Violence against women in Pakistan: Perceptions and experiences of domestic violence. *Asian Studies Review*, *32*(2), 239–253. https://doi.org/10.1080/10357820802062181

Khoshnami, M. S., Mohammadi, E., Addelyan Rasi, H., Khankeh, H. R., & Arshi, M. (2017). Conceptual model of acid attacks based on survivor's experiences: Lessons from a qualitative exploration. *Burns*, *43*(3), 608–618. https://doi.org/10.1016/j.burns.2016.10.003

Kuriakose, F., Mallick, N., & Iyer, D. K. (2017). Acid violence in South Asia: A structural analysis toward transformative justice. *ANTYAJAA: Indian Journal of Women and Social Change*, *2*(1), 65–80. https://doi.org/10.1177/2455632717708717

Law Commission of India. (2009). *The inclusion of acid attacks as specific offences in the Indian penal code and a law for compensation for victims of crime* (226). https://cdnbbsr.s3waas.gov.in/s3ca0daec69b5adc880fb464895726dbdf/uploads/2022/08/2022081066.pdf

Mujeeb, A., & Kamal, A. (2018). Interpersonal relationships, psychological effects, and coping strategies among acid burn female victims. *Pakistan Journal of Psychological Research*, *33*(2), 575–590.

Mumtaz, K., & Shaheed, F. (1987). *Women of Pakistan: Two steps forward, one step back?* Zed Books.

Nair, A. R. (2014). Acid attack-violence against women: Need of the hour. *Journal of Innovative Research and Solution*, *1*(1), 107–117.

Patel, M. (2014). A desire to disfigure: Acid attack in India. *International Journal of Criminology and Sociological Theory*, *7*(2), 1–11. https://ijcst.journals.yorku.ca/index.php/ijcst/article/view/39702

Singh, M., Kumar, V., Rupani, R., Kumari, S., Shiuli, Yadav, P. K., Singh, R., & Verma, A. K. (2018). Acid attack on women: A new face of gender-based violence in India. *Indian Journal of Burns*, *26*, 83–86.

Social Policy and Development Center. (2012). *The socio-economic cost of violence against women: A case study of Karachi* (Report 5). The Times Press Pvt. Limited.

Solberg, K. (2010). Pakistan moves to tackle acid violence. *The Lancet*, *376*(9748), 1209–1210. https://doi.org/10.1016/s0140-6736(10)61863-6

Song, M., Armstrong, A., & Murray, A. (2020). Acid attacks: Broadening the multidisciplinary team to improve outcomes. *Burns*, *46*(3), 514–519. https://doi.org/10.1016/j.burns.2019.03.018

Swanson, J. (2002). Acid attacks: Bangladesh's efforts to stop the violence. *Harvard Health Policy Review*, *3*(1).

The state of human rights. (2013). https://hrcp-web.org/hrcpweb/wp-content/uploads/2020/09/2014-State-ofhuman-rights-in-2013-EN.pdf

Weissman, D. (2007). The personal is political and economic: Rethinking domestic violence. *Brigham Young University Law Review*, 387–450. https://digitalcommons.law.byu.edu/lawreview/vol2007/iss2/3
World Economic Forum, Global Gender Report. (2022). https://www3.weforum.org/docs/WEF_GGGR_2022.pdf
Zia, T. (2013). *Acid violence in Pakistan*. Center for the Study of Women. https://escholarship.org/uc/item/65v958z1

3 "Those Experiences While Good Also Made Me Feel Uncomfortable and Broken"

A Male's Perspective of Living with Facial Eye Disfigurement

Zali O'Dea and Jane Southcott

Faces are central to communication and living with a facial disfigurement (FD) can have negative impacts on communication (Cingi et al., 2020). People society view as beautiful are thought to be more trustworthy (Sofer et al., 2017), and those who live with a disfigurement are often portrayed as bad, evil, or pathetic.

The Anomalous Man aired on 4 May 2023 by Saturday Night Live, a production of NBC. This skit reinforced old tropes that people living with FD put up with on a daily basis. In this skit, a grotesquely facially disfigured man was shown with a crablike claw for a hand, horns stemming from his forehead, an obvious skin tag on his lip, a piglike nose, and an extra eye in his back which blinked and could see. This eye was repugnant, meant to shock the viewers, and heighten the entertainment value of the skit at the expense of the FD and facially eye disfigured (FED) community. Online response to this skit from members of the FD community was swift, angry, and condemnatory. On 7 May, the activist group FaceOut Project responded with a public letter in which they stated that the skit was "profoundly problematic, in ways that were likely unintended, but still serious" (DeGuire et al., 2024). The letter continued:

1. The Anomalous Man is characterized as isolated and mocked, with terrible self-esteem.
2. It is implied that the woman who loves him is saintly for doing so and he is terribly fortunate to be desired at all.
3. His appearance is insulted relentlessly.
4. The idea that he could be sexually active is revealed as the ridiculous punchline of the sketch. (DeGuire et al., 2024).

O'Dea expanded on this critique with a special announcement on her regular YouTube channel supporting the critique and raising additional concerns for the FED community (O'Dea, 2024).

A person can be born with a FD or acquire it through trauma or disease. One in 111 people live with facial disfigurement (Disfigurement in the UK, 2017). FD is an umbrella term which encompasses varying conditions that affect the appearance of the face, such as cleft lip and craniofacial syndromes like moebius syndrome.

DOI: 10.4324/9781003535591-5

These have been researched in several ways, generally through a medical/psychological lens (Bogart et al., 2017; Bogart & Hemmesch, 2016; Demir, 2011; Feragen et al., 1999; Hamlet & Harcourt, 2015; Millar et al., 2013; Millard & Richman, 2001). In 2020 an extensive report was conducted by Lancet Global Health that identified the impact of the ever-growing issues of eye disease and the costs of vision loss to society (Burton et al., 2021). It is imperative that these phenomena are researched and the voices of people living with FED are shared because the frequently heard dismissive comment, "it is only an eye" implies that an eye is a small thing without significance. However, the loss of an eye and FED has long-term effects on people's quality of life regardless of being born with FED or having acquired it through disease/trauma. This chapter will look at one section of the FD, FED, which is "any condition or trauma which disfigures the eyes, either to the eye itself, eye lid or surrounding area. This can pertain to either one or two eyes" (O'Dea, 2023, p. 345). There is little research on understanding the lived experiences of people living with FED (LwFED), particularly the experiences of males.

We present a case study of Derek (pseudonym), a 32-year-old male from North America and his lived experience of LwFED. Derek lives with monocular vision (vision in one eye only) which, according to many governments, worldwide is not deemed as vision impaired, including the USA, UK, and Australia. Although statistics on the prevalence of monocular vision are hard to locate, in Australia, approximately 11/1000 people live with monocular vision (Keel et al., 2017). In the USA between 3–4/1000 people have removal of the eye (enucleation) and 3–4/100,000 people have an acquired third nerve palsy (this figure increases with age) (Erie et al., 1992; Fang et al., 2017). Given the prevalence and impact of FED on both individuals and society, it is important to have a clear understanding of what constitutes living successfully with FED, such as the four foundational blocks offered by O'Dea (2018, 2023): Active Intentional Decisions, Forgiveness, Healthy Self-esteem, and Resilience. This is discussed in more detail in this chapter in reference to our participant, Derek.

Literature Review

Recently, LwFED has become the subject of research. An autoethnographic article by the first author of this chapter is believed to be the first of its kind concerning LwFED (O'Dea, 2018). Other research has explored a mother with LwFED acquired by trauma or rare cancer and her family, and a non-FED mother's experiences parenting her child with LwFED (O'Dea & Southcott, 2023a, 2023b). Another study explored the complexities of a family spanning three generations with four members simultaneously LwFED (O'Dea & Southcott, 2024). LwFED is not only issue for an individual, but an entire family can be affected, including, but not limited to, parents and siblings (Berger & Dalton, 2011; Bogart et al., 2017; Grollemund et al., 2020; Payakachat et al., 2011; Upadhyaya, 2014; Zelihić et al., 2021). People living with FED and FD speak predominantly about the psychosocial distress of being stared at and avoided whilst in public (Gagnon, 2016; O'Dea,

2023; Rumsey et al., 1982). People living with FED are "five times more likely than the general population to have no paid work" (Williamson, 2023, p. 63) and are the least preferred candidate for the job and less likely to obtain promotions (Stevenage & McKay, 1999; Williamson, 2023). People LwFED/FD people are treated as if they have an infectious disease, experience cyber bullying, bullying at school and in the workforce, are stigmatized, experience anxiety and depression, and may withdraw from society (Al Bdour & Mohamed, 2018; Bonanno & Esmaeli, 2012; Frances, 2004; Jones et al., 2021; Ryan et al., 2012).

While there has been a sudden influx of lived experience with FED, this mostly has been written about from a female perspective of either parenting a child LwFED or mothering whilst LwFED. To our knowledge, there is not a case study looking at a male's experience into this phenomenon. This chapter offers a glimpse into a male's expert understanding of LwFED.

Methodology

This inductive qualitative case study of Derek employs Interpretative Phenomenological Analysis (IPA), which empowers the subject as the expert of his lived experience, permitting personal expression, knowledge, and experience (Eatough & Smith, 2006; Smith, 2017; Smith et al., 2009). With ethical approval, data were gathered by the first author via a single semi-structured online interview with Derek. Although there was an option for a follow-up interview, Derek felt that he had said all he wished to. Semi-structured interviews are conversational in style and "are often the best way for learning about the *motivations* behind people's choices and behaviour, their *attitudes and beliefs,* and the *impacts on their lives* of specific . . . events" (Italics in original) (Raworth et al., 2012). The first author is an insider, an individual LwFED, she is also a published researcher within the field. She is well-versed in interviewing as she is also a specialist counselling within the field. The second author is an experienced IPA researcher who brings an ethical perspective to this study. The interview transcription was read, re-read, and analysed independently by both authors to enhance the credibility of our findings. Both authors independently analysed the interview transcripts to enhance the credibility of the analysis (Fade, 2004). Following debate and negotiation, the outcome of the sharing of understandings and interpretations was agreed upon and a composite analysis was generated (Wagstaff et al., 2014). The table of codes, emerging themes, and overarching themes follows our introduction of our participant. Throughout the text, verbatim quotations foreground Derek as the expert in his own experiences.

Introducing Derek

Derek is 32 and lives in North America. His family of origin consisted of his mother, father, and two sisters. Derek is the middle child. Before the accident, Derek considered himself to be an average young man who had just graduated from high school and was a keen motorbike rider. Derek acquired his FED at the age of 19 in a motorcycle accident. He recalls:

> A car went through a stop sign, and I hit the side of her car. I broke all the bones in my face, several vertebrae and several bones in my arms and legs, and so breaking my cheeks, that caused me to lose vision in my left eye and to essentially disfigure around my face.

His family "were very supportive." His injuries were so severe that "at first the doctors didn't think I was going to survive." After a week, they knew he would survive with a long recovery ahead of him due to "a lot of facial and head trauma and damage." His family "just kind of rallied and supported." At the time of the accident, his sisters were 22 and 17 and all siblings were living in the family home.

Derek admits it is a struggle knowing that if someone had not been careless, he wouldn't be LwFED. He explains that,

> the lady that caused my accident had acknowledged having several glasses of wine that morning, and they also found marijuana in her car under her driver's seat. She survived [and]. . . she was totally fine. She had advanced stages of multiple sclerosis . . . and she shouldn't have been driving in the first place. Her disease had progressed to the point where a year and a half later she passed away from it.

Derek experienced a great deal of frustration and anger towards her, which "disappeared when I saw her obituary. The anger towards her just disappeared because she was dead, there was no conversation anymore, she was gone." His anger dissipated quickly because at the time:

> I didn't have the time or energy to focus on being angry or frustrated at her because I had a lovely girlfriend, I was going back to school, I was working out a lot, I was feeling healthy and strong, so I was kind of at a good place mentally, which kind of helped me get through.

Analysis

We begin with a table of our initial coding, identified emergent themes, and the overarching themes we developed.

We explore each overarching theme in turn.

Minimizing

Derek minimises his appearance and the effect that it has and continues to have upon his life. He speaks candidly about losing his vision and the changes to his face, which "weren't the significant portions of my injuries." He explains that,

Table 3.1 Codes, Emergent Themes, and Overarching Themes.

Initial coding	*Emergent themes*	*Overarching themes*
Face already damaged (sports)	Already damaged face	Minimising
Face different but people recognised him	Appearance not that noticeable/bad	
Girlfriend/wife glossed over		
Less noticeable (sunglasses)		
Not a lot of staring/will explain		
Vision "not that bad"	Vision acceptable	
No expectation of survival (lucky)	Surviving and Life Trajectory	Rationalising
Just kept going		
New career (wheelchairs/prosthetics)		
Guys don't have to look nice	Appearance and gender	
Injury an asset in new job	Benefit	
Talking to son	Responding to family	Coping
Reaction of niece		
Extended family		
Friends' reactions		
Online community Lost eye involvement (meeting others)	Finding community	
Getting drivers licence back (not motorbike)	Independence	

> I had significant damage to my arms and legs, so as much as losing sight in one eye was traumatic, there was a lot of other pain, a lot of other surgeries to go through, so I kind of just glossed over it and it was the new normal and I just kind of kept going.

Already Damaged Face

Derek minimises the impact of his facial scarring because his face was already damaged. Derek felt that his face has "become just the new normal." Before the accident, Derek already had "noticeable damage" to his face with some facial scarring. He explained that as an 18-year-old boy, he was proud of these scars:

> I already had several scars on my forehead, and a couple around my eyebrows and around the cheek of my eye from hockey, sports and different activities, so I already had a couple of significant [scars]. [A year before his accident] I ended up with almost twenty stitches to my forehead from wave boarding and some water sports when I'd fallen.

Derek was accustomed to having scars on his face and felt proud stating that his son plays hockey now and "I'm waiting for the day that he has his first scar." He says he still plays sports but admits that he isn't the same athlete that he used to be because, "it is fast-moving sport with just one eye, I'd run into people a lot more, so it became a little dangerous with less peripheral vision in such a fast-moving sport, it became dangerous."

Appearance

Derek took some time to adjust to "a new normal." Initially, he explained that he had significant other damage to his body and that whilst "losing sight in one eye was traumatic, there was a lot of other pain . . . so I kind of just glossed over it, and it was the new normal and I just kind of kept going." Although he glossed over, his appearance "was a significant adjustment, kind of accepting my face looked different and I looked different in a mirror than I used to. I looked different in a picture than I used to." He considers that his saving grace was that he had met a bunch of old friends who he hadn't seen for a while in the community and "they recognised me, they still knew who I was, so it made me feel as though I didn't look that different." He described that event as helpful: "they still recognised me, that they still knew who I was despite the . . . what I thought was significant damage to my face."

Derek describes having a hard time "wondering would I be able to get married? Would a girl be interested in me in that sort of way, so that was hard." He started dating a girl who became his wife and "she kind of glossed over some of the visual differences as well." His now-wife had known Derek before the accident for a significant amount of time; however, it wasn't until after the accident during "four major surgeries – two on my cheeks, one on my skull and one on my knee" that they began dating and eventually married. He describes this as "quite the introduction."

Derek says he doesn't experience stares or avoidance of people in public very much because he wears sunglasses throughout the year. He explains, "I wear sunglasses a lot so that . . . they're wraparound and they pretty much fully cover my face, so that might be part of the reason it's not as obvious or as noticeable." All these circumstances help Derek believe his appearance is not that noticeable or bad.

Derek has nieces and nephews who have noticed that his face is different. He has graciously allowed them to "touch and look from one eye to the other, and we've been able to talk about how Uncle Derek's eye is broken and how it doesn't see and how it doesn't work." In those instances, "while [they were] good also made me feel uncomfortable and broken because that's kind of the first people noticing that it's not right." He confesses that within society he may have just ignored any "funny looks," although when children point and look "it makes me feel a little uncomfortable that they're noticing when adults don't necessarily seem to . . . as much."

Derek continues to accommodate the changes to his appearance. After his initial big adjustment of

> get[ing] used to with meeting new people with my new face was [difficult] because I had lost complete vision in my left eye, but I still had the physical

> eye, it had gone lazy per se. So my left eye, even though it's blind, it looks like it is the healthier eye, even though it's not. So I had to get used to . . . if I was looking at someone and talking to them, I had to get used to them thinking I was looking at someone over their shoulder because they would look at my bad eye and see it pointing off to the side, so they would think that I was talking to someone next to them, and I still experience that fairly often, but I've learned to compensate.

Rationalising

Derek uses rationalisation to help him. He rationalises that he is very lucky to have survived, that there is a difference between genders and that males don't care about their appearance as much as females, and he further stated that LwFED has its benefits.

Surviving and Life Trajectory

After the accident, Derek's chances at survival were uncertain. Derek explains, "at first the doctors didn't think I was going to live." However, "after about a week they knew I was going to survive but they knew there was a lot of facial and head trauma and damage."

Derek's life trajectory was changed due to the accident. His aspirations of joining the Coast Guard and becoming an ocularist were thwarted by his ongoing physical issues after the accident and monocular vision, respectively. Derek did complete three years of a prosthetic and orthotic design course. A friend of his worked for a prosthetic company and he found a job as a wheelchair and seating specialist where his lived experience is beneficial to his customers because he can empathise and help them in their journey.

Gender Differences

Derek rationalises that as a male, his LwFED was not that bad because appearance is less important for guys. He explains, "as a guy my looks aren't something that I'm raving about on a regular basis." Derek speaks about his understanding about women LwFED. He has formed personal relationships through an online community,[1] and has realised that women experience LwFED differently. He speaks about a young girl who he befriended who also was in a car accident sustaining trauma to her cheek and face:

> she took it a lot harder than I did. She used a lot of make-up, a lot of growing her hair long, wearing large sunglasses, using a patch and different things to try and hide and disguise the scarring. Guys can't throw on make-up and foundation quite as easily as girls can. So that kind of covering and hiding that wasn't so much of an option for me.

Derek realises that his experience was very different. Prior to the accident, he already wore proud sporting scars on his face due to being a "fairly skilled athlete [who was] quite accomplished at all of them." Derek seemed to wear his "sporting scars" as a sign of physical prowess, which he saw as being acceptable for a young man like himself. So when he was scarred in the accident, he felt that his new scars were just an additional layer to what he already had.

Benefit

Before the accident, Derek planned on joining the Coast Guard but couldn't due to the damage he sustained. Then he expressed interest in getting into ocular prosthetics with the view of becoming an ocularist while being monocular and

> having an iris that lets in more light than it should, I have a hard time differentiating between depth and colour . . . different shades of white, different shades of yellow, some of those light colours . . . I can't distinguish between several whites, so picking white shading for eyes wouldn't work.

After the accident, Derek went back to college and completed studies in prosthetic and orthotic design. Whilst he was there:

> there were two people in our class who were amputees, so I didn't feel as though I was alone in being different or handicapped or disfigured because part of the other students in the class were as well.

Derek was offered a job with wheelchairs and custom seating where his lived experience "has been quite an asset to be able to share my experiences, my accident." He is grateful he can support people with "yes, I understand, I've spent time in a wheelchair myself, I've been there done that . . . so it's been nice to be able to share my experiences and explain how I ended up working with wheelchairs as well."

Coping Mechanisms

Derek has various coping mechanisms. Some he found beneficial such as finding community. Responding to family comes with mixed feelings and coping mechanisms which leave him feeling supported yet broken. Others, such as his independence, have had a variety of issues since LwFED.

Finding Community

Derek found an online community called Lost Eye on Facebook which was "really influential." He joined and realised that "meeting some other people that were monocular as well or had vision issues" was beneficial. He recalls "[it was] really significant, really influential because I realised [that] I wasn't the only one that had some of these difficulties and struggles." He explains it was helpful "to engage with and talk to other people who had facial issues."

Responding to Family

Derek's family of origin consisted of Mum, Dad, and two sisters, one older than Derek and one younger. All children (aged 17–22) were living at home when the accident happened. His family "just kind of rallied and supported" him several times, both initially and when he lost his licence because of LwFED. The support of his family is not only comforting but also highlights his facial disfigurement, which leaves him feeling broken.

Derek doesn't "like taking pictures with people near as much as I used to because I always look like I'm looking off away from the camera." He shares this dislike with an aunty who dislikes her photo being taken. He explains:

> she always makes a big deal of hiding her face and turning away and she's perfectly fine, she's a beautiful lady, but she always avoids having her picture taken, and it irritates us because we always try to remind her these pictures aren't for you to look at, they're for our kids and grandkids to look at when you are dead and gone . . . she's personally insecure.

He supports her by saying, "I always tell her, I don't want my picture taken either so come do it with me [laugh] and kind of make it a team event."

Derek has a niece and nephews. They were aged 2–5 at the time of interview. They noticed that their uncle's face looks different than their other aunts and uncles and their parents. Derek explains:

> They've all kind of looked at my face, touched it, looked from one eye to the other, and we've been able to talk about how Uncle Derek's eye is broken and how it doesn't see and how it doesn't work. And those experiences while good also made me feel uncomfortable and broken I guess because that's kind of the first of the people noticing that it's not right.

Derek recalls a recent incident where he had surgery to take a screw out of his cheek which was causing infection, and straight after the surgery they went to his sibling's house where he could recover from surgery before driving home. He tells us that,

> my niece who was about three and a half at the time . . . she was very worried about me, very concerned about how my eye was bleeding, and she still talks about that, how my eye was bleeding, and my eye needed to be fixed.

He says that it reminds him that "even at a very young age they notice." His niece was very helpful, "which it was very special that she noticed, that she paid attention, that she tried to help."

At the time of the interview, Derek had a five-year-old son. He described how he and his wife had explained to him:

> And he's seen pictures of me like within a few months after my accident, and I've had two or three surgeries in the last five years, so he's been through that process with me where daddy's been sick, where daddy's been ill, daddy's face is bleeding because he had a screw taken out of his cheek.

Derek has had supportive family members, members who have gone through many surgeries with him, including his son, family members who he "teams" with to support each other to take family pictures for future generations, through to family members who have pointed out his facial disfigurement and made him feel broken despite being caring.

Independence

One of the biggest issues that Derek faced was the loss of his driver's licence and regaining it. Originally Derek didn't quite meet the requirements: "I was able to eventually get my licence back because of how close I was to meeting the requirements, I was able to get a waiver, but every year now I have to reapply for my driver's licence." He explains that being a "young man, having your driver's licence, especially in the area where we live where it's fairly rural, it's been quite important." The loss of his license he attributes as being a "significant barrier for me, and that was . . . mentally some of the hardest fights that I had."

Discussion

Derek offers a different male perspective to expand how we think about LwFED. Derek has noted this himself, speaking of the differences he perceives between himself and females. He is proud of his sporting scars and tries to view the additional scarring from his accident as less impactful than they otherwise might have seemed. However, beneath the surface, Derek offers occasional glimpses of how he continues to be challenged, feeling broken. Derek continues to both minimise and rationalise the damages to his face and body, finding ways to cope and, if possible, see the changes to himself as a positive part of his life journey, rather than roadblocks. It may be that Derek is being male contribute a different perspective to the existing accounts of LwFED by females (O'Dea, 2018; O'Dea & Southcott, 2023b; Pileggi et al., 2018; Sharratt et al., 2019).

Regardless of sex or gender, those LwFED need to find ways to live successfully. On his own, Derek developed strategies (minimising, rationalising, and coping) to LwFED, but developing a framework that all could use would be beneficial and hopefully encourage those LwFED to feel that they are not alone on their journey. O'Dea (2018) explains her four foundational blocks that she believed contributed towards living successfully with FED:

1. Active Intentional Decisions,
2. Forgiveness,
3. Healthy self-esteem, and
4. Resilience.

These foundation blocks are not stand-alone silos, rather dovetail in and out of one another. It is important to note that whilst we make a delineation for the purpose of this discussion, the reality of these four foundational blocks is more complex. Derek uses all of the four foundational blocks, and it could be argued that although he has not said it outright, he has expressed and experienced forgiveness towards the woman whose decision to drive left him LwFED.

Foundation Block 1: Active Intentional Decisions

Throughout the analysis of Derek, we encounter many times where Derek has made active intentional decisions about how he LwFED. An active intentional decision is where a person actively and intentionally decides to create the lifestyle they desire. O'Dea (2018) gives an example from her own life: "for me, forgiveness acts as a release to be able to live life without burden and bitterness. It is an active intentional decision [stating she] believes people are intentional with what they want to accomplish" (p. 2327).

Derek uses an array of active intentional decisions, such as the intentional use of sunglasses to protect his eye and as a form of camouflage to make his FED less noticeable. Another active intentional decision discussed is his ability to allow his nieces and nephews to explore his FED, looking, touching, and being concerned about his wellbeing.

Foundation Block 2: Forgiveness

As discussed earlier, there is an inference that Derek may have forgiven the woman who caused the accident as she died a year and a half later, or it could be interpreted as him finding relief as she "got her just desserts." After her death, the anger and frustration over her negligence disappeared. LwFED disappeared almost suddenly after reading her obituary. After reading about her death, he wasted no more time being angry or frustrated because he was "alive," had many good things in his life to be "grateful for such as a wife, family and a job."

Foundation Block 3 and 4: Healthy Self-Esteem and Resilience

Derek's ability to pick himself up and keep moving forward despite LwFED is a sign of resilience (Bonanno, 2004; Tugade & Fredrickson, 2004). For him to be resilient, he relied on a good support system around him, namely his wife, family of origin, online community, and a friend who found him a meaningful job whereby he can use his lived experience to help others. Having meaningful employment is important, particularly for people LwFED who often find difficulty getting a job (Williamson, 2023). Derek's reportedly healthy self-esteem can be attributed to situations such as his old friends glossing over his appearance and being able to see that he was the same Derek despite his facial disfigurement. Regaining his licence was another boost which assisted Derek's healthy self-esteem. Despite his worries, Derek found and married a woman who was happy to be his wife. Derek's family, friends, and having one of his deepest fears (although he did not say it was a fear) answered within a relatively quick time, even during four surgeries, have allowed him to build a healthy self-esteem and be able to buffer stares or not take any notice of them from the community.

Conclusion

Ultimately, Derek has found ways to negotiate the changes to his life after the accident that left him with monocular vision and LwFED. He has found and maintained an effective support network; has a fairly robust sense of self-esteem; and uses active intentional decisions to create a better future for himself and family. He has married, gained qualifications and meaningful employment, and ostensibly forgiven the woman who caused the car accident. Despite these achievements, there remains an undercurrent of unresolved issues. It appears that this mask is only so deep. From the outside looking in, Derek has a great family, friends, and work life but there appears to be a deep form of insecurity residing within him because he is LwFED. This is glimpsed through his awkwardness when family members point out his differences, which he says makes him feel "broken." For example, he admitted that he has a difficult time when children stare and point out his disfigurement because, to him, adults do not do this often.

This singular qualitative case study of Derek, who is LwFED, adds to existing research, offering expert insight into how one male has come to terms with his FED. Each case study that we do expands what we know of how people accommodate and negotiate impactful change in their lives LwFED. This increases the lived experience voice of this marginalised community, utilising *their* voices instead of looking through a medical lens which is often published, and is instead researched by an insider, adding a level of trustworthiness that other research may not have. More studies are needed to expand understanding, particularly in how the presence of O'Dea's Four Foundational Blocks within the individual person can support people LwFED in a healthy manner.

Note

1 Supporting communities and professional support include Karibu Anawim meaning "Welcome to The Way of Victory" (https://www.karibuanawim.com) and Lost Eye (https://www.facebook.com/groups/losteye).

References

Al Bdour, Z., & Mohamed, E. A. (2018). Anxiety and depression in a sample of disfigured orofacial cancer patients at Khartoum Teaching Dental Hospital, Sudan. *Journal of Advanced Medical and Dental Sciences Research*, *6*(2), 59–65. https://doi.org/10.21276/jamdsr

Berger, Z. E., & Dalton, L. J. (2011). Coping with a cleft II: Factors associated with psychosocial adjustment of adolescents with a cleft lip and palate and their parents. *The Cleft Palate-Craniofacial Journal*, *48*(1), 82–90. https://doi.org/10.1597/08-094

Bogart, K. R., Frandrup, E., Locke, T., Thompson, H., Weber, N., Yates, J., Zike, N., & Hemmesch, A. R. (2017). "Rare place where I feel normal": Perceptions of a social support conference among parents of and people with Moebius syndrome. *Research in Developmental Disabilities*, *64*, 143–151. https://doi.org/10.1016/j.ridd.2017.03.014

Bogart, K. R., & Hemmesch, A. R. (2016). Benefits of support conferences for parents of and people with moebius syndrome. *Stigma and Health*, *1*(2), 109–121. https://doi.org/10.1037/sah000018

Bonanno, A., & Esmaeli, B. M. D. (2012). Cancer and facial disfigurement: Reducing survivors' stigma in social interaction. *Clinical Journal of Oncology Nursing*, *16*(2), 153–159. https://doi.org/10.1188/12.CJON.153-159

Bonanno, G. A. (2004). Loss, trauma, and human resilience: Have we underestimated the human capacity to thrive after extremely aversive events? *American Psychologist*, *59*(1), 20–28. https://doi.org/doi.org/10.1037/0003-066X.59.1.20

Burton, M. J., Ramke, J., Marques, A. P., Bourne, R. R., Congdon, N., Jones, I., Tong, B. A. A., Arunga, S., Bachani, D., & Bascaran, C. (2021). The Lancet global health commission on global eye health: Vision beyond 2020. *The Lancet Global Health*, *9*(4), 489–551. https://www.thelancet.com/journals/langlo/article/PIIS2214-109X(20)30488-5/fulltext

Cingi, C. C., Yüksel, E., & Shahin, O. O. (2020). Communication disorders due to facial deformities. In C. Cingi & N. Bayar Muluk (Eds.), *All around the nose* (pp. 931–936). Springer. https://doi.org/10.1007/978-3-030-21217-9_105

DeGuire, L. et al. (2024). Letter to NBC universal in response to SNL "anomalous man" sketch. *The FaceOut Project*. https://www.faceoutproject.com/activism

Demir, T., Karacetin, G., Baghaki, S., & Aydin, Y. (2011). Psychiatric assessment of children with nonsyndromic cleft lip and palate. *General Hospital Psychiatry*, *33*(6), 594–603. https://doi.org/10.1016/j.genhosppsych.2011.06.006

Disfigurement in the UK. (2017). *Changing faces*. https://www.changingfaces.org.uk/wp-content/uploads/2021/05/disfigurement-in-the-uk-report-2017.pdf

Eatough, V., & Smith, J. (2006). "I was like a wild wild person": Understanding feelings of anger using interpretative phenomenological analysis. *British Journal of Psychology*, *97*, 483–498. https://doi.org/10.1348/000712606X97831

Erie, J. C., Nevitt, M. P., Hodge, D., & Ballard, D. J. (1992, February 15). Incidence of enucleation in a defined population. *American Journal of Opthamology*, *113*(2), 138–144. https://doi.org/10.1016/s0002-9394(14)71525-9

Fade, S. (2004). Using interpretative phenomenological analysis for public health nutrition and dietetic research: A practical guide. *Proceedings of the Nutrition Society*, *63*, 647–653. https://doi.org/10.1079/pns2004398

Fang, C., Leavitt, J. A., Hodge, D. O., Holmes, J. M., Mohney, B. G., & Chen, J. J. (2017). Incidence and etiologies of acquired third nerve palsy using a population-based method. *JAMA Ophthalmology*, *135*(1), 23–28. https://doi.org/10.1001/jamaophthalmol.2016.4456

Feragen, K. J., Semb, G., & Magnussen, S. (1999). Asymmetry of left versus right unilateral cleft impairments: An experimental study of face perception. *The Cleft Palate-Craniofacial Journal*, *36*(6), 527–532. https://doi.org/10.1597/1545-1569_1999_036_0527_aolvru_2.3.co_2

Frances, J. (2004). *Educating children with facial disfigurement creating inclusive school communities*. RoutledgeFalmer.

Gagnon, S. (2016). My biggest wish as a mom who sees people stare at her child's differences. *The Mighty*. https://themighty.com/2016/08/mom-responds-to-staringcomments-about-her-son-with-goldenhar-syndrome/

Grollemund, B., Dissaux, C., Gavelle, P., Carla Pérez, M., Mullaert, J., Alfaiate, T., Guedeney, A., team, C., & palate Infant, P. (2020). The impact of having a baby with cleft lip and palate on parents and on parent-baby relationship: The first French prospective multicentre study. *BMC Pediatrics*, *20*, 1–11. https://doi.org/10.1186/s12887-020-02118-5

Hamlet, C., & Harcourt, D. (2015). Older adults' experiences of living with cleft lip and palate: A qualitative study exploring aging and appearance. *The Cleft Palate-Craniofacial Journal*, *52*(2), 32–40. https://doi.org/10.1597/13-308

Jones, A., Plumb, A. M., & Sandage, M. J. (2021). Social media as a platform for cyberbullying of individuals with craniofacial anomalies: A preliminary survey. *Language, Speech & Hearing Services in Schools (Online)*, *52*(3), 840–855. https://doi.org/10.1044/2021_LSHSS-20-0019

Keel, S., Xie, J., Foreman, J., Taylor, H. R., & Dirani, M. (2017, November 1). The prevalence of vision loss due to ocular trauma in the Australian national eye health survey. *Injury*, *48*(11), 2466–2469. https://doi.org/10.1016/j.injury.2017.09.020

Millar, K., Bell, A., Bowman, A., Brown, D., Lo, T.-W., Siebert, P., Simmons, D., & Ayoub, A. (2013). Psychological status as a function of residual scarring and facial asymmetry after surgical repair of cleft lip and palate. *The Cleft Palate – Craniofacial Journal, 50*(2), 150–157. https://doi.org/10.1597/10-222

Millard, T., & Richman, L. C. (2001). Different cleft conditions, facial appearance, and speech: Relationship to psychological variables. *Cleft Palate Craniofacial Journal, 38*(1), 68–75. https://doi.org/10.1597/1545-1569_2001_038_0068_dccfaa_2.0.co_2

O'Dea, Z. (2018). The Ayes have it! *The Qualitative Report, 23*(10), 2313–2336. https://doi.org/10.46743/2160-3715/2018.2897

O'Dea, Z. (2023). *What are the lived experiences of people living with facial eye disfigurement (FED) and their family members?* [Doctoral dissertation, Monash University]. https://bridges.monash.edu/articles/thesis/What_are_the_lived_experiences_of_people_living_with_Facial_Eye_Disfigurement_FED_and_their_family_members_/23812791

O'Dea, Z. (2024). *The anomalous man skit May 2024: Karibu Anawim "Welcome to The Way of Victory"*. https://www.youtube.com/watch?v=Iah6149gnFE

O'Dea, Z., & Southcott, J. (2024). "Everything seems to be the right eye in our family": Intergenerational family living with facial eye disfigurement: An interpretative phenomenological analysis. *The Qualitative Report, 29*(1), 162–182. https://doi.org/10.46743/2160-3715/2024.5993

O'Dea, Z., & Southcott, J. (2023a). "I'm his mum and it is my job to keep him safe": Mothering a child living with facial eye disfigurement. *Applied Research in Quality of Life*. https://doi.org/10.1007/s11482-023-10199-4

O'Dea, Z., & Southcott, J. (2023b). "My mummy has a hole in her face": Living with facial eye disfigurement. *The Qualitative Report, 28*(11), 2995–3015. https://nsuworks.nova.edu/tqr/vol28/iss11/1/

Payakachat, N., Tilford, J. M., Brouwer, W. B., van Exel, N. J., & Grosse, S. D. (2011). Measuring health and well-being effects in family caregivers of children with craniofacial malformations. *Quality of Life Research, 20*(9), 1487–1495. https://doi.org/10.1007/s11136-011-9870-2

Pileggi, V., Rice, C., Stead, S., & Atkinson, K. (2018). Resistance in relationship: Mothers' armoring of their adolescent daughters living with facial difference. In S. Pashang, N. Khanlou, & J. Clarke (Eds.), *Today's youth and mental health: Hope, power, and resilience* (pp. 247–263). Springer International Publishing. https://doi.org/10.1007/978-3-319-64838-5_14

Raworth, K., Sweetman, C., Narayan, S., Rowlands, J., & Hopkins, A. (2012). *Conducting semi-structured interviews*. Oxfam.

Rumsey, N., Bull, R., H., & Gahagan, D. (1982). The effect of facial disfigurement on the proxemics of behaviour of the general public. *Journal of Applied Social Psychology, 12*(2), 137–150. https://doi.org/10.1111/j.1559-1816.1982.tb00855.x

Ryan, S., Oaten, M., Stevenson, R. J., & Case, T. I. (2012). Facial disfigurement is treated like an infectious disease. *Evolution and Human Behavior, 33*(6), 639–646. https://doi.org/10.1016/j.evolhumbehav.2012.04.001

Sharratt, N. D., Jenkinson, E., Moss, T., Clarke, A., & Rumsey, N. (2019). Experiences of living with visible difference: Individual and social reflections. *Health Psychology Update, 28*(2). https://uwe-repository.worktribe.com/output/848451

Smith, J. A. (2017). Interpretative phenomenological analysis: Getting at lived experience. *The Journal of Positive Psychology, 12*(3), 303–304. https://doi.org/10.1080/17439760.2016.1262622

Smith, J. A., Flowers, P., & Larkin, M. (2009). *Interpretative phenomenological analysis: Theory, method and research*. Sage.

Sofer, C., Dotsch, R., Oikawa, M., Oikawa, H., & Todorov, A. (2017). For your local eyes only: Culture-specific face typicality influenes perctptions of trustworthiness. *Perception, 46*(8), 914–928. https://doi.org/10.1177/0301006617691786

Stevenage, S. V., & McKay, Y. (1999). Model applicants: The effect of facial appearance on recruitment decisions. *British Journal of Psychology, 90*, 221–234. https://doi.org/10.1348/000712699161369

Tugade, M. M., & Fredrickson, B. L. (2004). Resilient individuals use positive emotions to bounce back from negative emotional experiences. *Journal of Personality and Social Psychology, 86*(2), 320–333. https://doi.org/10.1037/0022-3514.86.2.320

Upadhyaya, C. (2014). Psychosocial effect of common skin diseases. *Indian Journal of Health and Wellbeing, 5*(6), 764–766. https://pubmed.ncbi.nlm.nih.gov/12046366/

Wagstaff, C., Jeong, H., Nolan, M., Wilson, T., Tweedlie, J., Phillips, E., & Holland, F. (2014). The accordion and the deep bowl of spaghetti: Eight researchers' experiences of using IPA as a methodology. *The Qualitative Report, 19*(47), 1–15. https://doi.org/10.46743/2160-3715/2014.1216

Williamson, S. (2023). Chapter 4: Stigma related to sight loss and psychosocial care. In S. Watkinson & S. N. Williamson (Eds.), *Ocular disease and sight loss: Meeting psychosocial needs* (pp. 57–80). Springer International Publishing. https://doi.org/10.1007/978-3-031-21728-9_4

Zelihić, D., Williamson, H., Kling, J., & Feragen, K. B. (2021). "It's tough because I see that it's upsetting her . . .": A qualitative exploration of parents' perceptions of talking with their adolescents about having a visible difference. *Body Image, 38*, 306–316. https://doi.org/10.1016/j.bodyim.2021.05.006

Interlude

Living Louder

Uncovering and Unlearning the Lessons of Rejection Stories

Jasmine "Jaz" Gray

The school cafeteria was as loud as lime green and hot pink. The sound of kids crescendoed as we scurried in class by class. After waving vigorously at friends in other seventh grade classes that I had not seen since yesterday, I grabbed a plastic tray, set a cup of apple juice on top, and proceeded through the lunch line. I cannot remember what was on the menu that day. Maybe our famous pizza. Shaped like a brick and sprinkled with squares of pepperoni, it tasted a lot better than it looked.

When I reached our long, wood laminate table, other students from my class had already started to sit. Somehow all the girls typically ended up on the left end of the table and all the boys on the right. I put my tray down in the middle of the girls' section. As I ate my meal and chatted, I could see the boys out of the corner of my eye. About halfway through lunch, one of the boys pulled out one of those white sheets of notebook paper with the blue lines. Using his snub of a pencil, he started writing on the paper, glancing over at the girls' end of the table periodically. Then, he folded the paper tightly and passed it to another boy sitting next to him. One boy would cup his hands to receive the paper, unfold it under hunched shoulders, make jots down the page, and then quickly refold and pass the paper to the next boy. None of the other girls seemed to notice or maybe they just had no reason to worry.

Looking back, I can remember only one of the girls who sat around me. She was not the most popular girl in school, but she had some stature with the cool kids. And she was a cute girl – a perfectly round head and a curved Nubian nose. Her lips were neither too small nor too big, like my oversized bottom lip with its keloid scar underneath. Most importantly, she had that hair. We both wore our naturally kinky-curly coils straightened. While I thought my hair was thick, lengthy, and styled with more creativity, hers was longer. Every now and then, smiling and talking like the rest of us, she would use her fingers to comb her tresses back. I would eventually start to comb mine forward, swooping it over the right side of my face like a blackout curtain, blocking stares rather than sunlight.

As the paper came around to the girls' side of the lunch table, I could see each girl unfold the paper, take a look, refold the paper, and pass it on. The girl I can remember was sitting to my left with one person in between us. After scanning down the paper, she rolled eyes and folded the paper back. As she handed it to the

DOI: 10.4324/9781003535591-7

girl sitting next to me, she said with disgust, "A seven." Then motioning to herself dramatically, placing her hand over her heart, she yelled down to one of the boys, "I'm a SEVEN?!" And that's when my stomach knotted.

Before I knew it, the folded paper was in my hands. I had a split second to decide whether I would unfold it or simply pass it on. I should have just passed it on. Instead, like a kid cautiously winding a jack-in-the-box, I slowly pulled the paper open. On the far left side of the page were the names of each girl in our class. Next to each name was a series of numbers. Circled in the top right corner was, "1–10." As I put the pieces together, I realized that the boys had all rated us on a scale from one to ten. My eyes started scanning the page for my name before my brain could stop me. Of course, I had to know. I had to know how they saw me.

Zero. Zero. Zero. They rated me with zeroes and a couple of ones. On the outside, I played it cool. I raised my cheeks, one larger than the other and becoming increasingly misshapen, into a fake smile. I had not yet endured the devastating procedure that would paralyze my face, preventing me from ever fully smiling again. After refolding and passing the scores, I sipped my juice, slowly raising the cup to my mouth and taking a deep breath. I had not yet had sections of my tongue and lips removed, rendering me unable to drink without a straw. Head down, picking at the remainder of the food on my plate, I had a little time to digest what had just happened.

"Don't they know the difference between having a condition and being ugly?" I thought. It just felt unfair to put someone with a facial disfigurement on the same list as those with "normal" faces. *Of course* I would be rated low. I would have rather been left out altogether. I wanted to yell over to the boys, "Why even put my name on the list!?" This would not be the only time the rating game would be played during lunch. In some act of self-preservation, I must have blotted the details of these experiences from my memory. I can only remember the nauseous feeling of knowing that the game was rigged against me. I did not realize that, throughout my life, I would be forced to play the game time and time again.

For any human being, the face is integral to our story. The story of how we want to be perceived, how others interpret us, and how we connect to the experiences happening within and around us are all communicated through and connected to our faces. The shape and texture of each part – foreheads and ears, eyes and noses, jawlines and mouths – resound like sirens penetrating the social atmosphere, calling ourselves and others toward the importance of our existence or affirming our invisibility. For those with a facial disfigurement, each misshapen crevice and curve, every scar or distortion on our face somehow signals that we are not only unattractive but damaged goods. We are the bruised fruit, the dented can, the almost expired condiment marked "reduced price."

In adulthood, I have been on a journey to unlearn what decades of invalidating experiences have communicated to me about my worth. Recently, I told my therapist that I had a problem comparing and devaluing myself next to other women when it came to physical attractiveness. "I always allow this sizing up to change how I feel about myself and how I want to interact with someone I like," I shared.

Eventually, I started to couple greater self-awareness with reflection through writing blog posts which allowed me to both externalize my past experiences and interrogate them. In one of my posts during graduate school, I wrote:

> I was in a class with a guy I thought was . . . interesting (insert sly smile). . . . He was making some really thoughtful, passionate point, had his lil square matte black glasses on, fresh out somebody's barber's chair. And perhaps it had crossed my mind, you know, maybe I should make a point to speak after class, maybe it could be someth-and then I looked around the room. I counted – 1, 2, 3, 4, 5, 6 – at least six other women in our class checked all the boxes. Smart, nice enough, lots of personality, and all naturally pretty. I thought we had a lot of the same qualities but some key differences. They had no asymmetrical face, no visible signs of illness, no impairments. And almost immediately, I was just not as interested in this guy as I had been a few seconds before. Just like that, I burst my own bubble. I could almost hear the pop. I could almost feel the splat of gum stuck to my nose. Just like that, I figured I don't really even know this person. He could be a complete jerk, and why was I thinking about my classmate anyway. Tsk, tsk #sorrytothisman. That now fleeting feeling, a barely lit flame, I had pinched right out. Let the heat sizzle between my fingers. Just like that . . .

At some point, I had a realization that the years I had spent feeling inadequate and desperately desiring to be "normal" were a form of internalized inferiority rooted in a lack of societal acceptance that in turn propelled a lack of self-acceptance. In another blog post, I explained:

> For many, the unusualness of these "different" faces – slopping where faces should not, stretched here, pinched there – can just be plain uncomfortable to look at. It rarely occurs to those we encounter that instead of wishing, praying, or asking about some forthcoming change to our appearance, the change should be in them. That maybe they could practice disciplining themselves so that they no longer react to us based upon their own uncomfortability.

In a social world, the unlearning we must do as disfigured people begins anew every time we decide to leave our home. Each day brings with it the opportunity for yesterday's progress to be challenged by today's new slights. However, each day also brings a chance for the world to "change its heart" in the words of Alessia Cara's song "Scars to Your Beautiful."

Those of us with facial disfigurements dream of and fight for the day when we can live unencumbered by the barriers that bias breeds. In the meantime, we can learn to embrace the beauty of consistently seeking self-understanding, uncovering the distortions we have believed about ourselves and replacing them with new truths – loving what we see when we look in the mirror, expecting decency and kindness from those we encounter, anticipating relationships with significant others who adore us and think we look good on the *outside* too, successfully navigating education and employment fields, and finally accepting our divine path of being different. We can allow wholeness to rest on us every morning like new mercies, fortifying us to face whatever comes. May our lives be lived as loud as a lunch room full of school children, knowing that our presence tints a sepia world with neon colors.

Pretty Disability

A Collection of Essays from a Black Girl Who Has Contemplated Her Beauty and Worth

Rasheera D. Dopson

Essay 1: Pretty Woman

"There is more than one way to be a woman."

I grew up with this idea of what a woman should be or look like. When I was a little girl, I envisioned a woman as someone who shopped in the women's section at Macy's and wore colorful clothes on the mannequins. A woman went to work every morning in a suit and heels. Her hair was pulled back into a bun, and you knew she was about her business. In my teenage years, a woman was someone who was educated, pretty, and smart. She floated through life like a flower in the breeze, and she always kept a smile on her face. She wore feminine-looking clothes like summer dresses, a woman was someone who always smelled nice. In adulthood, a woman was someone who had her stuff together; she hits all the major life milestones such as graduating from college, buying a house, getting married, and having babies. If you had done all these things as a girl, in my mind you were officially a grown woman. Grown women didn't fail, they were perfect. They are the perfect cooks, the perfect wives, the perfect mothers, etc. This woman and failure are never acquainted and she never appears to be broken.

Talk about jarring – how these images of perfection conflict with the sobriety of reality! Nevertheless, I learned over time that the aesthetic of perfection is not an indication of womanhood. The essence of womanhood is far from perfect – it's actually quite messy. The more women I've talked to over the years, the more I began to understand that the blueprint we were all given to imitate is deeply flawed. Womanhood had nothing to do with being perceived as being pretty or perfect. Womanhood was being brave enough to face the vulnerability and nuances of life. When I finally came to this epiphany, I thought, "now, finally, I had a chance to become a woman, too, because I didn't have to fit into the impossible mold of perfection."

I think about the famous title from Sojourner Truth "Ain't I A Woman"[1] and how she meant what she said. I've realized over the years that being a woman has less to do with the external makeup we put on. Womanhood is our internal structure and the inward belief system that tells us we are ready, and that we have arrived

DOI: 10.4324/9781003535591-8

at the space of full maturation. Womanhood has less to do with a look and more with the concept of being ready. Coming into womanhood also has to deal with the big question of what the 'it' is that you're ready for? It asks questions like, "what tools do you need to get there; do you need support or steady flow of finances; does this mean I need to pursue an education?" All of these questions and more present themselves over time as we navigate womanhood. Most importantly, I know now that womanhood isn't a single story or path. She has many different expressions and is unique to each person who graces her threshold. When the girl is ready and mature – the woman will come forth.

Essay 2: Pretty Privilege

priv·i·lege/ˈpriv(ə)lij/

Noun: a special right, advantage, or immunity granted or available only to a particular person or group.

What do disabled people and pretty girls have in common?

People often make assumptions about them based on their looks. Pretty privilege denotes a lived experience solely based on the attractiveness of one's physical appearance (Cellerino, 2003). Pretty privilege is unique because the privilege starts at the foci of the face. If the face passes the screening of beauty, then prettiness is applied to the rest of the body. Those who are considered pretty have been marked by society as the go-to standard of beauty. Culture has taught us that being pretty has a particular look. Whether it's an heir or an aesthetic or attitude, 'pretty' distinctly separates itself differently from other appearance-based words such as beautiful, stunning, gorgeous, or even cute. Some scholars on the subject of beauty have written that "having pretty privilege comes with many benefits and awards because when you're labeled 'pretty,' conversations are centered around you, standards are based upon you, and people tend to pay attention to you because humans have been systematically trained to give attention to things that are stamped with beauty" (Adam, 2017). Prettiness is proximal to centrality – pretty privilege is the illusion that everything revolves around or is a response to your beauty.

What a great privilege the pretty girl holds – to have a world that is hyper-fixated on her beauty. Does nothing bother her, does she not suffer? Well, according to online conversations, there can be a downfall to pretty privilege, such as false assumptions and low expectations, perceived low intelligence, superficial relationships, etc. While part of me empathizes – because it must be hard to have low expectations projected onto you – the backlash of pretty privilege pales in comparison to the stigma that people on the other end of the spectrum experience.

Take people with disabilities: we face all the stigma without the privilege. But what happens when you're disabled and happen to have aesthetically pleasing features? Does the stigma cancel out the privilege? These are questions I've wrestled with over the years. Although I don't claim the pretty privilege, I have been told that I don't act like I have disabilities, which is code for "you're too pretty to be Disabled."

This statement reveals the narrow expectations people hold about disability and beauty. It's as though my appearance – my style, my nails, my hair – disrupts what they think a disabled person "should" look like. For a long time, I internalized this ableist mindset: Why bother dressing up? Why put on makeup? People won't notice my lipstick – they'll just stare at my disabled ear.

It's torturous to engage in beauty rituals that are traditionally tied to femininity and prettiness, while simultaneously justifying why you do them because of your visible disability. It wasn't until my late 20s that I met other disabled women who dared to call themselves pretty – or even cute. We often demoted ourselves to 'cute' because 'pretty' felt off-limits, almost like an act of theft. Pretty had a gate around it. In my effort to escape the gatekeeping, I started using the word 'beautiful.' Beauty felt more inclusive, more expansive. To be called beautiful seemed like a step above – it wasn't just a compliment about external appearance, but about the soul. Still, as I spoke with other disabled women, I realized that many of us wanted to be called pretty. Or sexy. Or stunning.

I remember the first time reading *A Face for Picasso,* a memoir by Disability writer Ariel Henley. The first few chapters in her book describe her first encounters with learning about the origins of beauty standards. I too shared a similar experience. Senior year taking Philosophy. As my teacher began to illustrate what Plato described as beauty, I felt disrupted. Apparently, the more symmetrical your features are, the more you are considered to be beautiful. Can you imagine how unsettling this knowledge can be, being a person with a facial difference? We are the poster children of anti-symmetry. On hearing how beauty was the object of perfect lines, I left class that day feeling very ugly.

As a woman with a facial difference, I often felt at odds when engaging with any content related to prettiness or beauty. In my own eyes, I felt attractive enough, yet I constantly questioned my position in the pretty-girl community. I had heard all my life that prettiness was perfect, straight, symmetrical. Never in my life had I ever heard anyone say prettiness was disfigured. Could the two exist in the same space, being both pretty and disabled, beautiful and disfigured?

> The golden ratio had been used to create an attractiveness ranking system for women. Women were rated on a scale of one to ten based on the symmetry of their facial structure. How many times do you see a magazine article about the most attractive celebrities? We celebrate their beauty – their facial proportions as if that is all they are.
>
> (Henley, 2021)

Culturally, disability is the antithesis of perfection. Does one's imperfection overshadow a girl's ability to be considered pretty? It shouldn't, yet it does. I believe that, underneath the pretty umbrella there is enough room to include disfigurement. One does not have to cancel out the other.

The quote that says *beauty is in the eye of the beholder* indefinitely merits critical inquiry of whoever holds the gaze of beauty determines its value. If prettiness is based on perception, and perception is grounded in opinion, then why is it that the majority of culture leans towards an opinion that excludes the many? I'm not sure if you've noticed, but pretty privilege is only given to the select few. The rest of us hang on the mercy of being seen as ordinary beings. It is funny how this privilege works and how it can even at times be revoked. I always say that the pretty girl and the disabled have so much in common. For one: people make assumptions about both groups that aren't necessarily true. Number two, at any point and time, you can become a part of the Disability community and at any time and point, you can be rejected from the pretty privileged community. No space is secluded from ultimate security or protection.

If prettiness is subjective and aided by design, then what do we say to those who are "born with it?" Or those who obtain it? Through biological and social phenomena – if you're born with the 'right' set of genes or have resources that can make you pretty – you have access to this invisible world of acceptance and social exclusivity. Is pretty privilege right? Is it fair? Is it just? How can we on the other side of the pretty spectrum honor those with extraordinary features without diminishing the ordinary? It's almost like a cultural war between the beautified and the not. My solution is equity. Privileges shouldn't be reserved for the few but extended to the many.

In having pretty privilege, we can be direct partakers and decision-makers in either maintaining or abolishing the status quo of societal beauty standards. If we wield our pretty privilege for good, we can transform and break the glass ceiling of beauty. However, if we harness our privilege for personal gain, we then become responsible for the harmful standards it has on future generations. The decision is ours.

Will we allow our prettiness to be used as a tool to empower others? When we partner together and use our pretty privilege for good, we can single-handedly dismantle the societal standard of beauty, giving all of us the space and opportunity to come together and bestow beauty on others, extending the privileges and perks that come with being pretty. If we as a society could band together to find prettiness in all people, then perhaps every woman could feel that she is beautiful and receive the gaze of appreciation from her peers not because she is perfect, but because her worthiness is based on where her strength lies.

Essay 3: Pretty Desirable

I was knee-deep in feminist theory one semester. The readings were dense, each one leaving me with a big, unclosed sigh. One chapter on the history of porn had me blushing and Googling terms I'd never encountered. My late-bloomer, never-dated, extremely sheltered upbringing had not prepared me for the realities I was now confronting.

I had signed up for this feminist theory class hoping to learn the history of women's struggles so I could better advocate for disabled women. What I didn't expect was to stumble into a personal reckoning.

The semester was an education in more ways than one. I learned about women, yes, but I also learned how often disabled women are excluded from conversations about feminism, sexual health, reproductive rights, and empowerment.

One of the most eye-opening moments came when we were assigned *A Right to Sex* by Amia Srinivasan. It was a thought-provoking, critically engaging read – until I reached chapter four: "The Politics of Sexual Attraction." That chapter ripped me to shreds. Up until then, I had never thought deeply about the intersection of desirability, sexuality, and disability. Suddenly, I was face-to-face with a conversation I had buried deep within myself, a taboo I hadn't dared to confront.

On some level as a then-32-year-old woman, I had an awareness of sexual attraction and who society did and did not deem as sexy and desirable. I grew up during the early 2000s, when shows like *America's Next Top Model* dominated the airwaves and entrenched unrealistic beauty standards on adolescent teen girls' views. This cultural trend heightens the need for women to be seen as sexy. Women who did not embody these sexy characteristics were considered unsexy. I acquiesced myself to the non-sexy attributes. I simply didn't see myself as attractive because somehow my mind associated disability and attractiveness on two different planets. I was unsure how my worldview of sexiness got this way – I knew it wasn't just *America's Next Top Model* – but overall there seemed to be a message that erased my sexuality and attractiveness just because I was disabled.

Amia Srinivasan did an excellent job on capturing the essence of how we view desirability in North American culture. She laid a clear foundation that who we consider to be desirable and undesirable, attractive and unattractive, was all informed by an able-bodied lens that made whiteness the epicenter of beauty, and all other skin tones and body types as othered. The more compounded you identify, the more you fall outside the scale of desirability. A book I never read before by a global scholar I never met or had coffee with laid bare the worst of my subconscious fears. Not only was I not desirable, but society thought so as well. "Preferences are political. Desire actively shapes systems of power and oppression. People who are considered less desirable in a world that is built around and actively centers on whiteness: black, fat, disabled, poor, and gay people stand on the fringes of society (https://archives.documentwomen.com/the-politics-of-desirability/).

As a Black Disabled woman, it was deeply unsettling to read, on the pages of a widely circulated book, research and public opinion claiming that I was not desirable. Those words felt threatening. While the author didn't write anything society hasn't already affirmed, it still felt like a form of public shaming. This raises an important question for researchers and scientists: how do we shed light on issues for the sake of knowledge and awareness without inadvertently weaponizing that knowledge or embedding it into harmful belief systems? There's a kind of violence that occurs, whether intentional or not. I believe Amia's exploration of public attitudes was not intended to cause harm – but on the other hand, it amplifies and reaffirms beliefs that people often use to justify their biases. If we continue to write about Disability from an undesirable gaze, then we will continue to view it as such.

The harder truth was that I didn't need Amia to tell me I wasn't desirable – society reminded me of that every day. From the absence of Disabled women in beauty ads, campaigns, entertainment, media, and movies; to their neglect in women empowerment spaces; to their exclusion from narratives surrounding key milestones of womanhood – marriage, dating, motherhood, intimacy, travel, and education – the message was clear: Disabled women do not belong. We are often forced to carve out spaces for our own narratives instead of being included in the mainstream. Silos are only effective when they are not the only option. Without bridges to connect those who are marginalized to the center, the silos become prisons by design – keeping those who are deemed desirable and wanted at the top, while the rest of us are left to drift to the bottom.

Nevertheless, this book liberated me in a strange way, forcing me to confront a bitter reality I'd known deep down all along. Once freed from the fantasy, I could finally begin to actualize the dream – my dream of seeing Disabled women recognized in society in meaningful ways. Not with contempt or pity, but celebrated for who they are: robust, unapologetic, and making a difference in the world.

Yes, according to cultural standards, Disabled women are not considered desirable. But somehow, this bitter truth led me to a new revelation about myself. If sexiness was the prize to win, I forfeited my right to compete. I didn't want to be sexy – not if it meant conforming to their narrow definition of desirability. I'd rather be accepted for who I am, authentically, than be loved for a shallow version of myself.

But to be honest, that's easier said than done. Who wants to be marginalized and not seen as desirable?

Knowing how society views desirability is deeply painful. I hope for a day when Disabled women are intentionally included in conversations about desirability – not as a contrast to attractiveness, but as worthy contenders in their own right. Until Disability is seen differently, I must remain steadfast in redefining what desirability means to me. I hold on to the higher truth that having a disability does not equate to being undesirable.

Essay 4: Pretty Black Barbie

Netflix recently came out with a documentary called *Black Barbie: A Documentary*. While scrolling one night it came on my Netflix feed and my fingers rushed to press play. What girl with a massive Barbie collection throughout her childhood would not sit and watch a 90-minute documentary on Barbies? As the film played across my TV screen, I had my phone close by because I wanted to take notes. The launch of this documentary excited the scholar in me to know that finally this conversation was being made available to the masses. Not only on the popularization of Barbie, but how Barbie stood in proximity to Blackness. In my mind, this documentary – although I was watching it for entertainment purposes – could very well inform my academic journey. Because I too was curious about how societal standards of beauty influence little girls – especially little Black girls, especially little Black girls with disabilities. It was somehow a sign from God to say, "Daughter, keep writing because the world is seeking answers to the questions you ask."

I'll be honest, the first time I heard the word *Barbie* in the context of Black beauty was through the female rap artist Nicki Minaj. Of course, I'd heard through the cultural references of the *Barbie* look being the most desired aesthetic. Like all other beauty standards, I typically rejected them because they screamed unattainability. Yet somehow Nicki Minaj caused this beauty phenomenon to reappear – causing a wave of Black women to seek out blonde hair, perfect edges and remarkable bodies – hello BBL trend. Now, although I had rejected this notion of the *Barbie* look, I will admit it had an influence on me – yes, yes I went through my blonde hair phase too. However, I'm not sure if I wanted blonde hair to look like a *Barbie* or to prove to the world that Black girls looked good in blonde hair too. On some level, I was subconsciously fighting colorism and racism that said Black girls were too dark to wear blonde hair. Or having certain hair colors made us unnatural or ghetto.

I recall in high school my sister also went through a blonde phase. This was before Nicki Minaj. She was criticized for her blonde locks. Despite her hair being super cute – it was unacceptable in our predominantly white school that Black girls could have Blonde hair – somehow that was only reserved for white girls and not us. As you can imagine, I was completely thrown when blonde hair on Black women started to become acceptable and no longer taboo.

The emergence of the *Black Barbie* aesthetic infiltrated our communities. Forcing Black women to take on these personas juxtaposed to perfection: Black women who displayed perfect skin, perfect hair, perfect bodies, perfect fashion choices, perfect job, perfect romantic partner. This aesthetic of perfection made me want to vomit – it seemed so unearthing that young girls were aspiring to something so unattainable. It also seemed deeply unethical because this perfection came with a high price tag attached to it. A price that, historically, Black women had always been behind the curve of.

This tension between the *Barbie* aesthetic and Black beauty caused a lot of internal conflict. On the one hand, it was an undoing of what I believe to be the epitome of Black beauty. Growing up, I saw Black beauty as perfect – I saw Black beauty as withstanding excellence despite of hardship, struggle, poverty, sickness, etc. To me, Black beauty wasn't perfect, but it was excellent, and excellence was not blonde. It was very disorienting of culture to take a turn in embracing a form of beauty that seemed so counter-cultural to Black culture.

When I thought of Black beauty, I thought about women like Michelle Obama – she was not a video vixen but she was excellent. Even Beyonce – a bona fide beauty queen to me wasn't beautiful – she was excellent in her singing, her craft, her skill, and her performance. Beyonce is who she is not because she rests on beauty standards alone – her excellence is a driving force. However, with both figures of Black beauty presenting as perfect or excellent, none of them equated to disability. Yet, Black spaces often fail to embrace disability, reinforcing the notion that disability is incompatible with excellence.

I was once asked, "What is the proudest moment or thing you've accomplished?" After a moment of reflection, I replied, "Graduating with my master's from Morehouse School of Medicine." As I walked across the stage, I felt an immense sense of pride – not just as a graduate of a Historically Black College and medical school, but as someone openly embracing two integral identities: being Black and being Disabled. That moment was a testament to both my resilience and the richness of my intersecting identities. Yet, I couldn't help but wish that the Black community would more intentionally hold space for women with disabilities, celebrating our contributions and recognizing our experiences.

Barbie has always symbolized something larger than herself – a reflection of society's evolving ideals. The creation of Black Barbie was a milestone for inclusion, representing Black beauty and excellence. But while Barbie's representation holds significance in shaping societal perceptions, it isn't everything. If Barbie can evolve, so too must Black Barbie – expanding beyond perfection and excellence to embrace the full spectrum of Blackness, including disability. The future of representation demands nothing less.

Note

1. McKissack, P. 1944–2017. (1992). *Sojourner truth: Ain't I a woman?* Scholastic.

Works Cited

Cellerino, A. (2003). Psychobiology of facial attractiveness. *Journal of Endocrinological Investigation*, *26*(Supp 3), 45–48.

Esel, E. & Esel, G. S. (2017). The neurobiology and evolutionary foundations of the perception of beauty. *Dusunen Adam the Journal of Psychiatry and Neurological Sciences*, *30*, 368–388.

Falaiye, A. (2016, November 21). *Everyday Feminism*. Accessed 2024. https://archives.documentwomen.com/the-politics-of-desirability/.

Henley, A. (2021). *A face for Picasso: Coming of age with Crouzon syndrome*. Farrar, Straus and Giroux (BYR).

Section 2

Interventions

4 Psychosocial Interventions to Support People Affected by Visible Differences

Diana Harcourt, Maia Thornton, Pippa Tollow, Fabio Zucchelli, and Alex Clarke

Having an appearance that is different to 'the norm' because of an injury, health condition or treatment can potentially have a varied, extensive, and enduring psychosocial impact. Although the intensity of that impact varies from one individual to another, there is considerable commonality in the types of challenges being reported, regardless of the nature or cause of their difference. These common challenges include being confronted with difficult and uncomfortable social situations due to the reactions and behaviours of others, including staring, avoidance, intrusive questions, and an absence of friendly behaviour, with many experiencing stigma and discrimination (Changing Faces, 2019; Rumsey & Harcourt, 2012). For some, this leads to depression and anxiety, negative self-perceptions, self-esteem issues, and avoidance of social situations, including romantic and intimate relationships (Rumsey & Harcourt, 2004; Sharratt et al., 2018).

Some people could clearly benefit from psychosocial support, ranging from relatively low level psycho-education and information to intensive therapeutic interventions aimed at behaviour change, but it is important to acknowledge that people with a visible difference are not a homogenous group and that support needs are not consistent over time. Someone who is managing well now might still want support in the future. Some people manage the challenges they face very well, they might not be unduly worried by how they look and might place little importance on it (i.e., they have low levels of appearance investment), and some demonstrate positive growth from their experiences (see Egan et al., 2011).

In an online survey of 550 adults with a range of visible differences (Clement et al., 2025), more than 60% of respondents wanted help accepting their appearance and similar proportions wanted support with confidence, self-esteem and mental health. Almost half (41.9%) sought guidance on communicating about their appearance, addressing questions and reactions (31.8%), and managing social situations (30.2%). Preferred sources of support included healthcare professionals (reported by 89.3%) and online/digital platforms (websites 65.8% and online support groups 47.6%). Key factors influencing support-seeking included wanting access to condition-specific information, knowing it was evidence-based, and healthcare professionals' awareness both of the issues being faced and the availability of therapeutic approaches that address them.

DOI: 10.4324/9781003535591-10

This chapter introduces a range of psychosocial interventions to support people whose lives are impacted by a visible difference. Importantly, the interventions we focus on are evidence-based and have been developed with extensive input from people with relevant lived experience, either as a person with a visible difference or a parent/carer of a child or young person with a condition or injury that has affected their appearance.

The primary focus is on interventions that are generic, meaning they are deemed applicable to people whose lives have been impacted by any kind of visible difference, whether that is something they were born with (congenital) or developed later (acquired). Generic resources are relevant and useful because research has repeatedly shown that although individuals would, ideally, prefer condition-specific support (Clement et al., 2025), they report similar challenges and coping strategies, despite the source of their visible difference. Generic resources are efficient when limited resources preclude the production of multiple versions of the same intervention. However, some circumstances present additional challenges, for example post-traumatic stress after burn injuries, or difficulty eating or speaking after facial paralysis. Some people might, therefore, benefit from additional resources or organisations offering help with the issues that are unique to their particular condition.

Therapeutic Approaches

Historically, Cognitive-Behavioural Therapy (CBT) and Social Skills Training (SST) have been the therapeutic approaches most commonly used in this field (see Harcourt et al., 2018). CBT is based on the theory that anxiety can be maintained through negative automatic thoughts and can lead to enacting safety or avoidant behaviours (e.g., avoiding social situations, appearance-fixing behaviours such as reliance on wigs or camouflage make up; Clarke et al., 2014). CBT usually involves changing behaviours and thinking patterns to allow and encourage alternative explanations and management of the difficulties encountered in day-to-day life. SST is a behavioural approach based on the premise that repeated exposure to a challenging situation can reduce anxiety and associated avoidant behaviour (Clarke et al., 2014). It combines social skills acquisition, exposure to social situations, and opportunities to practice social skills, and has typically been provided through an in-person group format (for example, Robinson et al., 1996).

Given that challenging thoughts, avoidant behaviours and difficult social interactions are all commonly reported by individuals with visible difference, it is understandable why CBT and SST have been popular approaches. However, there is only limited evidence for their effectiveness in this context (see systematic reviews by Costa et al., 2021; Jenkinson et al., 2015; Muftin & Thompson, 2013; Norman & Moss, 2015; Waite et al., 2024). Whilst the limited evidence of effectiveness may, in part, be due to methodological issues with the research that has been conducted, it highlights the importance of considering alternative therapeutic approaches. A criticism of a CBT approach has been that the focus on challenging thoughts can be problematic when an individual's lived experience provides evidence to support the thoughts which they are being encouraged to change. For example, it can be difficult to challenge thoughts such as "People will stare, because I look strange" when the person is experiencing these reactions on a regular basis.

In recent years, psychosocial clinicians and researchers have been examining the use of Acceptance and Commitment Therapy (ACT) as an alternative approach, for example with people with burn injuries (Shepherd et al., 2019) and within a specialist Disfigurement Support service (Zucchelli et al., 2018, 2021). Described as a third-wave cognitive-behavioural approach, ACT offers a key conceptual contrast to CBT. In ACT, the target is to change the *function* of thoughts and feelings – specifically the extent to which they aid or hinder personally defined quality of life – rather than the thoughts and feelings themselves (the target of CBT) (Hayes, 2004). By encouraging the individual to observe and acknowledge their thoughts in a non-judgemental way, ACT avoids the need to challenge the legitimacy of thoughts (more akin to the CBT approach; Hooper & Larsson, 2015).

The CAR Framework of Appearance-Related Interventions

During this chapter we refer to a stepped care framework developed by members of the Centre for Appearance Research (Rumsey & Harcourt, 2012), shown in Figure 4.1, and use hypothetical case studies to illustrate a range of support needs and potentially suitable interventions. Stepped care frameworks such as this, where interventions become more intense as one moves up the framework, with highly specialised interventions at the highest level, are common in other areas, including support for depression or eating disorders. People can enter the framework at any level and move to other levels as required. At any level of intensity on the framework, interventions can be provided through a range of formats and based on a variety of therapeutic approaches. This variety is important since people's preferences for support differ (as shown in the support needs survey conducted by Clement et al., 2025). The important thing is that support is accessible (e.g., online) when in-person interactions and interventions are not possible, as was the case during the COVID-19 pandemic and whilst lockdown measures were in force (Tollow et al., 2023).

The triangular shape of the framework reflects how the numbers of people represented is smaller at the peak whilst the expertise and training of those delivering the interventions at this highest level is greater (far fewer people are likely to require specialist one-to-one interventions delivered by a highly trained psychosocial specialist (level 5) compared with the numbers who could benefit from targeted information (at level 1)). Level 0 interventions are intended to inform the general population, and promote greater acceptance and shift negative attitudes towards visible disfigurement.

Level 1 interventions are targeted to a specific patient group. They can be useful for patients with lower levels of appearance distress and may offer benefits more broadly to a given population. For example, the website www.SupportingChildrenWithBurns.co.uk offers information for parents of children with burn injuries (Heath et al., 2020) and www.healthtalk.org uses in-depth qualitative research

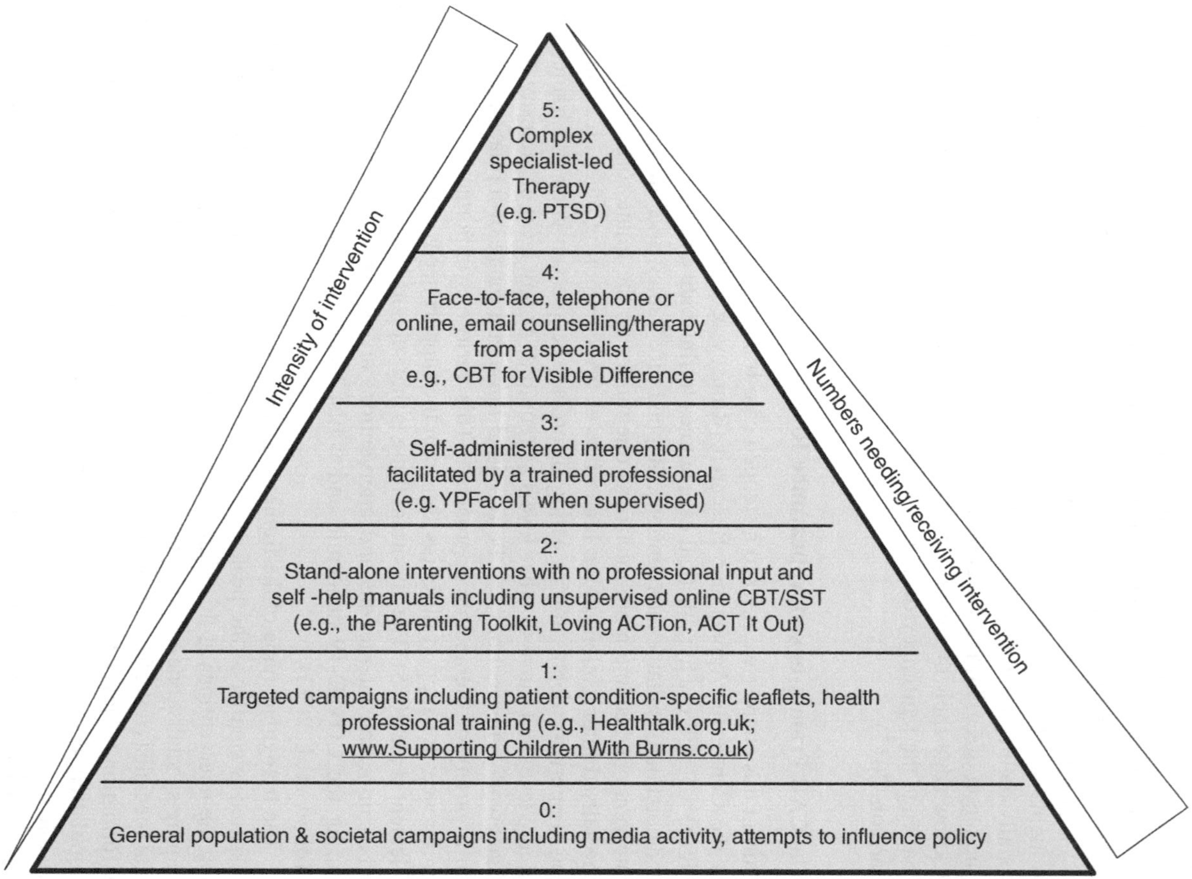

Figure 4.1 The CAR Framework (adapted from Rumsey, N., & Harcourt, D. (Eds.). (2012). *The Oxford handbook of the psychology of appearance*. Oxford University Press)

to create condition-specific modules where people can access the stories and lived experiences of others with their same condition, helping them to feel connected to others, less isolated, and better informed. To date, modules on the site include those specific to burn injuries, cleft lip/palate, alopecia, skin conditions including eczema, psoriasis and acne, and life-changing injuries (which may impact appearance). Interventions at levels 2 and above are designed for those who experience distress as a consequence of their visible difference and whose day-to-day lives are negatively impacted as a result.

We can therefore use the CAR framework to describe a range of evidence-based interventions and their application. Most of the interventions outlined in this chapter are self-guided and would sit at Level 2 on the CAR framework, a level at which interventions are easily accessible and relevant for large numbers of users. Since we can only include a selection of interventions in this chapter, we encourage readers to also examine the range of interventions reported in recent systematic reviews as well as those that are provided by support organisations but might not have a published research evidence base.

Support for Adults

ACT It Out: An ACT-Based Intervention

Many of the new and emerging self-guided psychological interventions for adults with visible differences (some included in this chapter and elsewhere in this text) are web-based. User preferences for self-management have evolved over the past 10 years, with smartphones surpassing laptops as the primary device for most people (Ofcom, 2020). This technology has led to growing interest in mobile health and mental health applications (collectively referred to as mHealth apps), alongside more traditional web-based solutions. MHealth apps can provide a greater level of user functionality to cultivate daily skills training and self-monitoring, including real-time feedback, notifications and all-day access (Yuen et al., 2012). As a skills-focused approach to psychosocial adjustment, ACT is well suited for mHealth delivery. Tailored mindfulness practices, values-based action planning and SST can all be built into mHealth interventions. For these reasons, an app has been developed to deliver an ACT-based intervention known as ACT It Out – a six-session mHealth intervention, co-developed by researchers, specialist clinicians and user representatives. A feasibility study has demonstrated preliminary effectiveness and clinical safety of this new app (Zucchelli et al., 2022), which will be freely available for use on both android and iPhone devices. Aniya's case study that follows details how it could be helpful.

ACT It out is a Level 2 intervention on the CAR framework – a self-guided intervention with low-intensity therapeutic content. However, it does require considerable motivation and engagement from the user if it is to be used to its full potential.

Case Study 1: Aniya

Aniya is 58 years old. Six months ago, she underwent cardiac surgery for a life-threatening heart condition. The surgery caused visible scarring along her sternum. Prior to her surgery she loved spending time with her young granddaughter, and particularly enjoyed taking her swimming. She recently went to the pool with her granddaughter but thought that people were staring at her scarring. She felt embarrassed, and now spends a lot of time and energy worrying that people think she looks "damaged" and "unfeminine". She has always taken great care over her appearance and now only wears clothes that will conceal her scar, even in hot weather. She often compares herself unfavourably to other women of a similar age who she passes on the street or sees on social media on her phone. She has not taken her granddaughter swimming again because she hated feeling embarrassed. Her granddaughter is upset because she loves swimming and her parents aren't able to take her because of their work schedules.

Aniya's love of spending time with her granddaughter suggests that 'nurturing' (or similar) is an important personal value for her. Stopping their shared activity of swimming due to fears about how others perceive her appearance is clearly obstructing her from living in line with this value. Helping Aniya to clarify this value and set goals towards connection with her granddaughter – *value clarification* and *committed action* in ACT parlance – is a key focus for intervention. Aniya routinely uses her phone for social media use, so it is likely that she is familiar with app use.

In ACT It Out, users are asked to choose a particular life area they would like to focus their actions towards, as a priority. In Aniya's case, she may choose 'Relationships'. Users are then presented with a series of values and asked to rate how important each one is to them (e.g. assertiveness, kindness, intimacy etc.) This helps to shortlist and clarify which are most important to them. Users are then invited to set achievable value-based goals for the day, week and year. For Aniya, such goals might involve speaking to her granddaughter to find another activity she would like to do together, doing this (e.g. taking her to the playground), and ultimately working towards taking her swimming again.

We are also told that Aniya stopped going swimming because she "hates" feeling embarrassed. Behavioural avoidance like this, to get rid of or avoid unpleasant feelings or situations, is known as experiential avoidance (Hayes, 2004). ACT It Out could help Aniya open up to these difficult thoughts and feelings and hence reduce their power, by developing mindfulness (of which experiential *acceptance* is part) via tailored mindfulness practices that are included in the app. Greater experiential acceptance is likely to help her open up to feeling embarrassed at the pool in order to nurture her relationship with her granddaughter.

Support Around Romantic and Intimate Relationships

Adults with visible differences have reported that appearance-related concerns can impact their experiences of developing and maintaining romantic relationships (Griffiths et al., 2012; Sharratt et al., 2018). Disclosing or revealing a visible difference can be particularly challenging, with individuals reporting fears of negative evaluation from potential or current romantic partners (Sharratt et al., 2020). Adults have also reported that concerns related to their visible difference can impact their ability to engage with and enjoy sex and physical intimacy, with many reporting a reduction in sexual desire and avoiding situations where sex or physical intimacy might occur (Sharratt et al., 2018). The research conducted by Sharratt et al. (2018; 2020) and Griffiths et al. (2012) indicates a need for targeted psychosocial support but, until recently, there has been a lack of interventions specifically focussed on intimacy and romantic relationships and aimed at adults with a visible difference of any kind.

Loving ACTion is a new intervention delivered via a podcast series and focussed specifically on improving appearance-related distress in romantic relationships for adults with a visible difference (see Case Study 2: Sam). It was developed utilising a rigorous and iterative Participatory Action Research approach. A Delphi consensus study including specialist clinicians and researchers identified ACT as the optimal therapeutic approach, and key areas for intervention content including internal shame, appearance-related concerns and avoidant behaviours. The intervention was then co-produced alongside adults with lived experience through a series of feedback discussions and recording sessions. It consists of seven episodes, covering topics including appearance anxiety, communication and disclosure, values in relationships, and sex and physical intimacy. It is a Level 2 intervention on the CAR framework – a self-guided intervention with low-intensity therapeutic content.

The podcast modality of Loving ACTion means that individuals can privately engage in content at their own pace, which is a particularly important consideration for content that could be considered sensitive and emotive and possibly challenging to raise with a healthcare professional. However, Loving ACTion may not be suitable as a standalone intervention for adults with more complex support needs (who may require a higher level of support, for example Level 4 or 5 interventions provided by a specialist such as a clinical psychologist with expertise in working with people with visible differences). Loving ACTion is the first evidence-based intervention focussed specifically on concerns related to intimacy and romantic relationships, thereby addressing a gap in previous support provision.

Case Study 2: Sam

Sam is 25 years old and was born with a bilateral cleft lip and palate which has been surgically repaired. They have a visible scar and some ongoing speech difficulties. Sam recently invited Charlie, who they met on an online dating app, to go on a date. Sam is worried about when and how they should disclose their visible difference and has been wondering whether to tell Charlie in a text before they meet or mention it in person. Thinking about this conversation has made Sam very anxious and consider cancelling the date.

Sam could benefit from engaging in the Loving ACTion content related to identifying and clarifying their values in relationships. If Sam feels that pursuing a relationship is important, they could listen to the episode on difficult thoughts and feelings, and try some of the mindfulness exercises to help manage their anxiety about talking about the scar. Whilst walking to work, Sam could listen to the episode about disclosure and try the exercise on preparing for disclosure conversations to help decide how and when to talk to Charlie about their visible difference.

An Intervention Focused on Body Appreciation and Functionality

In recent years, researchers in the broader field of body image have been increasingly focussed on 'positive body image' and considering how to harness this construct to improve psychosocial outcomes in the general population. 'Positive body image' is distinct from 'negative body image' and includes elements of body appreciation (including an appreciation of one's functionality, health and features), body acceptance and the filtering of information in a body-protective manner (Tylka & Wood-Barcalow, 2015). A variety of interventions to promote positive body image have been developed and tested with general population samples, and researchers are now considering how it could help individuals with visible differences.

Relevant interventions might include intuitive eating, CBT, self-compassion, exercise and functionality exercises – a recent review found evidence that each of these are associated with improvements in positive body image (Guest et al., 2019). Particularly strong evidence has been found for an online writing-based functionality intervention, 'Expand your Horizon', which encourages participants to focus on what their body can do (i.e. body functionality) rather than how it looks. Developed by Alleva and colleagues, 'Expand your Horizon' does this by asking participants to complete three 15-minute writing exercises over the course of a week. This intervention has been found to improve multiple domains of positive body image in general population samples, including increased levels of body satisfaction, body appreciation and body functionality (Alleva et al., 2015, 2018a).

With evidence suggesting the effectiveness of 'Expand your Horizon' in the general population and in individuals with rheumatoid arthritis (Alleva et al., 2018b), researchers (Guest et al., 2024) adapted the intervention to explore its utility with individuals who have a visible difference. Case Study 3: Geeta illustrates a scenario in which this approach could be beneficial.

Whilst other interventions aiming to improve appearance-related distress in individuals with a visible difference may focus on addressing existing negative beliefs or experiences in relation to their condition, positive body image interventions aim to protect the individual from negative messaging and encourage them to foster more positive feelings towards their body (Harcourt & Williamson, 2019). Inviting adults with dermatological conditions to complete this functionality-based writing exercise Adkins et al. (2022) found improvements in body appreciation and functionality when compared to a control group. Their research did not, however, find an impact on appearance-or skin-related distress, suggesting the intervention had influenced elements of positive body image, but had not necessarily reduced negative body image. These results were echoed by Guest et al. (2024), who found significantly higher functionality appreciation in a group of adults who completed an online version of the programme adapted to suit people with visible differences (known as 'More than my Appearance'). However, although participants enjoyed the intervention, the study did not find an effect on body appreciation, depression or anxiety.

These studies demonstrate the potential benefits of using positive body image interventions with individuals with a visible difference and how distinct these are from traditional interventions targeting psychological distress or negative body image. Whilst neither observed change in these negative body image domains, Guest et al. (2024) suggested that positive body image interventions such as this could be most useful within a toolbox of interventions to support individuals with a visible difference. For example, combined with SST- or ACT-based interventions, such as those outlined in this chapter, as well as population level interventions to address societal attitudes and stigma. It is a Level 2 intervention on the CAR framework: self-guided intervention with low-intensity therapeutic content.

Case Study 3: Geeta

Geeta is 37, married with two children, and works as an office administrator. Five years ago she sustained a burn injury that has left her with facial scars. Her eyesight, speech, hearing and swallowing are unaffected, but she has become very self-conscious of her appearance. She feels her body has let her down and blames that for her discontent with her current job. She would rather be a receptionist in a doctor's surgery but doesn't feel confident to apply for a new job because she thinks nobody would employ her looking as she does.

Completing the guided writing tasks within the 'More than my Appearance' intervention (available at www.uwe.ac.uk/research/centres-and-groups/appearance/resources) would involve Geeta reflecting on what her body can do in terms of sensations (e.g. feeling pleasure), physical capabilities (e.g. walking), internal processes (e.g. digesting food), creative endeavours (e.g. singing), self-care (e.g. sleeping), and relationships and communication with others (e.g. hugging). These reflections could help Geeta to think about her body in a more holistic way and to appreciate it for what it can do, not what it looks like. This holistic appreciation could increase her confidence to apply for the career she aspires to.

High Level Specialist Therapy

The highest levels of interventions (Levels 4 and 5) are delivered by psychosocial specialists, such as clinical psychologists or social workers with particular expertise and training and capable of supporting patients with the most complex needs or comorbidities. These interventions could include those with suicidal ideation, debilitating levels of anxiety or depression related to appearance changes, inability to make treatment decisions that affect appearance, or with traumatic responses to body image-related treatment changes. Whilst historically delivered face-to-face, the COVID-19 pandemic saw this level of support being provided through online video conferencing platforms. The effectiveness of online versus in-person support at these levels warrants investigation.

A CBT-based manual to guide psychosocial specialists working at this highest level was developed by Clarke et al. (2014), informed by research into the factors and processes that influenced psychosocial adjustment amongst 1,265 adults with a range of visible differences (Rumsey et al., 2014). The manual offers session-by-session outlines, from the initial assessment that explores the value the individual places on appearance, the impact of appearance-related concerns on cognitions, feelings and behaviour on day-to-day life, and the coping strategies that the individual has/has not been using to date. Targeting and challenging beliefs about appearance is then achieved by focussing on recognizing and changing maladaptive behaviour, building social skills, using graded exposure in social settings and using the results of these behavioural experiments to modify prevailing beliefs and underlying assumptions. Whilst the manual (illustrated by Case Study 4: Paolo) has been widely used by psychosocial specialists, it has yet to be evaluated.

Case Study 4: Paolo

Paolo is 37. Eight months ago he was diagnosed with Bell's Palsy which affected his facial appearance. He was initially told that around 70% of people recover from Bell's Palsy within six months, and he is now very distressed and worried that his facial paralysis will be permanent. His GP has referred him to an experienced clinical psychologist with expertise in appearance-related issues. In a careful, in-depth assessment, the psychologist established that Paolo's anxiety centred on his worries around meeting new people and fearing that they would not understand him when he spoke. He felt that he was no longer the person he had been before the paralysis and was worried that he would lose his job as an estate agent. The psychologist worked with him to set out a formulation of his difficulties and to explain how the different emotions, beliefs and behaviours that he experienced made sense given his history. Over several weeks, they challenged his fears that he could no longer function by agreeing on specific tasks that he would complete at home. The outcome of these tasks and his feedback on the experience of completing them were then fed back into the formulation to challenge his beliefs and revise his expectations about himself. At the end of therapy he was less preoccupied with his speech, was able to be more accepting of his facial appearance, was considering dating again and was more confident at work. This is the highest level intervention on the CAR framework involving one-to-one evidence-based CBT sessions with a psychosocial specialist.

Support for Parents/Carers

Caring for children and young people with appearance-affecting conditions and injuries can require parents/carers to take on unique challenges and responsibilities, in addition to the 'typical' experiences of parenting. These can include emotional distress related to initial diagnostic processes (Stock et al., 2019), guilt following an accidental injury (Heath et al., 2018), and actual or anticipated social stigma, such as worries about teasing and bullying (Oliver et al., 2020; Thornton et al., 2024) or unwanted attention (Ablett & Thompson, 2016).

Historically, there has been a gap in cross-condition evidence-based support for parents/carers of children and young people with visible difference. Previous interventions have tended to focus on skills training to help them manage their child's condition, rather than emotional support for the parents themselves. In contrast, The Visible Difference Parenting Toolkit is an ACT-based e-book which aims to improve the psychosocial wellbeing of parents/carers of children with a visible difference of any kind and of any age. This self-guided intervention contains low level therapeutic content, so it aligns with Level 2 (a stand-alone intervention) on the CAR framework of interventions.

The Visible Difference Parenting Toolkit was informed by a series of studies. First, a qualitative study with 20 parents of children with a wide range of visible differences and 11 health professionals. This study found that parents/carers reported worries about potential future challenges related to their child's visible difference and concerns about how to best prepare them to manage these effectively and independently (Thornton et al., 2021). A cross-sectional online survey with 209 parents then found that parent-reported teasing was associated with greater psychological distress and greater self-compassion, and open parent-child communication and knowledge of the child's condition or injury was associated with reduced psychological distress (Thornton et al., 2024). These findings indicated an unmet support need and identified several important psychosocial constructs for intervention development. Finally, the intervention was co-produced with experts-by-experience (parents/carers and clinicians) during a series of iterative collaborative workshops.

Section one of The Visible Difference Parenting Toolkit focuses on the core principles of ACT and aims to teach skills for managing difficult thoughts and feelings, known as "helper skills". Section two is comprised of advice, guidance and exercises based on key topics identified in the qualitative study and survey outlined earlier: managing social challenges, communication, finding information and finding the right support. Case Study 5: Grace is an example of when The Visible Difference Parenting Toolkit could be useful.

The accessible nature of the e-book format makes The Visible Difference Parenting Toolkit quick and easy to access and use. Given the low intensity and self-guided nature of the resource, it is not appropriate for parents or carers experiencing high levels of psychological distress. However, the content could be adapted by healthcare professionals (e.g., clinical or health psychologists) to support parents with more complex needs alongside additional intervention.

Case Study 5: Grace

Grace is 11 years old and was born with a rare birthmark condition called Congenital Melanocytic Naevi (CMN) on her face. Her birthmark doesn't bother her, she is generally happy and has lots of friends at school. She loves singing and dancing at home and with her friends at school. She would love to join a local theatre group for young people and then study musical theatre at college. Her dream is to be a professional actor. Grace's parents worry about what the future will hold for her, that people will stare at her, that she will be teased at the theatre group and never chosen for roles on stage. They are finding the situation very stressful and feeling very anxious, but don't want to Grace to miss out on her love of musicals so they have subscribed to more TV channels so that they have a big selection to watch together at home, although Grace would like to go to the theatre.

Grace's parents might benefit from The Visible Difference Parenting Toolkit to help them to manage their difficult thoughts and feelings about receiving unwanted social attention, and explore how this is impacting the family. Following the principles of ACT in Section one of the toolkit, they could use values clarification exercises to better understand what is important to them as a family and learn skills to live in line with these values, even when difficult thoughts and feelings do come up. They could also use the tools in Section two on managing social challenges to develop some strategies to manage unwanted attention from others, if the situation arises. They might also find it helpful to look for positive media representations of people with visible differences, including successful actors with visible differences, and to be aware of support that could be helpful to Grace, if she should need it in the future (see next section).

Support for Young People

Young people with a visible difference experience unique challenges relating to this period in their lifespan, and various interventions have been specifically developed to help those experiencing appearance-related distress or challenges associated with their visible difference at this time. A recent systematic review (Waite et al., 2024) suggests that these interventions can broadly be grouped into residential camps, social skills training and CBT-based programmes, with most having been developed for young people with a specific visible difference (e.g. residential burn camps (Armstrong-James et al., 2018)). Whilst qualitative evidence suggests these interventions are highly acceptable and popular with young people, further high-quality studies are required to demonstrate their effectiveness and the factors that influence this.

One example of a successful cross-condition intervention designed for young people with visible differences is YP Face IT, an online psychosocial intervention with a focus on teaching adolescents self-management skills (Williamson et al., 2015). YP Face IT's key mission was to provide easy access and reduce barriers to support for young people with a visible difference. It was built on a similar intervention, 'Face It', developed to support adults with a visible difference of any kind (Bessell et al., 2010). Based on the key therapeutic components and chronology of 'Face IT', researchers used a participatory action research approach to adapt the intervention to meet the specific needs of adolescents and maximise acceptability in this age group. This process was evidence-based and highly collaborative, involving adolescents, healthcare professionals and the research team in face-to face workshops and usability analysis (Williamson et al., 2015). Like Face IT, the final content of the YP Face IT programme was based on social skills training and CBT techniques. It consisted of seven interactive weekly sessions, with embedded outcome measures and tailored feedback for users.

Feasibility and acceptability studies of YP Face IT in the UK and the Netherlands yielded promising results (Williamson et al., 2019; van Dalen et al., 2022), with two large scale studies going on to explore the effectiveness of YP Face IT in Norwegian and Dutch populations. These trials suggested positive outcomes in adolescents' scores on social anxiety and body esteem measures (Zelihić et al., 2022; Kling et al., 2022), with the intervention more suitable for those with greater levels of psychological distress pre-intervention. Recently, the Norwegian version of YP Face IT ('Ung Face IT') has been adapted and updated for its target population (for example, by including sections on social media) and now exists as a standalone intervention.

YP Face IT is an example of a widely accessible standalone intervention that young people could access at home. This is a Level 3 intervention on the CAR framework, since it is self-directed but requires a level of ongoing commitment to complete the full programme. Whilst not intended to replace more targeted one-to-one psychological support provided by a therapist, interventions like this provide an alternative form of support for those who require a less intensive solution or who may otherwise face barriers to accessing support. Similar interventions could also be used alongside support from a psychosocial specialist for those with a higher level of need. As knowledge about the support needs of young people with a visible difference grows, more support for this demographic will no doubt be developed in the future. The rigorous development and evaluation of YP Face IT offers a template for co-produced and rigorously tested interventions, with international collaboration extending its reach far beyond the original UK audience.

Considerations for Health Professionals and Support Organisations

Across the globe, charitable organisations and NGOs, many of which are small and under-resourced, play an invaluable role in supporting people affected by visible differences. They, and health professionals, are key in identifying and meeting people's support needs and we believe that a targeted, appearance-specific stepped care framework can help them achieve this. They also play an important role in supporting, motivating and encouraging people to engage with and complete the interventions outlined here.

Low level interventions such as clear communication, appropriate language use and information provision can be beneficial for everyone impacted by visible difference, not only those deemed to be struggling. Screening tools could help to identify those who might benefit from further support and then direct them towards reputable evidence-based interventions, but these tools must not be onerous for either patients or professionals if they are to be used as part of routine care.

Some staff could benefit from training to raise their awareness and understanding of the possible psychosocial impact of visible difference, so that they feel equipped and confident in discussing, managing and addressing individuals' concerns. For example, training packages such as those developed during a range of European-funded projects led by the team at Triskelionnorway.org can be useful, whilst many burn care teams within the UK use a specialist training package developed by the charity Changing Faces. Health professionals also have an invaluable role to play in creating an ethos in which appearance-related concerns and their consequences can be routinely and easily discussed within consultations, just as physical issues such as pain, fatigue or sickness are.

Looking Ahead

To date, the majority of interventions in this field have focussed on supporting the individual with the visible difference themselves. Whilst some, for example The Visible Difference Parenting Toolkit detailed earlier, are intended for parents/carers, there is still a need to understand more about any specific support needs of others including siblings, grandparents, other family members or romantic/intimate partners, and interventions to meet any specific needs they may have. Researchers and clinicians should be open to the possibilities of using (and adapting, where necessary) interventions in the broader body image field. For example, Lewis-Smith et al. (2018) adapted a theoretically based body image intervention to meet the needs of women who had been diagnosed with breast cancer. Perhaps this could form a basis for a new group-based intervention for adults with visible differences, either online or in person. The timing of interventions also needs further consideration. For example, the potential benefits and challenges of providing early intervention as part of routine care after burn injuries is being explored (see Shepherd et al., 2024).

The potential for social media to be used as a means to support people with visible differences, for example by connecting with others with similar lived experiences and by promoting broader acceptance of diversity of appearance, is significant. However, whilst online interventions can conveniently offer access to support at a time and place of the individual's choosing (and were clearly popular choices in the survey reported by Clement et al., 2025), it is important to ensure that other modes of support are still available for those without access to the internet, who lack confidence online or would benefit from higher-level intense specialist support (see Clarke et al., 2014).

Interventions to raise awareness and understanding of how others around the individual (for example teachers and employers) might support people with visible differences could also be of benefit. A number of freely available resources can be accessed on Face Equality International's resource hub at https://faceequalityinternational.org/resources/, and ensuring that all resources have been suitably evaluated would be a valuable addition to the field.

As is the case for body image research more broadly (see Landor et al., 2024), most visible difference interventions have been developed by researchers based in majority white, high income, English-speaking countries (particularly the UK and US). Work to establish the need, and appropriate, acceptable, feasible and effective interventions in other settings, particularly in low and middle income countries, should be a priority. Likewise, many groups are currently under-represented in visible difference intervention research, including people who identify as LGBTQIA+, men, older adults, military veterans, people with disabilities and those with limited language comprehension which makes accessing and using current interventions a challenge at best, impossible at worst. This work requires the use of appropriate and pragmatic designs. Randomised controlled trials are not necessarily appropriate or feasible in this situation, and establishing ways to maximise the implementation and impact of research-based interventions is imperative.

Conclusion

The survey by Clement et al. (2025) showed that individuals with a range of visible differences have wide ranging yet similar support needs, requiring holistic support from various providers, delivered in a range of formats. This chapter has outlined a range of psychosocial interventions aiming to meet some of their needs, and those of parents/carers of children and young people. Given the complexity of visible differences, we do not claim or anticipate that these alone will suffice, but we hope it demonstrates how support can be tailored to meet individuals' differing needs. These needs may change over time, and the relevance of interventions is not static. We have concentrated mostly on examples of self-guided interventions since they provide greatest access and are relevant for the largest numbers of users. Easy access to a range of interventions could give individuals multiple tools to draw upon to meet their evolving support needs. Work to continue to develop and evaluate new sources of support is imperative, as is making sure they are easily available to those who could benefit from them, and ensuring key stakeholders, such as health professionals and staff in support organisations, are confident and able to use and signpost to them. Whilst much progress has been made in recent years, there is still much work to be done.

References

Ablett, K., & Thompson, A. R. (2016). Parental, child, and adolescent experience of chronic skin conditions: A meta-ethnography and review of the qualitative literature. *Body Image, 19*, 175–185.

Adkins, K. V., Overton, P. G., & Thompson, A. R. (2022). A brief online writing intervention improves positive body image in adults living with dermatological conditions. *Frontiers in Medicine, 9*, 1064012.

Alleva, J. M., Diedrichs, P. C., Halliwell, E., Martijn, C., Stuijfzand, B. G., Treneman-Evans, G., & Rumsey, N. (2018a). A randomised-controlled trial investigating potential underlying mechanisms of a functionality-based approach to improving women's body image. *Body Image, 25*, 85–96.

Alleva, J. M., Diedrichs, P. C., Halliwell, E., Peters, M. L., Dures, E., Stuijfzand, B. G., & Rumsey, N. (2018b). More than my RA: A randomized trial investigating body image improvement among women with rheumatoid arthritis using a functionality-focused intervention program. *Journal of Consulting and Clinical Psychology, 86*(8), 666.

Alleva, J. M., Martijn, C., Van Breukelen, G. J., Jansen, A., & Karos, K. (2015). Expand your horizon: A programme that improves body image and reduces self-objectification by training women to focus on body functionality. *Body Image, 15*, 81–89.

Armstrong-James, L., Cadogan, J., Williamson, H., Rumsey, N., & Harcourt, D. (2018). An evaluation of the impact of a burn camp on children and young people's concerns about social situations, satisfaction with appearance and behaviour. *Scars, Burns & Healing, 4*. https://doi.org/10.1177/2059513118816219

Bessell, A., Clarke, A., Harcourt, D., Moss, T. P., & Rumsey, N. (2010). Incorporating user perspectives in the design of an online intervention tool for people with visible differences: Face IT. *Behavioural and Cognitive Psychotherapy, 38*(5), 577–596.

Changing Faces. (2019). *My visible difference*. https://www.changingfaces.org.uk/wp-content/uploads/2021/01/CHANGING-FACES-Report-My-Visible-Difference.pdf

Clarke, A., Thompson, A. R., Jenkinson, E., Rumsey, N., & Newell, R. (2014). *CBT for appearance anxiety: Psychosocial interventions for anxiety due to visible difference*. John Wiley & Sons.

Clement, C., Roberts-Mills, W., Thornton, M., Clarke, A., Mathews, A., Zucchelli, F., White, P., Slater, A., & Harcourt, D. (2025). Supporting individuals with a visible difference: A UK survey of needs and preferences, *Body Image, 52*, 101840, ISSN 1740-1445. https://doi.org/10.1016/j.bodyim.2024.101840

Costa, B., Thornton, M., Guest, E., Meyrick, J., & Williamson, H. (2021). The effectiveness of interventions to improve psychosocial outcomes in parents of children with appearance-affecting health conditions: A systematic review. *Child: Care, Health and Development, 47*(1), 15–30.

Egan, K., Harcourt, D., Rumsey, N., & The Appearance Research Collaboration. (2011). A qualitative study of the experiences of people who identify themselves as having adjusted positively to a visible difference. *The Journal of Health Psychology, 16*, 739–749.

Griffiths, C., Williamson, H., & Rumsey, N. (2012). The romantic experiences of adolescents with a visible difference: Exploring concerns, protective factors and support needs. *Journal of Health Psychology, 17*, 1053–1064.

Guest, E., Costa, B., Williamson, H., Meyrick, J., Halliwell, E., & Harcourt, D. (2019). The effectiveness of interventions aiming to promote positive body image in adults: A systematic review. *Body Image, 30*, 10–25.

Guest, E., Halliwell, E., Mathews, A., Alleva, J. M., & Harcourt, D. (2024). More than my appearance: A pilot evaluation of the expand your horizon online functionality-based writing programme for adults with visible differences. *Health Psychology and Behavioral Medicine, 12*(1), 2349004.

Harcourt, D., Hamlet, C., Billaud Feragen, K., Garcia-Lopez, L-J., Masnari, O., Mendes, J., Nobile, F., Okkerse, J., Pittermann, A., Spillekom-van Koulil, S., Stock, N. M., & Williamson, H. (2018). The provision of specialist psychosocial support for people with visible differences: A European survey. *Body Image, 25*, 35–39.

Harcourt, D., & Williamson, H. (2019). Positive body image in people living with visible differences. In T. L. Tylka & N. Piran (Eds.), *Handbook of positive body image and embodiment: Constructs, protective factors, and interventions* (pp. 255–262). Oxford University Press.

Hayes, S. C. (2004). Acceptance and commitment therapy, relational frame theory, and the third wave of behavioral and cognitive therapies. *Behavior Therapy*, *35*(4), 639–665.

Heath, J., Williamson, H., Williams, L., & Harcourt, D. (2018). Parent-perceived isolation and barriers to psychosocial support: A qualitative study to investigate how peer support might help parents of burn-injured children. *Scars, Burns & Healing, 4,* 1–12.

Heath, J., Williamson, H., Williams, L., & Harcourt, D. (2020). www.SupportingChildrenWithBurns.co.uk: A website developed with parents and professionals for the psychosocial support of parents of burn-injured children, *Burns, 46,* 1232–1233.

Hooper, N., & Larsson, A. (2015). The research journey of acceptance and commitment therapy (ACT). In *The research journey of acceptance and commitment therapy (ACT).* Palgrave Macmillan.

Jenkinson, E., Williamson, H., Byron-Daniel, J., & Moss, T. P. (2015). Systematic review: Psychosocial interventions for children and young people with visible differences resulting from appearance altering conditions, injury, or treatment effects. *Journal of Pediatric Psychology*, *40*(10), 1017–1033.

Kling, J., Zelihić, D., Williamson, H., & Feragen, K. B. (2022). Is it safe? Exploring positive and negative outcome changes following a web-based intervention for adolescents distressed by a visible difference (YP Face IT). *Body Image*, *43*, 8–16.

Landor, A. M., Ramseyer Winter, V. L., Thurston, I. B., Chan, J., Craddock, N., Ladd, B. A., Tylka, T. L., Swami, V., Watson, L. B., & Choukas-Bradley, S. (2024). The sociostructural-intersectional body image (SIBI) framework: Understanding the impact of white supremacy in body image research and practice, *Body Image, 48*. https://doi.org/10.1016/j.bodyim.2023.101674

Lewis-Smith, H., Diedrichs, P. C., & Harcourt, D. (2018). A pilot study of a body image intervention for breast cancer survivors. *Body Image, 27,* 21–31.

Muftin, Z., & Thompson, A. R. (2013). A systematic review of self-help for disfigurement: Effectiveness, usability, and acceptability. *Body Image*, *10*(4), 442–450.

Norman, A., & Moss, T. P. (2015). Psychosocial interventions for adults with visible differences: A systematic review. *PeerJ*, *3*, e870.

Ofcom. (2020). *Communications market reports*. https://www.ofcom.org.uk/research-and-data/multi-sector-research/cmr

Oliver, J., Dixon, C., & Murray, C. D. (2020). Being the parent of a child with limb difference who has been provided with an artificial limb: An interpretative phenomenological analysis. *Disability and Rehabilitation*, *42*(14), 1979–1986.

Robinson, E., Rumsey, N., & Partridge, J. (1996). An evaluation of the impact of social interaction skills training for facially disfigured people, *British Journal of Plastic Surgery*, *49*(5), 281–289.

Rumsey, N., Bryon-Daniel, J., Clarke, A., Clarke, S. A., Harcourt, D., Jenkinson, E., Lindenmeyer, A, McBain, H., Moss, T., Newman, S., Newell, R., Saul, K., Thomas, E., Thompson, A. R., & White, P. (2014). Factors and processes associated with psychological adjustment to disfiguring conditions. In A. Clarke, A. R. Thompson, E. Jenkinson, N. Rumsey, & R. Newell (Eds.), *CBT for appearance anxiety* (pp. 194–271). Wiley Blackwell.

Rumsey, N., & Harcourt, D. (2004). Body image and disfigurement: Issues and interventions. *Body Image, 1*(1), 83–97.

Rumsey, N., & Harcourt, D. (2012). Where do we go from here? In N. Rumsey & D. Harcourt (Eds.), *The Oxford handbook of the psychology of appearance* (pp. 679–692). Oxford University Press.

Sharratt, N. D., Jenkinson, E., Moss, T., Clarke, A., & Rumsey, N. (2018). Understandings and experiences of visible difference and romantic relationships: A qualitative exploration. *Body Image*, *27*, 32–42.

Sharratt, N. D., Williamson, H., Zucchelli, F., & Kiff, J. (2020). Becoming known: Disclosure and exposure of (in) visible difference. *Stigma and Health*, *5*(4), 413.

Shepherd, L., Reynolds, D. P., Turner, A., O'Boyle, C. P., & Thompson, A. R. (2019). The role of psychological flexibility in appearance anxiety in people who have experienced a visible burn injury. *Burns, 45*(4), 942–949.

Shepherd, L., Sirois, F., Harcourt, D., Norman, P., & Thompson, A. R. (2024). The acceptability of early psychological interventions for adults with appearance concerns after burns. *Burns*. https://doi.org/10.1016/j.burns.2024.07.038

Stock, N. M., Costa, B., Williams, J. R., & Martindale, A. (2019). Breaking the news: Parents' experiences of receiving an antenatal diagnosis of cleft lip. *The Cleft Palate-Craniofacial Journal*, *56*(9), 1149–1156.

Thornton, M., Harcourt, D., Deave, T., Kiff, J., White, P., & Williamson, H. (2024). Cross-condition risk and protective factors for psychosocial distress in parents and carers of children and young people with appearance-affecting conditions and injuries. *Body Image*, *51*, 101768.

Thornton, M., Harcourt, D., Deave, T., Kiff, J., & Williamson, H. (2021). "Have we done enough?" A cross-condition exploration of the experiences of parents caring for a child with an appearance-affecting condition or injury. *Developmental Neurorehabilitation*, *24*(6), 418–428.

Tollow, P., Hamlet, C., Zucchelli, F., Williamson, H., & Harcourt, D. (2023). Experiences and impact of the UK lockdown amongst adults who have a facial visible difference. *Current Psychology*. https://doi.org/10.1007/s12144-022-04089-5

Tylka, T. L., & Wood-Barcalow, N. L. (2015). What is and what is not positive body image? Conceptual foundations and construct definition. *Body Image*, *14*, 118–129.

van Dalen, M., Pasmans, S. G. M. A., Aendekerk, E. W. C., Mathijssen, I. M. J., Koudstaal, M. J., Williamson, H., Hillegers, M. H. J., Utens, E. M. W. J., & Okkerse, J. M. E. (2022). Acceptability and feasibility of an online psychosocial intervention for Dutch adolescents with a visible difference: A mixed-methods study. *Body Image*, *41*, 298–307.

Waite, E., Jenkinson, E., Kershaw, S., & Guest, E. (2024). Psychosocial interventions for children and young people with visible differences resulting from appearance-altering conditions, injury, or treatment effects: An updated systematic review. *Journal of Pediatric Psychology*, *49*(1), 77–88.

Williamson, H., Griffiths, C., & Harcourt, D. (2015). Developing young person's Face IT: Online psychosocial support for adolescents struggling with conditions or injuries affecting their appearance. *Health Psychology Open*, *2*(2). https://doi.org/10.1177/2055102915619092

Williamson, H., Hamlet, C., White, P., Marques, E. M. R., Paling, T., Cadogan, J., Perera, R., Rumsey, N., Hayward, L., & Harcourt, D. (2019). A web-based self-help psychosocial intervention for adolescents distressed by appearance-affecting conditions and injuries (young persons' face it): Feasibility study for a parallel randomized controlled trial. *JMIR Mental Health*, *6*(11). https://doi.org/10.2196/1477

Yuen, E. K., Goetter, E. M., Herbert, J. D., & Forman, E. M. (2012). Challenges and opportunities in internet-mediated telemental health. *Professional Psychology: Research and Practice*, *43*(1), 1.

Zelihić, D., van Dalen, M., Kling, J., Pripp, A. H., Nordgreen, T., Kvalem, I. L., Pasmans, S. G. M. A., Mathijssen, I. M. J., Koudstaal, M. J., Hillegers, M. H. J., Williamson, H., Utens, E. M. W. J., Feragen, K. B., & Okkerse, J. M. E. (2022). Reducing social anxiety in adolescents distressed by a visible difference: Results from a randomised control trial of a web-based intervention. *Body Image*, *40*, 295–309.

Zucchelli, F., Donnelly, O., Rush, E., White, P., Gwyther, H., Williamson, H., & VTCT Foundation Research Team at the Centre for Appearance Research. (2022). An acceptance and commitment therapy prototype mobile program for individuals with a visible difference: Mixed methods feasibility study. *JMIR Formative Research*, *6*(1), e33449.

Zucchelli, F. A., Donnelly, O., Sharratt, N. D., Hooper, N., & Williamson, H. M. (2021). Patients' experiences of an acceptance and commitment therapy-based approach for psychosocial difficulties relating to an appearance-affecting condition. *The European Journal of Counselling Psychology*, *9*(1), 29–40.

Zucchelli, F., Donnelly, O., Williamson, H., & Hooper, N. (2018). Acceptance and commitment therapy for people experiencing appearance-related distress associated with a visible difference: A rationale and review of relevant research. *Journal of Cognitive Psychotherapy*, *32*(3), 171–183.

5 Visible Difference and Social Media

Harnessing a Unique Tool to Increase Support and Reduce Stigma

Ella Guest, Abbi Mathews, and Amy Slater

This chapter discusses social media in relation to visible difference, including how individuals with visible differences engage with social media, the unique challenges they face online, and new research exploring whether social media can be used to reduce appearance-related stigma and increase acceptance of appearance diversity. The chapter ends with a discussion of the practical implications that arise from the current evidence and suggestions for future research in the area.

What is Social Media?

Social media refers to online platforms, like Facebook, Instagram, YouTube and TikTok that allow users to create and share visual and textual content with other users, and to communicate with networks of people (Kaplan & Haenlein, 2010). Social media has quickly become an integral part of daily life for most people, with approximately 5.24 billion worldwide active users as of February 2025, with this number continuing to rise (Petrosyan, 2025). In the United Kingdom (UK), for example, over 82% of the population are social media users (Dixon, 2024b). Social media users are spending considerable time on these platforms, with an average daily use time of approximately two and a half hours per day for users aged 16–64 years old (Dixon, 2024b). Higher usage is reported among women than men (Auxier & Anderson, 2021), and among younger than older generations (Hayes et al., 2015). Social media platforms continue to emerge and evolve and have different levels of uptake with users of different ages but, worldwide, the most popular platforms are Facebook (3.07 billion monthly active users), YouTube (2.50 billion), Instagram (2.00 billion) and TikTok (1.58 billion; Dixon, 2025).

Social media may provide positive benefits such as maintaining or strengthening existing relationships, offering an opportunity for self-expression, and the ability for individuals to form connections despite geographical barriers. However, there is now considerable evidence to suggest that social media use is associated with poorer body image (Saiphoo & Vahedi, 2019) and poorer wellbeing (Jarman et al., 2021). There are several salient features of social media that may play a role in this relationship. First, much social media content is known to be highly appearance focused, with images and content often promoting idealised and unachievable beauty ideals (e.g., thin and toned bodies, clear skin, Eurocentric facial features),

DOI: 10.4324/9781003535591-11

and standards and lives (Jung et al., 2022). Second, the normalcy and ease of digital alterations via apps and filters mean that many images portrayed are unrealistic. When users compare their own appearance to the appearance of the people they see portrayed in social media content (upward appearance comparisons), they are likely to feel that they do not 'measure up', and consequently feel more negatively about themselves (Fardouly et al., 2023). Third, the interactive nature of most social media platforms encourages 'feedback' on content created in the form of 'likes' and comments. These feedback features may serve to reinforce appearance ideals by indicating social approval where content is deemed to align with ideals and disapproval when it does not.

Theoretical Perspectives

There are several established theories and models that have been utilised to explain the influence of social media and body image. These include sociocultural theory (e.g., the tripartite influence model), social comparison theory, objectification theory, and uses and gratification theory. Of note, the vast majority of research has been conducted with young, white, and able-bodied individuals who do not have visible differences. Along with peer and family influences, sociocultural theory (Thompson et al., 1999) views social media as an additional channel for societal ideals of beauty to be disseminated which, when combined with social comparison, leads to the development of negative psychological outcomes. Applying the lens of objectification theory (Fredrickson & Roberts, 1997), social media affords an opportunity to sexually objectify bodies, which can encourage people to think about themselves from an observer's perspective. This external perspective of one's body and appearance is known as 'self-objectification' and has been shown to be associated with poorer psychological outcomes such as disordered eating and depression. Uses and gratification theory (Katz et al., 1973) suggests that individuals have different motivations for social media use, which lead to different types of engagement with social media platforms and, consequently, different outcomes for users as they experience different content and have different interactions (Rodgers et al., 2021).

Influencers

While social media may have started with a primary focus on connecting with friends or known acquaintances in a two-way interaction, many social media users are now also following content from unknown connections, such as celebrities. Indeed, as of 2024, nine of the top ten most followed Instagram accounts are of celebrities in sport (e.g., Cristiano Ronaldo, 636 million followers), music (e.g., Selena Gomez, 425 million followers), and media personalities (e.g., Kim Kardashian, 361 million followers). Social media users are also increasingly following 'influencers'. Social media influencers are content creators who have a status of expertise in a specific area and have cultivated a sizable number of followers across one or more social media platforms (e.g., Instagram, YouTube, or

TikTok). Contrary to celebrities or public figures who may be well known via traditional media, social media influencers are often 'regular people' who have become 'online celebrities' by creating and posting content on social media (Lou & Yuan, 2019). Influencers can attract very large audiences (often of young people) by sharing details about their personal lives, experiences, and opinions through their content (Ki & Kim, 2019). Audiences may trust the thoughts and recommendations of influencers who can shape followers' attitudes and behaviours (including buying behaviours from viewing influencer brand endorsements). In addition to influencing buying behaviours, some research suggests that social media influencers are also a significant alternative source of health-related information for young people (Engel et al., 2024). Others have noted the potential importance of social media influencers in bolstering advocacy efforts to combat stigma and unrealistic appearance ideals (Harriger et al., 2023).

How Do Individuals with Visible Differences Use Social Media?

In addition to using social media to connect with friends and family and view general content, many individuals with visible difference also use social media in relation to their condition or injury. Therefore, their motivations for using social media, and the challenges they face, can differ from the general population. To date, most research in this area has focused on the platform Facebook; however, explorations of other popular platforms such as Instagram, YouTube, and TikTok are increasing. One fundamental way in which individuals with visible differences, and their parents or carers, use social media is to connect with others with the same condition through closed Facebook groups (i.e., private groups that users are granted access to join), which are often hosted by charitable and support organisations. Research with individuals with cleft lip and/or palate and various skin conditions has found that these groups are commonly used to gain condition and treatment-related information and advice, for practical and emotional peer support, and to share personal stories and experiences (Kaundinya et al., 2023; Keim-Malpass & Steeves, 2012; Stock et al., 2018). Moreover, for conditions that are stigmatised, anonymous discussion forums, such as those on the platform Reddit, provide a space to connect and receive support while maintaining privacy and anonymity (Giordano, 2014; Merolli et al., 2013; Amaya et al., 2021).

Social media is used as a source of condition and treatment-related information, and individuals with visible differences report finding it to be a more efficient way to receive answers to their questions than arranging an appointment with a health professional or reading information published on webpages (Kaundinya et al., 2023; Merolli et al., 2013; Montgomery & Elbuluk, 2020; Stock et al., 2018). Furthermore, adults with a range of visible differences interviewed by Guest and colleagues (in preparation) felt that the treatment-related information shared by other social media users went beyond typical, procedural information by providing further context based on lived experience. For example, one participant with cleft lip and/or palate discussed how cleft-related personal stories included additional contextual information about the physical and emotional impact of undergoing surgery, practical tips, and information about what to expect during the longer-term recovery process.

Although the availability of condition and treatment-related information is highly valued by social media users with visible differences, it is largely shared by non-medical experts and is unregulated (Kaundinya et al., 2023). Unfortunately, this lack of regulation can lead to the distribution of potentially harmful misinformation and impact treatment-related decisions made by individuals with visible differences (Kaundinya et al., 2023; Stock et al., 2018; Wilson et al., 2023). For instance, an analysis of social media content relating to cleft lip and/or palate identified that the quality of educational information is varied and can be unreliable (Korkmaz & Buyuk, 2020; Bozkurt & Aras, 2021), which is particularly concerning when misinformation relates to medical treatments. For example, Finnegan et al. (2023) identified misinformation about topical steroids (a treatment used to control flare ups in skin conditions) on social media sites including Facebook, Instagram, TikTok, and X (formerly Twitter), which contributed to significant cardiophobia (fear of topical steroids). Moreover, they identified that numerous treatments with limited evidence of efficacy, or that contained harmful ingredients, were promoted as alternatives. To address misinformation, researchers have highlighted the importance of trained health professionals working alongside organisations and individuals with a social media presence to act as 'digital first responders' by authenticating and correcting misinformation (see Bautista et al., 2021 for practical guidance). Positively, some social media companies are taking a proactive approach to health information, such as YouTube's Health Shelf initiative, which includes verified health information on a range of topics, including some appearance-altering conditions. Nevertheless, support organisations and content creators would benefit from clearer guidance on regulating health information on social media and collaborating effectively with health professionals online (Merolli et al., 2013).

Some qualitative research has also found that social media can help facilitate adjustment to visible differences (i.e., how well someone copes with and adapts to their condition). For example, adults with alopecia and vitiligo reported that connecting with others with the same condition online created a sense of community, belonging, and reduced isolation, which helped them to accept and appreciate their condition and appearance diversity more broadly (Iliffe & Thompson, 2019; Kaundinya et al., 2023; Montgomery & Elbuluk, 2020). Peer support via social media can be particularly useful for connecting and building a sense of community in individuals with rare conditions by overcoming financial and geographical barriers (Guest et al., in preparation; Keim-Malpass & Steeves, 2012; Merolli et al., 2013). Furthermore, participants in Giordano's (2014) study felt that having connections with other burn survivors helped them to make meaning out of the trauma they had experienced. Finally, participants in Guest et al.'s research (in preparation) felt that social media had provided a space for them to become more confident showing their visible differences, which had made them more accepting of their appearance both online and offline. In particular, seeing others with visible differences, including influencers and content creators with large followings, and receiving positive feedback through post likes and comments of support and encouragement aided this process.

While the numerous benefits of social media have been outlined, one significant challenge for individuals with visible differences is experiences of negative comments, trolling, and cyberbullying. Indeed, Jones and colleagues (2021) identified that approximately one third of their sample had experienced cyberbullying due to having a craniofacial condition. Moreover, a survey commissioned by the UK-based national charity Changing Faces found that adolescents with visible differences are three times more likely than their peers to receive negative comments relating to their appearance on social media (Changing Faces, 2018). As visible differences are not protected characteristics in many countries, negative comments are rarely flagged as hate speech even when reported by other users. Given that it is legal to have a social media account from age 13, there needs to be greater protections for young people online. Positively, the UK's recent Online Safety Act (2023) includes laws that protect social media users from harmful content including online bullying, and abusive or hateful content which will be enforced by large fines to social media companies who do not comply with the rules. Furthermore, various school-based interventions include social media literacy content to help children and young people think critically about appearance-related content online (e.g., SoMe, Gordon et al., 2020; Dove Confident Me, Diedrichs et al., 2021) and some also include educational content about visible differences (e.g., Everybody's Different: The Appearance Game, Guest et al., 2021).

Many popular social media platforms, including Facebook, Instagram, YouTube, and TikTok, are highly visual in nature, with their content mostly centring around photographs and videos of people. As with mainstream media, unrealistic beauty standards dominate these platforms, with content often including young, white, able-bodied individuals whose appearance aligns with sociocultural appearance ideals (Foster, 2022). In line with general social media research outlined earlier in the chapter, a key theme in our interview study was that social media creates immense pressure to portray a 'perfect' online self that aligns with sociocultural beauty ideals for all users. However, even with widely used beauty filters and photo-editing tools, these standards are often felt to be unachievable for individuals with visible differences, whose appearances deviate from societal 'norms', which can have a negative impact on body satisfaction, self-esteem, and mood. In addition, participants explained that there are also filters on social media that mimic facial differences, which perpetuates appearance-related stigma and discrimination towards visible differences.

How Can Social Media Be Used to Reduce Stigma Towards Individuals with Visible Differences?

As outlined earlier, individuals with visible differences often experience stigma and discrimination relating to their appearance, including on social media. Although most research to date has focused on the experiences of individuals with visible differences, there is an increasing focus on whether social media can be used as a tool to target the perceptions and behaviors of the general population in relation to visible difference. Specifically, research seeks to understand whether social media can be used to effectively educate about visible differences, thereby reducing stigma and discrimination towards them.

Stigma refers to negative emotions, thoughts, and behaviors towards an individual based on their perceived membership of a certain group (e.g., sexism, racism and ableism, Goffman, 1963). Some individuals with visible differences report being subjected to stigma on a daily basis, through social avoidance, exclusion, bullying, and harassment (Rasset et al., 2022). Research finds that individuals make snap judgements of others' warmth and competence based upon their physical appearance, suggesting that those with visible, and particularly facial, differences are more negatively evaluated than those without (Paruzel-Czachura et al., 2024; Stone & Wright, 2012). Research using eye-tracking software suggests the presence of a facial disfigurement not only attracts attention to the disfigurement, but also diverts attention away from the eyes (Rasset et al., 2022). As the eyes convey key information about emotion and mutual gaze plays a role in establishing relationships, this is likely to negatively impact communication between individuals with visible differences and those they interact with (Senju & Johnson, 2009).

A key source of stigma towards individuals with visible differences is traditional media (e.g., television, film, magazines, newspapers), where visible differences are often underrepresented (not included or visible) and misrepresented (perpetuating stereotypes; Guest & Daniels, 2024). Examples of misrepresentation of visible differences include using the acquisition of scarring to represent a villain's origin story in fictional television and film, or to signify that they are an evil or bitter character. In other cases, visible differences are used synonymously with characters being pathetic, unlovable, or unintelligent (Chen et al., 2022). These stereotypes often exist in children's media, which socialize individuals to fear and avoid those who look 'different' from a young age (Holcomb & Latham-Mintus, 2022). Positive and authentic representation of individuals with visible differences in media could challenge these harmful stereotypes; however, the visible difference community remains underrepresented in mainstream media (Wardle, Boyce & Barron, 2009).

These issues are also reflected in the *social* media landscape, whereby content that aligns with beauty ideals is more likely to receive higher engagement, resulting in underrepresentation of individuals with visible differences (Foster, 2022). However, social media differs from traditional media in many key aspects. First, unlike traditional media, in which the public are passive consumers, social media allows anyone to also be a creator, resulting in the ability for two-way communication between creators and consumers. Therefore, there is a potential for a far greater representation of appearance diversity than in traditional media. In contrast to the harmful stereotypes perpetuated within traditional media, on social media individuals with visible differences can take control of their own representation and portray themselves within an authentic and positive light (Guest & Daniels, 2024). For example, Raiche Mederick (@raichemederick_) has >8,500 Instagram followers and uses her platform to share her life, educate her followers about burn scarring and visible differences more widely and, more recently, share her experiences of pregnancy and motherhood. Influencers with visible differences could therefore have an important role to play in increasing the appearance diversity that the public are exposed to and providing education about visible differences. A benefit of using social media is that its wide reach provides easy access to many members of the public. Indeed, because many individuals are already using social media on a daily basis, viewing and interacting with this content requires little effort from the viewer and can fit into their lives with little cognitive burden. Given the significant time individuals spend on social media, it provides a unique avenue to administer these messages repeatedly.

There are multiple ways in which social media might be utilised to reduce stigma towards the visible difference community. Firstly, social media can be an effective way to provide exposure to appearance diversity in a positive manner. For example, a twice-daily intervention delivered remotely via mobile phone application, which exposed participants to images of individuals with facial differences presented with positive stories about them, reduced implicit biases (Bilici et al., 2022). More indirectly, social media can provide a space to expose individuals to neutral or incidental depictions of those with visible differences, i.e., individuals who happen to have visible differences but are not defined by them and therefore are represented as holistic, ordinary, relatable people (Wardle, Boyce & Barron, 2009). Moreover, incidental representation is more likely to reach a wider audience of people than accounts that are specifically focused on visible differences. Including representation of visible differences within these settings is easy to do and although representation is still lacking, it is increasing in some areas. For example, in advertising, a recent campaign by the leading global beauty retailer Sephora features individuals with visible differences as models. Additionally, there are also talent and modelling agencies that focus on models from diverse and underrepresented groups, such as those with visible difference and disabilities (e.g., Zebedee Talent in the UK).

Social media can also be used to provide information about visible differences to educate, correct misinformation, and challenge stereotypes. For instance, community-led Facebook groups have been used to share images and challenge stigma associated with ostomies (an artificial opening in an organ of the body, used to treat certain diseases; Frohlich & Zmyslinski-Seelig, 2016). In this study, images within a Facebook group were found to challenge ostomy stigma in multiple ways, including by showing that individuals can still feel attractive with an ostomy, challenging the perception that ostomates become recluses, and promoting the idea that ostomies do not hold people back. The positive language and support found in this support group actively encouraged other members to post their own images, providing further content to challenge stigmas associated with this visible difference. Further research has also investigated the impact of these types of content on users who are unfamiliar with the target condition. A recent study used psoriasis-sensitizing content consisting of pictures, text, and videos aiming to draw attention to the skin condition, increase knowledge, and target stigmatisation on the image-based platform Instagram (Maspero et al., 2023). Results suggested that individuals exposed to the psoriasis-sensitizing content had significantly less disease-related misconceptions and stereotype endorsement when compared to a control group. Finally, a study by Guest and colleagues (under review) found that following an Instagram profile containing images of the skin condition vitiligo and factual information in the form of personal stories over the course of one week decreased stigma towards visible differences and increased vitiligo-related knowledge. These studies support the use of social media to provide education and challenge harmful stereotypes associated with conditions affecting appearance, both within groups who are already engaged with the area and the wider public.

Social media is also a suitable platform for disseminating general awareness campaigns. Charity campaigns (e.g., 'I am not your villain' by the UK-based charity Changing Faces) can have a wide reach via social media platforms. Charities supporting those with visible differences have employed campaigns, including Face Equality International's 'Face Equality Week'. During Face Equality Week 2024, the charity encouraged individuals to share selfies (self-photographs) with the caption 'My Face is a Masterpiece' and use the hashtag #FaceEqualityWeek. Changing Faces has run various campaigns, such as 'Stop the Stare', which aimed to educate individuals about the harmful impact of staring at those with visible differences, and 'I Am Not Your Villain', which highlighted harmful stereotypes within film and television. These campaigns raise awareness of visible difference issues and spark viewers to identify injustice, thus, increasing their awareness of stigmatising attitudes and behaviours in future interactions with or concerning individuals with visible differences. Furthermore, having this information equips individuals with more confidence to challenge stigmatising behaviours and comments of others in future interactions. However, the impact and efficacy of these campaigns on the general public is rarely captured in research. Nonetheless, there have been evaluations of some campaigns that seek to increase positive representation of visible differences that have not taken place via social media. For example, after viewing a photography exhibition of individuals with the birthmark condition congenital melanocytic naevi (CMN), over 85% of attendees reported feeling more accepting of people with visible differences (Zolkwer et al., 2023).

Another key avenue through which social media may be able to effectively reduce stigma is through parasocial contact with influencers within the visible difference community. Developing a 'parasocial' or one-sided relationship through sustained engagement with an individual online may be similarly effective at reducing stigma as having direct interpersonal contact, with the additional benefit of reduced capacity of members of the community to build these bonds themselves (Bond, 2020). Social media may be an ideal platform for these bonds as influencers are presented alongside, and can be interacted with, in a comparable way to an individuals' own friends. Furthermore, there are increasingly calls for more diversity in social media influencers, particularly from members of Gen Z (born 1997–2012), suggesting that these audiences would find this intervention acceptable (Foster, 2022). The relationship between social media creators and their audiences are stronger than that of traditional celebrities and public figures because they share more intimate details of their personal lives in a candid way and are therefore perceived to be more authentic. Indeed, previous research has found that reductions in stigma are mediated by the perceived strength of the viewer's parasocial bond with the target individual (Lotun et al., 2022). These bonds can be strengthened through personal narratives that challenge negative perceptions of individuals with facial disfigurements, and can be delivered through written, audio, or video content online (Stone & Fisher, 2020). For example, a recent study investigated the impact of watching a short documentary about people with scars and found that viewers had significantly lower intentions to behave in a stigmatising way towards individuals with visible differences, and viewed a broader range of appearances as beautiful, after viewing the documentary (Mathews et al., 2023). Although this study did not use social media to administer the intervention, these types of content could easily be adapted to fit a social media format. Further research suggests that it is important for the viewer to perceive similarities with the target individual to effectively improve attitudes, suggesting these interventions may work best when target individuals are matched with the viewer on key attributes, such as gender (Neubaum et al., 2020).

Future Research Directions

There are various avenues for future research in relation to visible differences and social media. First, most research to date has focussed on social media use in adults with visible differences; however, young people form the largest group of users, with 91% of children aged 12–15 years in the UK reportedly using social media (Dixon, 2024c). In conjunction with this finding, whereas existing research has largely focussed on Facebook and Instagram, younger populations are more likely to use video-based platforms like TikTok and YouTube. Consequently, research needs to be carried out with these populations to understand their experiences and how they might differ from adults. Secondly, given that there are now a significant number of influencers and content creators with visible differences using social media, it would be beneficial to carry out qualitative research to understand their experiences and provide guidance on how they can use social media effectively, including how to work alongside health professionals and charitable organisations, and protect both themselves and their followers online. Additionally, anonymous discussion forums, such as Reddit, attract users from a wider range of socio-economic, educational, and racial backgrounds than other platforms, including those who wish to receive anonymous support (Luong & Lomanowska, 2022; Shatz, 2017; Guest et al., 2024). Therefore, to fully understand a full range of experiences of social media users with visible differences, it is necessary to broaden research to platforms including Reddit.

At present, there are numerous visible difference campaigns on social media; however, the vast majority have not been evaluated. Therefore, to understand how to effectively use social media to change public perceptions and attitudes towards visible differences, more controlled, experimental research needs to be carried out to identify which specific aspects of posts and campaigns are necessary to elicit meaningful change (e.g., educational information, photographs, personal stories) and the optimal level of engagement needed for these be sustained. Moreover, one key challenge with this kind of research is finding suitable ways to measure levels of stigma. For example, self-report measures are subject to social desirability bias and struggle to capture implicit or 'subconscious' bias. Additionally, there is a lack of validated measures for assessing visible difference stigma, particularly for those with multiple stigmatized identities. Future research should explore ways of measuring stigma, particularly for these groups, and develop measurement tools that are suitable for use by charities and non-profit organisations to evaluate their campaigns.

Practical Implications

There are also several practical implications relating to social media and visible difference. One key recommendation is to develop guidance on how influencers/content creators can best work with health professionals and charitable and support organisations to meet the needs of their followers and ensure that the information being shared is relatable, but also accurate. For example, it would be beneficial for health professionals to help regulate content relating to treatments to ensure that information is accurate and safe. Second, given the widespread instances of online harassment, abuse, and cyberbullying, it is necessary for academics and influencers to work alongside policymakers to develop more stringent guidelines for safe social media use that protects creators and users of social media and increases the social responsibility of social media platforms, such as Meta (owner of Facebook and Instagram), by holding them to account.

Given that the current evidence suggests that viewing visible difference and appearance diversity more generally on social media can have a positive impact on viewers, it is beneficial for charities and influencers to continue to share content that portrays visible difference in a positive and realistic light, and to include educational information about the conditions to inform the general public. Therefore, evidence-informed guidelines should be developed and made available for influencers and charitable organisations supporting people with visible differences to help them develop their social media content and campaigns.

Despite the benefits of social media as an avenue to reduce stigma towards the visible difference community, one issue is the presence of algorithms that limit content reach. Social media platforms use intelligent algorithms to feed viewers content that they are likely to be interested in, meaning that these messages predominantly reach those who are already engaged with the cause. Consequently, these messages are less visible to those who interact with them the least, and who are likely to benefit from these campaigns the most. Furthermore, social media content that aligns with beauty ideals receives more engagement, further promoting narrow beauty ideals and lowering the visibility of visible difference content on platforms (Foster, 2022). Social media platforms have a moral responsibility to monitor their algorithms so that their users are presented with diverse creators. Promoting influencers with visible differences encourages 'incidental' following (i.e., following visible difference influencers because of the type of content they produce. For example, individuals may follow Nikki Lily for fashion content, but she also happens to have a visible difference). As a result, incidental following exposes audiences to, and promotes engagement with, content about the influencers' visible difference and related experiences, as well as providing the basis for a beneficial parasocial relationship with an influencer with whom they have similar interests (Neubaum et al., 2020).

Conclusion

In summary, social media forms an integral part of the lives of many people, including adults with visible differences. Social media has numerous benefits for individuals with visible differences and can help them feel better supported and more confident and accepting of their conditions. However, much of the content on social media is unregulated and those with visible differences face challenges relating to appearance pressures online and with experiences of online bullying and discrimination. Nevertheless, social media can also provide a platform to target more broadly the negative attitudes of the general population in relation to visible difference and appearance diversity. Further research is needed to better understand how to utilise social media in a way to benefit individuals with visible differences.

References

Amaya, A., Bach, R., Keusch, F., & Kreuter, F. (2021). New data sources in social science research: Things to know before working with Reddit data. *Social Science Computer Review*, *39*(5), 943–960.

Auxier, B., & Anderson, M. (2021). *A majority of Americans say they use YouTube and Facebook, while use of Instagram, Snapchat and TikTok is especially common among adults under 30* (p. 8). Pew Research Center.

Bautista, J. R., Zhang, Y., & Gwizdka, J. (2021). Healthcare professionals' acts of correcting health misinformation on social media. *International Journal of Medical Informatics*, *148*, 104375. https://doi.org/10.1016/j.ijmedinf.2021.104375

Bilici, N., Workman, C. I., Humphries, S., Paruzel-Czachura, M., Hamilton, R., & Chatterjee, A. (2022). Normalizing anomalies with mobile exposure (NAME): Reducing implicit biases against people with facial anomalie. *Preprint*. https://doi.org/10.31234/osf.io/wr5bu

Bond, B. J. (2020). Parasocial contact and prejudice reduction. In *The international encyclopedia of media psychology* (pp. 1–4). John Wiley & Sons, Ltd. https://doi.org/10.1002/9781119011071.iemp0205

Bozkurt, A. P., & Aras, I. (2021). Cleft lip and palate YouTube videos: Content usefulness and sentiment analysis. *The Cleft Palate-Craniofacial Journal*, *58*(3), 362–368.

Changing Faces. (2018). *Looking different: The future of face equality*. https://www.changingfaces.org.uk/wp-content/uploads/2021/05/Looking-different-the-future-of-face-equality-18.pdf

Chen, M. K. Y., Shen, K. T., Arulthasan, S. P., & Sebaratnam, D. F. (2022). The spectre of visible difference: Semiotics of disfigurement and moral character in James Bond films. *Clinical and Experimental Dermatology*, *47*(4), 767–768. https://doi.org/10.1111/ced.15034

Diedrichs, P. C., Atkinson, M. J., Garbett, K. M., & Leckie, G. (2021). Evaluating the "dove confident me" five-session body image intervention delivered by teachers in schools: A cluster randomized controlled effectiveness trial. *Journal of Adolescent Health*, *68*(2), 331–341. https://doi.org/10.1016/j.jadohealth.2020.10.001

Dixon, S. (2025). *Global social networks ranked by number of users*. Statista. https://www.statista.com/statistics/272014/global-social-networks-ranked-by-number-of-users/

Dixon, S. J. (2024a). *Active social media users in the United Kingdom (UK) 2024*. Statista. https://www.statista.com/statistics/507405/uk-active-social-media-and-mobile-social-media-users/

Dixon, S. J. (2024b). *Most popular social networks worldwide as of April 2024, by number of monthly active users*. Statista. https://www.statista.com/statistics/272014/global-social-networks-ranked-by-number-of-users/

Dixon, S. (2024c). *Social media usage and profile ownership among children and teenagers in the UK as of October 2021, by age group*. Statista. https://www.statista.com/statistics/1301863/uk-children-social-media-presence-and-usage-by-age/

Engel, E., Gell, S., Heiss, R., & Karsay, K. (2024). Social media influencers and adolescents' health: A scoping review of the research field. *Social Science & Medicine*, *340*, 116387. https://doi.org/10.1016/j.socscimed.2023.116387

Fardouly, J., Slater, A., Parnell, J., & Diedrichs, P. C. (2023). Can following body positive or appearance neutral Facebook pages improve young women's body image and mood? Testing novel social media micro-interventions. *Body Image*, *44*, 136–147. https://doi.org/10.1016/j.bodyim.2022.12.008

Finnegan, P., Murphy, M., & O'Connor, C. (2023). #corticophobia: A review on online misinformation related to topical steroids. *Clinical and Experimental Dermatology*, *48*(2), 112–115. https://doi.org/10.1093/ced/llac019

Foster, J. (2022). "It's all about the look": Making sense of appearance, attractiveness, and authenticity online. *Social Media + Society*, *8*(4). https://doi.org/10.1177/20563051221138762

Fredrickson, B. L., & Roberts, T.-A. (1997). Objectification theory: Toward understanding women's lived experiences and mental health risks. *Psychology of Women Quarterly*, *21*(2), 173–206. https://doi.org/10.1111/j.1471-6402.1997.tb00108.x

Frohlich, D. O., & Zmyslinski-Seelig, A. N. (2016). How uncover ostomy challenges ostomy stigma, and encourages others to do the same. *New Media & Society*, *18*(2), 220–238. https://doi.org/10.1177/1461444814541943

Giordano, M. S. (2014). *The lived experience of young adult burn survivors' use of social media*. https://academicworks.cuny.edu/gc_etds/216/

Goffman, E. (1963). *Stigma; notes on the management of spoiled identity*. Simon & Schuster. https://doi.org/10.2307/2575995

Gordon, C. S., Rodgers, R. F., Slater, A. E., McLean, S. A., Jarman, H. K., & Paxton, S. J. (2020). A cluster randomized controlled trial of the SoMe social media literacy body image and wellbeing program for adolescent boys and girls: Study protocol. *Body Image*, *33*, 27–37. https://doi.org/10.1016/j.bodyim.2020.02.003

Guest, E., & Daniels, E. (2024.). Beauty, media representations and body image. In O. Sarpila & G. Kuipers (Eds.), *Handbook of beauty and inequality*. Springer (Part of Springer Nature).

Guest, E., Jarman, H., Sharratt, N., Williamson, H., White, P., Harcourt, D., & Slater, A. (2021). "Everybody's different: The appearance game". A randomised controlled trial evaluating an appearance-related board game intervention with children aged 9–11 years. *Body Image*, *36*, 34–44.

Guest, E., Roberts-Mills, W., Zarola, A., & Slater, A. (in preparation). *"It's swings and roundabouts with social media": Exploring the social media-related experiences of adults with appearance-altering conditions using photo-elicitation interviews*.

Guest, E., Treneman-Evans, G., Mikkola, A., Rush, E., & Slater, A. (under review). *Utilising social media to increase acceptance of appearance-altering conditions: A two-part experimental study*.

Guest, E., Williamson, H., & Harcourt, D. (2024). Congenital melanocytic naevus (CMN) through the lens: Using photo-elicitation interviews to explore adjustment in adolescents with a rare birthmark condition. *Body Image*, *48*, 101656. https://doi.org/10.1016/j.bodyim.2023.101656

Harriger, J. A., Thompson, J. K., & Tiggemann, M. (2023). TikTok, TikTok, the time is now: Future directions in social media and body image. *Body Image*, *44*, 222–226. https://doi.org/10.1016/j.bodyim.2023.01.005

Hayes, M., van Stolk-Cooke, K., & Muench, F. (2015). Understanding Facebook use and the psychological affects of use across generations. *Computers in Human Behavior*, *49*, 507–511. https://doi.org/10.1016/j.chb.2015.03.040

Holcomb, J., & Latham-Mintus, K. (2022). Disney and disability: Media representations of disability in Disney and Pixar animated films. *Disability Studies Quarterly*, *42*(1), Article 1. https://doi.org/10.18061/dsq.v42i1.7054

Iliffe, L. L., & Thompson, A. R. (2019). Investigating the beneficial experiences of online peer support for those affected by alopecia: An interpretative phenomenological analysis using online interviews. *British Journal of Dermatology*, *181*(5), 992–998. https://doi.org/10.1111/bjd.17998

Jarman, H. K., Marques, M. D., McLean, S. A., Slater, A., & Paxton, S. J. (2021). Social media, body satisfaction and well-being among adolescents: A mediation model of appearance-ideal internalization and comparison. *Body Image*, 36, 139–148.

Jones, A., Plumb, A. M., & Sandage, M. J. (2021). Social media as a platform for cyberbullying of individuals with craniofacial anomalies: A preliminary survey. *Language, Speech, and Hearing Services in Schools*, *52*(3), 840–855. https://doi.org/10.1044/2021_LSHSS-20-00159

Jung, J., Barron, D., Lee, Y.-A., & Swami, V. (2022). Social media usage and body image: Examining the mediating roles of internalization of appearance ideals and social comparisons in young women. *Computers in Human Behavior*, *135*, 107357. https://doi.org/10.1016/j.chb.2022.107357

Kaplan, A. M., & Haenlein, M. (2010). Users of the world, unite! The challenges and opportunities of social media. *Business Horizons*, *53*(1), 59–68. https://doi.org/10.1016/j.bushor.2009.09.003

Katz, E., Haas, H., & Gurevitch, M. (1973). On the use of the mass media for important things. *American Sociological Review*, 164–181.

Kaundinya, T., El-Behaedi, S., Bilimoria, S., & Choi, J. N. (2023). Characterization of online support group resources for patients with dermatologic conditions. *Archives of Dermatological Research*, *315*(6), 1547–1552. https://doi.org/10.1007/s00403-023-02528-2

Keim-Malpass, J., & Steeves, R. H. (2012, July). Talking with death at a diner: Young women's online narratives of cancer. *Oncology Nursing Forum*, *39*(4).

Ki, C.-W. 'Chloe', & Kim, Y.-K. (2019). The mechanism by which social media influencers persuade consumers: The role of consumers' desire to mimic. *Psychology & Marketing*, *36*(10), 905–922. https://doi.org/10.1002/mar.21244

Korkmaz, Y. N., & Buyuk, S. K. (2020). YouTube as a patient-information source for cleft lip and palate. *The Cleft Palate-Craniofacial Journal*, *57*(3), 327–332.

Lotun, S., Lamarche, V. M., Samothrakis, S., Sandstrom, G. M., & Matran-Fernandez, A. (2022). Parasocial relationships on YouTube reduce prejudice towards mental health issues. *Scientific Reports*, *12*, 16565. https://doi.org/10.1038/s41598-022-17487-3

Lou, C., & Yuan, S. (2019). Influencer marketing: How message value and credibility affect consumer trust of branded content on social media. *Journal of Interactive Advertising*, *19*(1), 58–73. https://doi.org/10.1080/15252019.2018.1533501

Luong, R., & Lomanowska, A. M. (2022). Evaluating Reddit as a crowdsourcing platform for psychology research projects. *Teaching of Psychology*, 49(4), 329–337.

Maspero, S., Ebert, C., Moser, S., Zink, A., Sichert, P., Schielein, M., Weis, J., & Ziehfreund, S. (2023). The potential of Instagram to reduce stigmatization of people with psoriasis: A randomized controlled pilot study. *Acta Dermato-Venereologica*, *103*, 3513. https://doi.org/10.2340/actadv.v103.3513

Mathews, A., Costa, B., Mikkola, A., & Harcourt, D. (2023). "Scars: How our wounds make us who we are": Improving appearance-based stigma, conceptualisation of beauty and body esteem through a documentary. *Scars, Burns & Healing, 9*. https://doi.org/10.1177/20595131231205398

Merolli, M., Gray, K., & Martin-Sanchez, F. (2013). Health outcomes and related effects of using social media in chronic disease management: A literature review and analysis of affordances. *Journal of Biomedical Informatics*, *46*(6), 957–969. https://doi.org/10.1016/j.jbi.2013.04.010

Montgomery, S. N. B., & Elbuluk, N. (2020). Evaluating population interest in vitiligo through an analysis of Google trends and social media. *J Drugs Dermatol*, *19*(6), 661–665.

Neubaum, G., Sobieraj, S., Raasch, J., & Riese, J. (2020). Digital destigmatization: How exposure to networking profiles can reduce social stereotypes. *Computers in Human Behavior*, *112*, 106461. https://doi.org/10.1016/j.chb.2020.106461

Online Safety Act 2023, UK Parliament. (2023).

Paruzel-Czachura, M., Workman, C. I., El Toukhy, N., & Chatterjee, A. (2024). First impressions: Do faces with scars and palsies influence warmth, competence and humanization? *British Journal of Psychology*. https://doi.org/10.1111/bjop.12719

Petrosyan, A. (2025). *Number of internet and social media users worldwide as of January 2025 (in billions)*. Statista. https://www.statista.com/statistics/617136/digital-population-worldwide/

Rasset, P., Mange, J., & Montalan, B. (2022). Look me in the eyes! A pre-registered eye-tracking study investigating visual attention and affective reactions to faces with a visible difference. *Body Image*, *40*, 67–77. https://doi.org/10.1016/j.bodyim.2021.10.010

Rodgers, R. F., Mclean, S. A., Gordon, C. S., Slater, A., Marques, M. D., Jarman, H. K., & Paxton, S. J. (2021). Development and validation of the motivations for social media use scale (MSMU) among adolescents. *Adolescent Research Review*, *6*(4), 425–435. https://doi.org/10.1007/s40894-020-00139-w

Saiphoo, A. N., & Vahedi, Z. (2019). A meta-analytic review of the relationship between social media use and body image disturbance. *Computers in Human Behavior*, *101*, 259–275. https://doi.org/10.1016/j.chb.2019.07.028

Senju, A., & Johnson, M. H. (2009). The eye contact effect: Mechanisms and development. *Trends in Cognitive Sciences*, *13*(3), 127–134. https://doi.org/10.1016/j.tics.2008.11.009

Shatz, I. (2017). Fast, free, and targeted: Reddit as a source for recruiting participants online. *Social Science Computer Review*, *35*(4), 537–549.

Stock, N. M., Martindale, A., & Cunniffe, C. (2018). #CleftProud: A content analysis and online survey of 2 cleft lip and palate Facebook groups. *The Cleft Palate-Craniofacial Journal*, *55*(10), 1339–1349. https://doi.org/10.1177/1055665618764737

Stone, A., & Fisher, V. (2020). Changing negative perceptions of individuals with facial disfigurement: The effectiveness of a brief intervention. *Basic and Applied Social Psychology*, *42*(5), 341–353. https://doi.org/10.1080/01973533.2020.1768394

Stone, A., & Wright, T. (2012). Evaluations of people depicted with facial disfigurement compared to those with mobility impairment. *Basic and Applied Social Psychology*, *34*(3), 212–225. https://doi.org/10.1080/01973533.2012.674420

Thompson, J. K., Heinberg, L. J., Altabe, M. N., & Tantleef-Dunn, S. (1999). *Theory assessment, and treatment of body image disturbance*. American Psychological Association. https://psycnet.apa.org/fulltext/1999-02140-000-FRM.pdf

Wardle, C., Boyce, T., & Barron, J. (2009). *Media coverage and audience reception of people with disfigurement or visible loss of function*. The Healing Foundation.

Wilson, N., Liu, J., Adamjee, Q., Di Giorgio, S., Steer, S., Hutton, J., & Lempp, H. (2023). Exploring the emotional impact of axial spondyloarthritis: A systematic review and thematic synthesis of qualitative studies and a review of social media. *BMC Rheumatology*, *7*(1), 26. https://doi.org/10.1186/s41927-023-00351-w

Zolkwer, M. B., Whitehouse, J., Sanderson, S. C., & Kinsler, V. A. (2023). Impact of public exhibition on the perception of birthmarks. *Pediatric Dermatology*, *40*(4), 615–620.

6 FaceIT@Home

An Online Support Tool for Adults with Visible Differences

Alyson Norman

My name is Aly Norman and I am a researcher in the UK specialising in work with individuals with visible differences. This chapter outlines my journey to becoming a psychologist, particularly my PhD process, and the development of an online support tool for individuals with visible difference that became my PhD thesis. It is hoped that this chapter will provide useful information about FaceIT but also serve as a guide to current or aspiring PhD students regarding the ongoing need or tenacity when embarking on such a process.

I started my psychology journey in 2000 when I started an undergraduate psychology degree at the University of Southampton in the UK. On completion of my undergraduate degree in 2004, I had little idea of where I wanted my psychology degree to take me. Research was an area that had always fascinated me, but I was yet to identify what type of psychological research I wanted to engage with. At this point I decided to leave academia for a while and worked for a period with individuals with profound learning disabilities as a support worker. This experience demonstrated to me that whatever I did in my career, I wanted it to be something that made a difference to people in need. The process also taught me that working with learning disabilities was rewarding but was not an area I was likely to be able to stay within. This was partly because I found the client group challenging, but also because I missed the academic challenge of being involved in research. Therefore, when a part-time research role was advertised at the University of Exeter, I took the opportunity to try and get back into academia, ultimately starting a MSc in Psychological research methods.

It was during this time that I started to become more interested in clinical research and the development of interventions that could provide support to people. My passion was, and still is, for working with people with acquired brain injuries (ABI). This was borne out of personal experiences with my brother, who had experienced a road traffic accident at the age of 22 and became severely disabled. However, I failed to secure PhD funding to pursue a project working in that area, so I started looking for other opportunities to undertake a PhD.

During my undergraduate degree, I designed and ran a cognitive-based experiment to look at how faces affected by visible difference are processed and recognised by the brain. The study found that the presence of a visible difference on the face disrupts the normal face processing and recognition processes, making

DOI: 10.4324/9781003535591-12

it more difficult for individuals to ascertain that faces with visible differences are in fact 'face-like'. This process can lead to the staring we observe in others when they see a face with a visible difference. The person's attention is drawn to the face as the brain attempts to incorporate this new 'different' version of a face into their face template. That left me with an interest in factors that affect those with visible difference.

Around this time, academics at the University of the West of England (UWE), along with the UK charitable organisation Changing Faces, were developing a basic PhD application to develop and test the effectiveness of an online support tool for adults with visible differences. Determined not to allow the setback at the University of Exeter to prevent me from starting a PhD, I applied for the role, went to interviewed and, due to my previous research experience in the area, was offered the role and began working on the FaceIT project.

What Is FaceIT?

Changing Faces is a charitable organisation that aims to support those with visible differences or disfigurements. Within the UK, service provision to support the psychological and social needs of those with visible difference is highly variable. In some locales, there are specialist services to which people have automatic access to. In others, there is no real service provision, and those experiencing difficulties are often forced to access support privately through generic services that are not specifically designed to support their needs. Generic services can be problematic as many therapists have not yet learned the underlying psychological mechanisms of how visible difference impacts people, and therefore struggle to provide tailored and effective support. As such, since its early beginnings, Changing Faces has aimed to bridge this gap by offering access to support through a third party or charitable sector.

While Changing Faces is a relatively large organisation within the UK, larger than many other condition-specific charities, it struggles to provide the same level of support for everyone with a visible difference across the UK. Therefore, they have always looked for alternative models of support that reduce costs and therapists' time. This cost and time reduction is often achieved through the dissemination of online informational resources and leaflets. While information resources are useful, there is still a need for more tailored and intensive psychological and social support that may not be available elsewhere.

At the time of the inception of the original FaceIT program, Changing Faces was led by their former Chief Executive and Founder, Dr. James Partridge. James very much understood the need for ensuring that information and support provided to others was evidence-based and worked closely alongside another UK organisation called the Centre for Appearance Research in Bristol, a research centre based within UWE in Bristol. It is one of the largest research centres internationally that focuses purely on research around appearance psychology and how to develop tools and models of support to help those with visible difference and other body image concerns.

From this professional collaboration, Dr. James Partridge saw an opportunity to produce a more sophisticated way of providing support online and worked with the lead researcher at the Centre for Appearance Research (CAR), Professor Nichola Rumsey and her colleagues Dr. Diana Harcourt and Dr. Tim Moss, to outline a possible model for support through development of an online tool to support adults with visible differences. As part of this project, Dr. James Partridge and Professor Rumsey enlisted the support of a previous Changing Faces employee and Clinical Psychologist from the London Royal Free hospital, Dr. Alex Clarke, who had worked as a specialist clinical psychologist in the field of visible difference for many years. They put together the PhD proposal noted earlier and I began to work on developing FaceIT.

FaceIT@Home is designed to support adults with visible differences to feel more confident in social situations and to be better able to manage their appearance-related distress. The programme has seven sessions and a 3-month review component and is built on cognitive-behavioural therapy (CBT) and social skills interaction training (SSIT) approaches. The tool is freely available internationally through the author or by visiting the website https://faceitonline.info/. Research and development of the tool began in 2005, with the first prototype being ready for evaluation in 2008. The tool was tested in a randomised controlled trial (RCT) in 2009 and was found to be effective in reducing appearance-related distress and anxiety among adults with visible differences. Since then, it has been used by a range of individuals and clinicians working with people with visible differences. This chapter will provide an overview of the evidence base for the tool and the process of development. More importantly, the chapter will outline the journey of the tool since the prototype was completed, including case study examples of individuals who have used the FaceIT tool and narratives from other individuals who played a role in its development as either people with lived experience or as clinicians with an aim to reflect on how the FaceIT tool can utilised in the future.

The Development of FaceITOnline

When developing an online intervention, it is important to ensure a strong evidence base for the approach, as well as considering the ways in which any effective material will need to be developed to make it remain suitable for delivery within an online environment. The first stage of the process was to understand what had already been done in the field of visible difference and to evaluate the current intervention models. This stage resulted in a systematic review of 12 papers that looked at various models of intervention for adults with visible difference (Bessell & Moss, 2007). The findings from our review highlighted a general lack of evidence for any one intervention type, mainly due to a dearth of studies that established a sufficient evidence base using satisfactory research approaches with sufficient populations. Overall, the systematic review identified that a combination of CBT with SSIT seemed to be the most effective approach at reducing appearance-related distress and anxiety.

The systematic review provided some support for an evidence-based approach, but due to the poor methodological quality of the included studies, the overall effectiveness of a CBT/SSIT approach could not be verified. The review also identified some high attrition rates within the individual studies that suggested the approaches were not always the most appropriate to all individuals. Therefore, the second stage of my research was to undertake a small interview study to understand the experiences of those with visible difference who had undergone psychological interventions in the past. These participants helped me to understand the ways in which approaches such as CBT and SSIT could work for individuals and identified some key aspects around appropriate goal setting that participants felt would be useful for inclusion within a new intervention. This study also incorporated participants who had chosen not to engage in psychological interventions or had found them broadly ineffective. These groups were important in understanding factors that had led to disengagement with interventions or that left people feeling unable to seek psychological support. One of the main barriers to seeking help appeared to be asking for referrals from health professionals, suggesting that a self-referral, self-help approach may be beneficial (Bessell et al., 2010). The final groups of participants in the study were health professionals with experience in working with clients with visible differences. Drawing on their knowledge base provided a more in-depth understanding of techniques and strategies that might make an online intervention effective for users.

Case Study 1: Evan

My name is Evan* and I first met Alyson in the summer of 2006 in London. I have psoriasis and get it real bad on my face, head and hands. We met for an interview at a local café. Alyson was kind enough to agree to come earlier and wait outside for me so I could be sure she was there. I hate sitting in places on my own. I feel everyone is staring. I turned up in a long thick trench coat. It was about 30 degrees Celsius that day. In our interview Alyson asked me about the coat. She described me wearing it as a safety behaviour, something you do to stop people staring. She then explained that these behaviours often make staring worse because people were likely to stare because of my choice of clothing on such a hot day. I think I already knew this but having someone express it to me kindly made such a difference. I know that Alyson used my hatred of cafes as one of the examples in FaceIT. She asked me the following year if she could use it and asked me to help her design different options in the scenario. I gave her permission to do this and to use bits of my story throughout FaceIT. When it was finished Alyson let me use it and I find it so helpful. I wish someone had designed something like this years ago. It would have made such a difference to my life.

*pseudonym used

The Importance of User Involvement in the Development of FaceIT

The information gained from the systematic review and the interview study described above formed the basis of the original programme, known as FaceITOnline. The tool originally consisted of eight sessions of a combination of CBT and SSIT approaches. The design process of the tool was complex as a manual had to be produced and then the website had to be coded appropriately.

In designing any online tool, there are various considerations that must be given to usability: the user interface, graphical design and the level of language comprehension used when disseminating the information. Software packages work best when they are aimed at the target audience and designed with their support and guidance. Therefore, the design process of FaceITOnline utilised an iterative action research approach where a prototype was designed, and participants were asked to provide feedback before subsequent changes were made over successive time points. This process enabled the team to develop a tool that provided suitable and supportive information in a language that was empathetic and compassionate in nature, whilst easy to understand. It also ensured that the tool was easy to interact with and navigate, especially for those less adept at using websites and computers. After engaging with this series of iterative user tests, the team settled on a prototype that was suitable for testing the effectiveness and acceptability in an RCT.

Case Study 2: Terry*

I met Alyson in the first study for FaceIT. I remember my daughter seeing an advert on the Thyroid Foundation website. She suggested I talk to Alyson about my experiences. I have always hated my appearance. I have thyroid eye disease which makes everyone stare. Talking to Alyson was difficult. I was 68 at the time and had never talked to a single other person properly about how it affected me. I had spent my whole life refusing to look in the mirror. Alyson asked me if I would be willing to have some of my stories shared in FaceIT. I agreed. Anything to help someone else who may feel the same. Because she had included elements of our conversation in it, I was keen to help her to test the programme so I can get a look at what she had produced. I was also aware that as an older person with no tech ability, my insights might be valuable. While the first prototype was clunky and difficult to interact with, I can see the potential of it straight away. Over the various stages of testing, the tool became easier to use and I was impressed at the work that had gone into it. I haven't seen the most recent version of the programme. Sadly, my eye disease has progressed to the point that I struggle with my vision so I haven't been able to look at it. But I did see the 2012 version when it was first made publicly available and thought it was remarkable. So sensitively expressed, supportive, caring and empathetic.

*Pseudonym used

Testing FaceITOnline: The Randomised Controlled Trial

In September of 2008, I embarked on an Randomised Controlled Trial (RCT) of FaceITOnline. The program was tested against a face-to-face delivery of a similar model of intervention and a no-treatment control group (for full details see Bessell et al., 2012). The RCT assessed the effectiveness of the tool at reducing anxiety and depression, appearance-related distress, quality of life and fear of negative evaluation. Recruitment took place through charities that represent different conditions that cause visible difference across the UK. These included Changing Faces, the Cleft Lip and Palate Association (CLAPA), the Psoriasis Association, the Vitiligo Society and the plastic surgery outpatient department at the Royal Free hospital in London. Overall, 83 participants took part in the trial, 28 in the face-to-face delivery, 28 using FaceITOnline under supervision and 27 in the no-treatment control group. Participants were assessed at pre-intervention, halfway through the intervention and again at post-intervention. Follow-up data were collected at 3 and 6-months after the intervention ended.

Overall, FaceITOnline was found to be similarly effective to face-to-face delivery and more effective than the no-treatment control. The data showed that while the tool was not a direct substitute for face-to-face engagement with a therapist, it was effective at reducing anxiety, depression and appearance-related distress, although not at improving body image-related quality of life or reducing fear of negative evaluation. On reflection, it seems likely that the reason for the lack of change in these variables is that body image is a much wider self-concept that encompasses not just the element of appearance impacted by the visible difference, but other areas too. The focus of the intervention is on the 'feature' and this may explain a reduced level of change overall. It is still something that needs further investigation, however, and it is possible that perhaps with time and increased confidence in social situations, people may also see improvements in general body image and wider self-concept.

As well as identifying that FaceITOnline was effective, acceptability measures were also taken to gain an understanding of how likely individuals were to use the tool. The acceptability ratings showed that out of a total score of 60, the FaceITOnline tool was rated 52.7, demonstrating a high level of acceptability. Usefulness and satisfaction scores were 8.79/10 and 8.38/10, respectively. Participants were asked which model of delivery was preferred overall (face-to-face or online), with 48% preferring online and 50% preferring face-to-face (2% had no preference). This preference seemed to relate more to personal preference rather than the approach they had been exposed to. Most importantly, 90% of those in the trial felt that they would use the tool if other support were not available to them.

Case Study 3: Naomi

In November 2002 at the age of 31, I sustained severe facial injuries, and other injuries to my body, following a road traffic accident in Kenya. Three people tragically lost their lives. I was on, what was supposed to be, a dream safari holiday to experience Kenya's amazing wildlife, away from my pressurised job in recruitment at that time.

I was airlifted to a private hospital in Nairobi and I underwent extensive reconstructive facial surgery over the next two weeks. I was in denial regarding the life-changing situation I was now in, and I avoided any mirrors at the risk of seeing my reflection.

When my discharge date approached, a counsellor within Nairobi hospital tried to prepare me for my new appearance and my visible difference. What I saw, was not me, I was horrified. I found it very difficult to comprehend what a dramatic turn my life had taken.

I endured a nervous flight back home to the UK and underwent further reconstructive facial surgery over the next eight years. The psychological impact of my life-changing injuries was significant. I had lost social anonymity and experienced high levels of social anxiety and appearance-related distress.

I live in Devon, an area based in the Southwest of the UK. There was and still is a lack of specialist psychological support available locally for people living with a visible difference.

My GP at the time offered me counselling with someone who dealt with divorce. I was disheartened and felt disadvantaged that due to where I live, I was unable to access the psychological support that I needed locally. I felt that a general counsellor was not appropriate, so I sought further support.

I made contact with Changing Faces in London and welcomed support from them. Following a referral by The Trauma Clinic in London, I was referred to Dr. Alex Clarke at the Royal Free hospital in London. This was so she could provide me with the specialist psychological support that I needed as an outpatient at the Royal Free hospital.

As it was necessary to travel to London, which takes a few hours by train from my home in Devon, my social anxiety was magnified. After multiple sessions with Dr. Clarke, she then introduced me to Dr. Alyson Norman and I became involved in the FaceIT trial in 2008.

I found FaceITOnline to be extremely supportive, interactive and beneficial with its stepped care approach relating to my difficulties with social avoidance. It is unique, easy to follow and the exercises you work through are relatable and practical.

The programme includes examples of everyday experiences, such as testing social situations and turning negative thoughts into positive thoughts. Including how to deal with others staring, their comments and assumptions due to having an altered appearance. The coping strategies assisted me with the tools that I needed to move forward. I have kept diaries to catalogue my difficulties and the progress I have made over many years.

Over time, I could refer to the FaceITOnline programme when I needed to. I found it invaluable. I have now regained my confidence to pre-accident levels.

I work for a charity (unrelated to FaceIT) which provides free, impartial and confidential advice to people regarding the problems that they face. I find it very rewarding, making a difference, whilst helping to improve the lives of others.

Since benefiting from FaceITOnline over many years, and following on from my initial introduction and participation in the trial, I have become an advocate for FaceIT. I am very passionate about the expertly developed programme.

On a voluntary basis, I have supported the development of the programme through the multiple stages of its journey. I have provided extensive feedback regarding the feasibility and usability of the programme, in addition to featuring within the programme's content.

I am now part of a FaceIT Steering Group in addition to being a member of the FaceIT@Home Together support group.

When given the opportunity, as a voluntary contributor via local television, radio and social media, I raise awareness of the FaceIT@Home programme. Anyone can acquire a visible difference at any stage of their life, because of many different situations. I am confident that if people seeking support who are facing challenges of living with an altered appearance became aware of FaceIT@Home, they could significantly benefit from the programme in the comfort of their own home. Users can benefit from it at any stage in their recovery or condition, over and over again.

FaceIT@Home is an incredibly comprehensive and easy-to-follow programme for anyone needing support with social situations relating to their visible difference. They can use the programme in the comfort of their own home. It may just be the 'lifeline' that they need to help them deal with challenges they face and reduce their anxiety.

While research has always been a driving force in my career, I have developed a passion specifically for applied research. Upon completing my PhD in 2009, I found myself with this hefty tome of a thesis that while impressive to friends and family, would be unlikely to ever see the light of day. I didn't go into academia for prestige or publications; I went into it to make a difference. Developing FaceITOnline as part of my PhD was an amazing experience, but for me it was not enough – I wanted the tool to get out there to people who needed it and to be used. This drive was to shape the next 15 years of my research career and will probably continue to do so well into the future.

Developing a Commercial Version of FaceITOnline

After completion of the RCT for FaceITOnline, I continued to work on various projects in the field of visible difference. In late 2009, with the support of the Centre for Appearance Research in Bristol, I was able to obtain some funding through the European Development Fund to turn the prototype version of FaceITOnline into a usable online version with the support of a tech company based in the UK. The process of designing a website is onerous and can take many months when the process is user led. We had spent so long engaging users in the original design of the protype that we wanted to ensure that the general look and feel of the final program remained like that suggested by users during the earlier research project, which meant working closely with the web designers to ensure that that the user voice was reflected in the final design.

A more exciting part of the development process was recreating the videos that are embedded within the FaceIT programme. In two sessions of the programme, the team had created a series of videos designed to support adults with visible differences work through challenging social situations. The first set of videos consisted of three films about a woman engaging in a series of situations that may cause social anxiety for those with appearance-related distress. These were a job interview, attending a social coffee with a friend and walking past a group of teenagers in the park. These videos were filmed with multiple endings in sections that allowed viewers to decide what they wanted the woman to do at each stage of the film. Feedback was then provided based on the choices users made. These were all created with the support of the web development company and featured some of the research team and one of our previous participants (see Case Study 1). The original prototype had the same videos but filmed locally using poor-quality video editing software. An additional three films appear in the FaceIT programmes and consist of a series of first-person videos where someone with social anxiety related to an appearance concern takes part in a form of exposure therapy of social situations. Exposure therapy is a psychological intervention that involves encouraging clients to face their fears of a social situation through direct exposure (Wolpe, 1958). These events are 'graded' on a 'hierarchy' so that individuals start with less fear-provoking situations and then engage in increasingly difficult situations until their fears have become more manageable across a range of activities and situations. The technique is based on the principle that exposure to fear-provoking stimuli reduces anxiety over time as the physiological response to the anxiety starts to return to normal levels with a natural dissipation of anxiety, particularly when paired with anxiety management techniques (Wolpe, 1958). Research has shown that vicarious exposure, watching other people being exposed to fear-provoking stimuli, can also be effective at reducing anxiety (Vincelli, 1999). Therefore, the films acted as a form of vicarious exposure to three different situations – buying items in a shop, going to a café and travelling on a bus. The scenarios for all six videos were taken from specific examples that participants in our earlier studies had given us of situations they found particularly difficult to manage because of staring, name-calling and unwanted questioning about their appearance, common problems faced by those with visible differences in public settings (Rumsey et al., 2004).

Alongside the launch of the adult version of FaceITOnline, I also worked alongside the Centre for Appearance research to support the development of a young person's version of the tool, called YPFaceIT. This tool would go on to be tested with young people across the globe.

The Launch of FaceITOnline

After months of development work, the tool was ready to be released for general use and was officially launched at a small event in November 2011 with the first training session for health professionals hosted in April 2012. At that time, the programmes were made available to health professionals to use in a facilitated fashion with their clients. During the RCT we had been unable to obtain ethical approval to test the programme as a self-help tool, so had only tested it using a facilitated model. Therefore, the original rollout of the programme involved providing organisations with licenses to use it with their clients through a similar model of delivery. Subsequent training was undertaken online by various health professionals, mainly within the NHS in the UK, but that included professionals from the United States and Australia.

At the initial stage, licenses were obtained through the University of the West of England to use the programme. These were available at a minimal cost. To extend the initial reach of the programme, we wanted to try and get the tool out to more users to be able to garner further detailed feedback about people's experiences of using FaceIT in the real world. During the summer of 2014, at the Appearance Matters conference in Bristol, we aimed to launch the programme more formally to health professionals attending the international conference. I have always been a keen believer in fate, and yet there have been points along the journey of FaceIT that have tested my positivity and resolve. I will talk more towards the end of this chapter about some of the difficulties we experienced along the way, but the first major hurdle came in that summer of 2014. Due to personal circumstances, I was unable to attend the conference. To this day, I suspect that the inability to present it to the world led to the project being set back many years.

Over the coming years, we discovered that while health professionals loved the FaceIT model, they were finding it difficult to use with their clients. This difficulty was partially due to the facilitated nature of the mode of delivery and partly due to the length and depth of the program. The real-world service user feedback suggested that clients struggled to engage with the material because it was too detailed. It was clear that further developments were needed to make FaceITOnline a successful tool for users.

Case Study 4:

J. Michael Murphy and his colleagues at Shriners Hospital in Boston, Massachusetts did a study that demonstrated that it was possible to make YPFaceIT available as part of usual care for adolescents being treated for burn injuries in an outpatient clinic (for details see Riobueno-Naylor et al., 2020)[1] Many burn injury survivors have facial scarring or other disfiguring conditions that are often a source of concern for the patients and their families, so having the FaceIT program available was enthusiastically accepted by most teens and their parents. The study also documented the difficulties inherent in trying to add another component to the already full schedule of medical procedures that most patients faced. Other impediments to full implementation were lack of access to computers in the clinic or at home for some patients and lack of basic computer skills for others. Study staff concluded that FaceIT could be an important tool for teens with disfiguring conditions, but that a number of logistical barriers needed to be overcome before use of the program could become more widespread.

Development and User Testing of FaceIT@Home

At the beginning of 2015, work started on redeveloping the tool based on feedback from health professionals. The aim was to make the programme shorter in length, lighter in content and easier to understand. By this point, YPFaceIT had been produced and we decided to go for a similar model with a small number of changes to the content that would make the tool more applicable to an adult audience.

A staple of the FaceIT project from inception has been the inclusion of the voice of experts by experience. As the YP version of the tool had not undergone user testing or received feedback from adult users, we started the process of evaluating the tool from an acceptability and usability perspective with an adult cohort. This study started in 2016 and consisted of three stages. The first involved giving participants one session of the new version of the tool, FaceIT@Home, to use in their own homes and then conducted telephone-based interviews with participants to garner their feedback on the content, structure, graphics and usability of the tool. From this process the research team, based at University of Plymouth, UK, then worked with the web development team to make changes to the tool based on participant feedback. We then invited a different group of participants to come to the university and engage in a user testing process, known as a 'think aloud' approach (Krahmer & Ummelen, 2004), where people use a web page or software package while being observed and provide verbal commentary on their experiences of using the tool throughout. This process was then followed up with a focus group with participants. Following this second phase, further changes were made to FaceIT@Home. In the final stage, the whole programme was made available to participants who engaged with the tool in their own homes and then completed a usability feedback questionnaire. Based on this final stage of feedback, the research team made a small number of changes to the programme before it was ready for use. This process ended in the summer of 2018. The full version of this research process is outlined in Norman et al. (2022)

Marketing FaceIT@Home

Throughout the years of working on the FaceIT project, the concept of generating profit from the tool could not have been furthest from any of our minds. To be frank, the programme has cost the organisations that have supported it – UWE, Bristol, Changing Faces and the University of Plymouth – thousands of pounds to develop and run. The goal overall has always been to reach a place where FaceIT@Home could be used by adults with visible difference easily at minimal or no cost, while ensuring the project had suitable funds to be sustainable long term. Part of the process of making it sustainable has been trying to identify potential partners that we could work with to provide a longer-term home for FaceIT@Home. In 2015, another member of the wider FaceIT research team and I made a connection with a large UK-based web company that owned a prestigious depression management tool named Beating the Blues. Beating the Blues was designed in the early 2000s to provide online support for people with depression (Proudfoot, 2004) and is still one of the few computerised CBT (CCBT) tools that have been approved by the UK National Institute for Health and Clinical Excellence (NICE). The company that owned Beating the Blues expressed an interest in gaining the license to distribute FaceIT in the UK and in the US as part of a growing portfolio of online interventions and other digital health solutions. This was an exciting time for the FaceIT team. UWE and the University of Plymouth worked hard to produce a legal contract that would enable FaceIT to 'fly the nest' to its new home.

Unfortunately, we then experienced our second major hurdle. The company had overstretched themselves financially, and in the late stages of finalising the contract with them in 2018, the company ceased trading. This was felt like a devastating blow. I had invested so much time in FaceIT and really thought we had found a way to reach the people who so desperately needed it. So to have that hope dashed was challenging and difficult to pick myself up from. Happily, at this stage, Changing Faces expressed renewed interest in acting as a home for FaceIT@Home as part of a growing suite of services they were developing.

Changing Faces Trial 2020

By 2019, work had begun on providing Changing Faces with the exclusive license to deliver FaceIT@Home in the UK as part of a service evaluation project. The concept of the trial was to offer FaceIT@Home in a range of different contexts. The tool was to be used to support people in their waiting list for face-to-face services, as an adjunct to their standard wellbeing service, but also as a top-up after completing therapy. To provide the tool as part of their services, extensive user testing and further development was required. The process took longer than planned due to staffing difficulties at the web development company. In February 2020, we were finally able to start the service evaluation trial and a soft launch was planned for early March with a full launch in the summer. At this point came the next major challenge for the FaceIT project and our small team. As the main driving force behind getting the programme designed and keeping it maintained, I have always been an integral part of the programme delivery.

Sadly, my father who has been diagnosed with cancer in 2017, died late February 2020, leading to a small delay in the soft launch. This would not normally have been an issue but as everyone reading this will know, the global COVID-19 pandemic had already started to affect countries across the world and led to a nationwide lockdown in March 2020 in the UK. This led to a distinct change in the landscape of all service delivery. Organizations providing support had to swiftly switch to online, move premises and take up home working practices. This led to multiple delays in kickstarting the FaceIT@Home evaluation.

Despite the initial delays, the team were confident that the global pandemic would work to the advantage of FaceIT@Home because we were now working in a time where online access to support was even more vital than ever before. While this was, and is, true, there were factors associated with the pandemic that made it difficult to launch a tool such as FaceIT@Home at that time. A major challenge was media focus on the pandemic to the detriment of all other local, regional or national news. Without a platform to have individuals hear our voice, the project was unable to reach those who may be interested in using the tool.

Further difficulties came when we finally recruited people who might benefit from the programme. These forms of online interventions come with high attrition rates as service users often struggle to find the motivation to stay engaged with online tools without facilitated support. This perfect storm of factors meant we had limited numbers come through for the evaluation and only one individual who completed all sessions. Changing Faces decided to pause the FaceIT@Home roll out while they took stock of their own service provision and financial situation in an economically challenging post-COVID landscape.

Reflections and the Future of FaceIT@Home

Since starting my PhD in October 2005, I have lived and breathed the FaceIT project. The completion of my PhD in 2008 was for me only the start of a much longer journey in offering support to those with visible differences who so desperately needed it. As discussed earlier, my goal was not just about an academic achievement. It was about making a difference and bringing about meaningful change. For this reason, I have always pushed forward with FaceIT@Home as a possible tool because I know that it has been found to be effective in a randomised controlled trial and I know that those who have used the programme over the years have provided amazing feedback about the positive changes the programme has brought about in their lives.

Yet, along this professional journey, there have been many hardships that have often left me wondering whether my passion and commitment to the tool was misplaced. In the last 19 years since starting my PhD, alongside a myriad of personal difficulties, I have been through the process of seeking research funding from various sources only to be rejected. I have teamed up with multiple organisations, watched Chief Executives and management teams of those organisations come and go, shift and change direction, and some organisations have even collapsed. Each step of the FaceIT journey has been fraught with problems, difficulties, trials and tribulations. Major obstacles that have had to be overcome.

As well as the major difficulties, there has always been the spectre of university systems and regulations. While the landscape of UK academia has shifted in the last 10 years, with more focus on the impact that comes from research rather than purely research outputs, projects such as FaceIT@Home often struggle to find internal support unless they are likely to be financially lucrative. I have been very lucky to receive support from UWE and the University of Plymouth, but the administrative processes within such organisations make running a tool that is designed to make a difference without financial output challenging.

Despite all the setbacks, I am still fighting the cause. I have nurtured my baby through its infancy, and it has grown into a disruptive teenager with all the strife that entails. But I am now seeing the light at the end of the tunnel. My baby is maturing and now more than ever before has the potential to make a real difference to those with visible difference.

In the last three years, I have worked with multiple different web development teams to find a sustainable long-term home for FaceIT@Home that would be cost effective to run. I have managed to wrestle back control of the programme from the large web development team previously running the tool and now have a new version of it that is content-managed, cheap to host and is easy for users to interact with. These factors are all crucial in making the tool a success long-term. Now that we have reached a stage where we have a tool that had been redesigned, I am excited to see what the future may hold.

We have already started collaborations internationally, with individuals and organisations in the US, Australia, Ireland and Norway showing interest in using the programme in its newest form. We have also had an uptake of interest among local UK-based charities and services within the NHS that work with people with visible difference. Furthermore, the new tool is more mobile compatible, which brings it into line with the needs of a younger, more mobile-savvy generation who do not want to sit at a desktop to engage in therapy. Finally, for the first time ever, we have a social media presence. We have a Facebook page (https://www.facebook.com/groups/611672430945553), a Twitter/X feed (https://x.com/FaceITOnline) and a YouTube channel (https://www.youtube.com/@faceit2362), with Instagram and TikTok channels soon to follow. This social media presence feels like an important part of bringing FaceIT@Home into the modern world and making it more usable and accessible to young people experiencing visible difference.

My vision for FaceIT@Home is that soon it will be a freely accessible programme that can be available to any English-speaking person with a visible difference across the globe. I want to see people using the programme in all sorts of different ways that suit their own needs. In similar ways to the previous projects outlined earlier in this chapter, I see FaceIT@Home as an important self-help tool that people can use in their own homes as a linear support tool. I also envisage it working as stand-alone, life-long support for individuals with specific difficulties. Even those who may feel broadly confident about their visible difference will come across situations where they may feel anxious. I want FaceIT@Home to be available to them for information purposes even if they do not need direct intervention. We have small numbers of people already using FaceIT@Home in this way, but by 2030 I hope to see it being used in volume. Finally, I hope that the tool can be used more widely as a source of information for both professionals and loved ones who may be supporting people with a visible difference, to help them gain a better insight into difficulties experienced by people and how to provide positive care.

My vision for the future also includes regular referral of people to the FaceIT@Home programme by health and social care professionals across the UK, and more internationally. Again, we are making small breakthroughs here with our recent collaborations, but there is still a long way to go. We are also beginning to trial new models of introducing FaceIT@Home to those who need it and new methods of supporting people to use it. One of the recent developments is the creation of the FaceIT@HomeTogether group, a support group that runs online once a month where people who are using FaceIT@Home, or would like to use it in the future, can come together for an hour and work together on a particular session of the programme. This is a model that has been suggested and implemented by my friend and colleague J. Michael Murphy from Boston, who has been a long-time supporter of FaceIT@Home along with other committed individuals.

Case Study 5: Jaime*

Jaime is a nurse who had used FaceIT@Home with several of his patients and then contacted us about using it for his own personal appearance concerns. As an adolescent, Jaime had had surgery to remove a tumor that had left a scar on his face. He was also very short and had been exposed to teasing and social stigma on both fronts. Although he was successful in many ways with a good marriage and career, his occasional experiences with being teased or left out because of his appearance had resulted in patterns of social avoidance. Despite trying out several different types of psychotherapy, he still found it very difficult to attend social events. Jaime found FaceIT@Home helpful but came to believe that it would be even more effective if it were used in a group setting with members reading some of the FaceIT@Home lessons each week and then discussing them together. Jaime is one of a number of people with lived experience who are helping Alyson to set up FaceIT@HomeTogether.

Conclusions

The journey of FaceIT@Home that I have been on over the last 19 years has not been an easy one. I am sure that had someone informed me in 2005 that I would still be trying to get FaceIT@Home established as a tool in 2024, I may have reconsidered my research options. However, I stand proud of the achievements that the team and I have made along the way. I am grateful to the Centre for Appearance Research and Changing Faces for the vision they had in seeing the need for such a tool, and I am grateful to all those who have supported its journey to where we are today: the participants who took the time to sign up to various studies, the people who have worked on the programme in other ways to support its journey and the amazing professionals who have shared my vision for FaceIT@Home. I am also grateful to University of Plymouth for investing the time, money and general resources in helping me to realise my vision. Despite the difficulties, I am proud of the difference we have made to people's lives, and this keeps me plodding on with the project. If you are reading this as either an adult with a visible difference or someone who supports them, either as a professional or as a loved one, please do look at FaceIT@Home as it may just be the lifeline that you or someone you know is in need of.

Note

1 Riobueno-Naylor, A., Canenguez, K., Kogosov, A., Drexler, A., Sadeq, F., DePamphilis, M., Holcomb, J., Stoddard, F., Lydon, M., Murphy, J. M., & Sheridan, R. L. (2019, April). Feasibility and implementation of the YP face IT online program for youth recovering from burn injuries. *The Journal of Burn Care and Research, 40*(Suppl. 1), S188–S189. https://doi.org/10.1093/jbcr/irz013.329

References

Bessell, A., Brough, V., Clarke, A., Harcourt, D., Moss, T., & Rumsey, N. (2012). Evaluation of the effectiveness of Face IT, a computer-based psychosocial intervention for disfigurement-related distress. *Psychology, Health and Medicine, 2*, 1–13.

Bessell, A., Clarke, A., Harcourt, D., Moss, T. P., & Rumsey, N. (2010). Incorporating user perspectives in the design of an online intervention tool for people with visible differences: Face IT. *Behavioural and Cognitive psychotherapy, 38*, 577–596.

Bessell, A., & Moss, T. P. (2007). Psychosocial interventions for visible differences: A systematic review. *Body Image, 4*, 227–238.

Krahmer, E., & Ummelen, N. (2004). Thinking about thinking aloud: A comparison of two verbal protocols for usability testing. *IEEE Transactions on Professional Communication, 47*(2), 105–117.

Norman, A., Veale, J., & Williamson, H. (2022). Assessing the usability and acceptability of FaceIT@home: An online CBT intervention for people with visible differences. *Cognitive Behavior Therapist, 15*, e41.

Proudfoot, J. G. (2004). Computer-based treatment of anxiety and depression: Is it feasible? Is it effective? *Neuroscience & Biobehavioral Reviews, 28*, 353–363.

Riobueno-Naylor, A., Williamson, H., Kogosov, A., Wang, S., Drexler, A., Canenguez, K., . . . & Murphy, M. (2019). 432 feasibility and implementation of the YP face IT online program for youth recovering from burn injuries. *Journal of Burn Care & Research, 40*(Supplement_1), S188–S189.

Rumsey, N., Clarke, A., White, P., Wyn-Williams, M., & Garlick, W. (2004). Altered body image: Auditing the appearance related concerns of people with visible disfigurement. *Journal of Advanced Nursing, 48*(5), 443–453.

Vincelli, F. (1999). From imagination to virtual reality: The future of clinical psychology. *Cyberpsychology & Behavior, 2*(3), 241–248.

Wolpe, J. (1958). *Psychotherapy by reciprocal inhibition.* Stanford University Press.

Interlude

Finding My Voice

Dina Zuckerberg

When I was growing up, I didn't want to share my story. If someone asked me about my facial difference, I would walk away.

I was born with a cleft lip, hearing loss and no vision in one eye. From the time I was three, I wore a hearing aid. I had six surgeries, years of orthodontics and speech therapy. For years I kept this piece of my life hidden away.

I would walk to the back of the school bus and sit by myself. I would sit alone in the cafeteria at lunch. At gym, I was picked last for team sports. Over and over, I was teased. Kids said mean things like I had "cooties." Those moments stay with me, even today.

In my early twenties, I was invited to join Inner Faces, a group for teens and adults who had craniofacial differences like me. At first, I didn't want to go. It forced me to face things that I spent so much of my life running away from. The group leaders persisted and didn't take "no" for an answer. But I didn't want to be part of this group. I had spent so much of my life wanting to fit in to be like the other kids. I didn't want to acknowledge that I looked different and how difficult life was for me. My script was to say everything was "fine."

Being in Inner Faces was transforming. We wrote an original musical called *Let's Face The Music*. Collaborating with visionary director and composer Elizabeth Swados and Jodie Berlin Morrow, we told the stories of our lives and what it was like to grow up with facial differences. In one powerful piece, we looked into a mirror and shared what we saw. We performed the show at the One Dream Theater in New York City. It was the first time I got up on stage and revealed, in my own words, what my life was really like. Yet, I still didn't feel I truly embodied myself or fully found my voice in the world.

Over a decade ago, I landed my dream job as the Director of Family Programs at myFace, a non-profit that supports children with craniofacial differences. For more than 70 years, myFace has worked with individuals and families to provide comprehensive critical team care. Every day, we deliver support, education and raise public awareness.

In my heart, I longed to do everything to make it easier for children living with facial differences. I wanted no child to experience what I went through growing up.

Soon after I began working at myFace, R.J. Palacio's young adult novel, *Wonder*, came out. The book is about Auggie, a ten-year-old boy born with Treacher

DOI: 10.4324/9781003535591-14

Collins Syndrome, and his journey to fit in at his new school where no one else looks like him. I read *Wonder* in one sitting and really connected with Auggie. Finally, there was a book in which I related to the story right from the first page. I will never forget Auggie's words:

> *If I found a magic lamp and I could have one wish, I would wish that I had a normal face that no one ever noticed at all. I would wish that I could walk down the street without people seeing me and then doing that look-away thing.*

I remember being around Auggie's age, maybe a little younger, blowing out the candles on my birthday cake. I wished I could look like the other kids so it would be a little easier for me.

In many ways, Auggie's middle school experience was a lot like mine. And the more my voice was silenced in school, the more powerless I felt. I withdrew.

Wonder was life changing. It inspired me to visit schools through a program we created at myFace called The Wonder Project. The program teaches students the importance of empathy, inclusivity and being an upstander against bullying. It includes an assembly, thought-provoking classroom materials and interactive teaching strategies that illustrate the importance of accepting differences and the power that comes with choosing to be kind! Through the program, I have told my story growing up with a craniofacial difference and have spoken to over 100,000 students.

Sharing my journey with students has helped me transform and discover my voice. I feel more powerful and have grown to understand how I need to use my voice to educate others. And the more comfortable I have become to divulge how my voice was silenced, the more I can make a difference.

Once, when I presented at a school and showed my hearing aid to the students, one boy raised his hand. He was so excited to share that he also wore hearing aids. I was the first young person he met who wore a hearing aid like him. That connection meant everything and he beamed with pride. It felt so good, knowing that he could share that with me and his classmates.

When I visit schools, I tell the students how I wish I had upstanders in my life when I was a child. I love that word: *upstander*. For me, it means when you witness an injustice, like someone being bullied, and you take a stand to make it right. When you see someone sitting alone in the lunchroom, you choose to sit with them. When you see a child being picked on, you take that child out of the situation and ask if they would like to walk to class with you. If you see someone standing alone, a simple smile and "hello" can make all the difference.

Once, during a school assembly, when I shared that I wished I had more upstanders in my life, a boy raised his hand. With tears in his eyes, he confessed that just the week before, he witnessed another student being teased. The boy regretted his decision not to stand up for the student. However, from that day forward, he would be an upstander and stand up for others.

Many times after presenting in schools, the students cheer and give me a standing ovation. I think of Auggie's wise words, "Everyone in the world should get a standing ovation at least once in their life because we all overcometh the world."

Sometimes I can't believe I am sharing my deeply personal story, the message of choosing kindness and what it means to be an upstander. What's more, I still love it. Here I am, wanting to visit more and more schools through the Wonder Project and to connect with students because I see the impact I have on them. As much as I teach them, they teach me so much too.

Looking back at when I was growing up, I wish that kids didn't tease and exclude me. I wish I didn't need surgeries. I wish that things weren't so hard. But if I didn't have those experiences, I would not be the person I am today. And then I think, maybe I am exactly where I was meant to be.

The Swan Fallacy

Sora J. Kasuga

My husband Josh and I had just left the theater where we'd performed our duo circus show in front of a packed audience. We were working on a cruise ship owned by one of the biggest entertainment companies in the world. Already a few contracts in, we weren't new anymore. Tonight, we'd given it our all and received thunderous applause, two standing ovations, and praise from the cruise director. As we walked around the ship, people now recognized us in this weird microcosm of celebrity-dom. Every interaction blended into the next.

"Great show!"

"Can we get a picture?"

"What got you into the circus?"

We finally reached the elevator which would take us up to our room. Exhausted, we anticipated collapsing on the bed and ordering room service. The elevator chimed, and we held our breath, hoping for an empty car. The doors slid open. No dice.

A stately older couple stood inside. We stepped into the car, and the wife lit up.

"You two really know how to put on a show!" She praised my strength and how Josh made her laugh until she cried.

Her husband remained silent but I could tell he was studying me.

We shyly said our thanks, then he jumped in. "What happened to your face?"

My mouth went slack. I tried to recover – to hide my reaction. "Did you . . .? Did you see our show?" I asked.

The wife could see my confusion. "Oh, he missed it tonight. He doesn't know."

A few weeks before the show, I'd made a decision. When Josh introduced me for my first aerial act, I asked him to tell my story: how I'd grown up with a facial difference, encountered challenges and setbacks in the entertainment industry, but despite it all, created a brilliant, sparkling career performing all over the world. I thought making the show personal like this would fit in well with the ship's inspirational branding. Also, I surmised, it would deter them from firing us because of any issue they had with my face. But that was secondary. I had a bigger agenda: This speech would be the key to easing my mental health during our weeks on the ship. It was my metamorphosis story. My chance to disclose my difference but also talk about how I *overcame*, how I *triumphed,* how I *rose from the ashes* to be here on this very stage tonight.

DOI: 10.4324/9781003535591-15

I thought that surely after the show, I wouldn't have to field questions about my face. It meant survival. And it seemed to be working – until now.

I steadied myself on Josh's arm, as if the ship was tipping sideways.

"What happened to your face?"

I had been interrogated like this my whole life. I was used to this question. It's just that . . . it wasn't supposed to happen now. The spell had been broken.

What? You mean, you don't see me as beautiful?

* * *

From the age of three, I grew up dancing, though Mom resisted putting me in lessons at first. I was born with vascular malformations in the left side of my face, a condition that caused swelling, discoloration, bleeding, and tearing from my left eye and pain from my temple down to my jaw. She was afraid dancing would exacerbate my condition. I begged until she caved.

Outside of class, I watched ballet productions – *Swan Lake*, *Sleeping Beauty* – and imagined myself as the principal dancer. As much as I longed for the spotlight, the stories were what mattered, especially the tales of transfiguration where the main characters morphed into princesses, good and beautiful in every way.

These stories shaped my belief that happy endings were inevitable . . . a guarantee. I looked forward to that magical moment that would transform me physically into the person I felt I was on the inside. I knew it was my destiny.

* * *

Though it didn't come from the world of ballet, *The Ugly Duckling* was my favorite story, both the Disney short and the *Little Golden Books* version. In this Hans Christian Anderson staple, a duckling who is physically different from his siblings is deemed ugly. He is cast out. When he grows up, he discovers that he is not a duck but a swan, revered by the world for his beauty. This was clearly me: othered because of my looks but soon to evolve into a creature envied. These fantasies were fed by the fact that I was constantly visiting doctors and plastic surgeons during my childhood. Each visit, a new promise:

"Your face will be more symmetrical!"
"We'll get you looking like a normal kid!"
"You'll be so pretty when we're done!"

After each surgery, I looked into the mirror expecting a new, symmetrical face. Instead I saw long scars, brightly colored bruises, more swelling. I didn't know if things were getting better. I felt more confident, but my face still looked lopsided. That confidence was influenced by my family and friends complimenting me on "how much better" my face looked. If they said I was becoming more of who I was meant to be, then that must be fact. But I continued to experience difficulties navigating my social surroundings.

* * *

I didn't know it at the time, but my struggles with stigmatizing attitudes toward my face were compounded by my racial identity: I was a Japanese American, growing up in a majority-white, small, rural, town in Arizona. These two things – race and face – felt insurmountable. I would forever be an outsider.

In an attempt to minimize my facial difference, I always smiled. I exuded constant happiness, acting like any "normal" kid would act. To counter any racism and xenophobia, I explained how I was born here and how "American" my family was, furiously defending our place in this country as rightful citizens. I told people I was a "banana"... yellow on the outside, white on the inside. My facial difference and Asian heritage were the opposite of the normative standard of beauty: white skin, blonde hair, blue eyes, symmetrical face. Of course, because these two features were visibly apparent, there was a limit to how far this could go.

Even as I tried desperately to push my core identities away from me, one theme of my childhood remained constant: a yearning for belonging. This sentiment was deeply felt not only by me and my sister, but by my mom and her side of the family.

* * *

On February 19, 1942, during World War II, President Franklin D. Roosevelt signed Executive Order 9066 which authorized the incarceration of around 120,000 Japanese Americans from the West Coast into concentration camps (no evidence exists that anyone who was imprisoned had ever plotted or committed crimes against the United States). In 1944, my mother was born in the Amache camp in Colorado where her mom's side of my family was imprisoned. My grandfather was serving as a doctor in the United States 442nd Infantry Regiment on the front lines in Germany. Of course, Mom didn't remember her time in the camp, as she was just an infant, but she often told stories of growing up after the war had ended. She remembered being called "jap." While many of her peers took no issue with her Japanese heritage, she remembered being taunted for eating rice out of a bowl with chopsticks. Still others yelled, "Go back to where you came from!"

My sister and I are Yonsei, or fourth generation Japanese American. Our family's trauma, passed down through the generations, resonated in our bones. Would we ever be accepted as full members of this country?

* * *

In 2020, I sat at a picnic table many mornings under a large oak tree in the quiet park across the street from our house. I wrote in my journal. As blue pen sketched thoughts onto lined yellow pages, I felt like I was being hit with one train after another, each one filled with distant memories, fears, grief, and rage previously buried for years, now brought up in a world stymied by a pandemic.

Asian hate was spiking; Xenophobia in raw, bestial form. I feared for my elders. For the first time in his life, my uncle, almost 80, felt unsafe in his grocery store. I could feel the stares and distancing as I walked down the street. I felt lucky to have Josh, who is white, with me in public. In childhood, I remember feeling othered, being made fun of for my culture and Asian features. Emotionally unsafe. This was the first time where I felt like the shape of my eyes, dark hair, and golden skin could incite violence. I wondered, if this hatred was so easily on public display now, how often had it shown up more subtly in my life previously, before it was "safe" to be openly racist? How often had I naively tried to shield myself from the truth?

Live entertainment was on pause, and thus, I had nothing but time to think. Distant memories from the early years of my career began slamming into me from behind at a rate and ferocity I couldn't control. I remembered standing frozen when a costume designer tried to hide the left side of my face for an ensemble number when no one else's face was covered. I remembered the threat of losing my aerial job at a nightclub if I didn't agree to wear masks to partially cover my difference. I remembered the year-long tour contract that was canceled because the founder of the circus feared the audience's reaction to how I looked. I was often made to feel like I was lucky to be hired onto shows, like I should be grateful for the generosity. In 2020, for the first time, I saw how those experiences – during the formative years of my career after circus school – sabotaged the next decade of my life.

To be fair, I also remembered all the producers, directors, and agents who hired me and never once brought up my difference. It was these individuals who kept hope alive in my heart. They were proof that for many, my appearance didn't matter . . . even in the looks-based field of entertainment. And yet, those experiences could not heal the damage that had already been done.

One memory after another flattened me against the tracks.

On our last cruise ship contract before the pandemic, Josh and I had performed six shows over two weeks and had received six standing ovations.

I was completely miserable the whole time.

My mental health was at an all-time low. I could not feel that success. It wasn't real to me. What I realized in 2020 was the extent to which I'd buried life-shifting experiences, minimized trauma, suppressed my pain in order to push forward and "get on with life." And now, it seemed like stigma had won.

I decided to end my performing career.

* * *

In 2023, I sat in front of my computer in Josh's parents' house, dressed in a gray, fitted blazer. From the waist-down in yoga pants and slippers. I logged onto Zoom where Phyllida Swift, CEO of Face Equality International (FEI), three other panelists, and I waited to go live. We were about to address the United Nations. Today, I would give testimony about the workplace discrimination I faced in the entertainment industry.

Two days earlier, I had sat on the floor of the United Nations attending the 16th Conference of States Parties (COSP) to the Convention of the Rights of Persons with Disabilities (CRPD). One by one, I witnessed representatives from around the world proudly stating what laws had been enacted in their countries to protect the rights of disabled people.

A month before the UN event, I'd chatted over Zoom with Phyllida and the other speakers to discuss the scope of our panel. We looked over a group document and decided what stories we would share.

"Does anyone have any questions?" Phyllida asked toward the end.

I raised my hand. "I looked at the UN's website and noticed that our panel is scheduled for the day after COSP ends. Is this a mistake?" I was hopeful and frustrated at once. We had all been dispirited that our panel had been denied an in-person spot at the UN, but now this?

"Unfortunately," she said, "that's correct."

The overarching theme of COSP 16 was *Harmonizing National Policies and Strategies with the CRPD: Achievements and Challenges*. Under that, there were three sub-themes. Our panel fell into the third: *Reaching The Under-Represented Groups of Persons with Disabilities*.

"Nothing screams 'underrepresented disability' like being pushed to Zoom and being scheduled on the day *after* the conference ends," I lamented to Josh after the call.

Now broadcasting live from a basement in New Jersey, I sat on the edge of the couch as Phyllida made opening remarks.

> Today, we believe that disfigurement has not been mentioned once in a universal periodic review to the Human Rights Council in over 90,000 recommendations. The CRPD extends to the Facial Difference community thanks to the human rights/social model, but we know that this is not adequately reflected in the laws and practices of some states who have signed up to the Convention. This includes the UK and the USA.[1]

After the two of us spoke, Christina Raj, a powerful activist from India, took the floor. Christina founded the *Center for Ichthyosis Related Members Foundation – India* which provides community, support, and resources for people living with Ichthyosis and their families across Asia and Africa. "Leave No One Behind," is her maxim. She was born with a rare combination of a number of different types of Ichthyosis, a condition that requires a high level of care to manage pain and appearance.

"I am the oldest survivor in Asia and Africa to date," she said. She is in her mid 50s. Her testimony began.

> Ichthyosis patients are highly ostracized, harassed, abused, spat upon, and even physically assaulted. We don't get admission in schools and colleges. We don't get jobs. And there's a huge disparity in salaries. We are expected to work more . . . more than others because society thinks that they are doing us a favor. The severe dry skin gives a very scaly appearance all over when skin keeps peeling which causes disfigurement and people address us as snake, reptile, crocodile. And we are subject to extreme mental torture because of these kinds of names. Rarely, they remember our names.

In under-developed and developing countries in Asia and Africa, she said, the whole family experiences humiliation. She detailed how her house and land had been illegally occupied for the past 36 years by people who told her, "You don't require a house because you will die any day." She sued to keep her property and had won her case in court, and yet, local law enforcement refused to help. On top of that, she experienced verbal and physical violence from her neighbors regularly. She testified that there is very little support for those with Ichthyosis.

The weight of her words highlighted what was at stake. The epidemic of international human rights violations surrounding those living with facial difference *must* be acknowledged. Extreme stigma surrounding visible difference leads directly to acts of violence and oppression. This fight is literally about life or death.

* * *

I am now in my early 40s. I am grumpier and more cynical. To hell with *The Ugly Duckling.* To hell with the idea of growing into white supremacist standards of beauty as the predominant goal, the societal aspiration, the inspiration porn[2] we should aspire to.

There is no moral to the story. No indictment of society for its terrible behavior. It's just another myth that links objective physical beauty with expansive personal worth.

As I got older, I realized that it didn't matter how many surgeries or procedures I underwent. I was never going to be treated like a "normal" person. I would never be able to force myself into the ideal of beauty, let alone grow into it naturally. My last facial surgery was near the end of college. I took forever to heal and my immune system was depleted. I resolutely made the decision that there would be no more surgeries, at least in the cosmetic department. There would be no "swan" moment. No matter what I did, the comments, the stares, the whispers . . . they would always be there.

Life will be extraordinary, Hans Christian Anderson promised. *Just become a swan.*

Mr. Anderson was not known for his realism.

* * *

I know stigma quite well. It has caused me to question my worth at every turn. Every time I was passed over, let go, shut out, I believed that I wasn't skilled enough, intelligent enough . . . just *enough.* Rarely did anyone admit to their prejudice. Otherwise, I never knew: was it because of my face? Race? Gender? Because of stigma, I've experienced severe anxiety, depression, suicidal ideation, and self-harm.

Through my family's history here in the US, I know stigma can incite the incarceration of 120,000 innocent people for years and create trauma deeply felt generations after. I know stigma can look like re-education in the camps to "Americanize" Japanese Americans (read: assimilate to white culture) with orders to abandon their communities and culture upon release.[3]

The message was clear: *Fix yourself, or else.*

I was lucky enough to be brought up in a nurturing, upper-middle-class household. This is not the reality for most in our worldwide community. For those who do not have safe households and communities, income security, guaranteed food and housing, access to healthcare, along with other vital supports, the risk is that much higher. From the stories gathered from my beloved Facial Difference (FD) community around the world, I know stigma causes dehumanizing questions, stares and comments, abandonment at birth or infanticide, violent attacks by strangers and family alike, scorn, pity, and mockery from the media, institutionalization, workplace discrimination, and most of all, a perceived depletion of worth . . . all exacerbated if intersectionality is at play.

Fix yourself, or else.

But what if we can't or *don't want to be* fixed?

* * *

I regret using my story as inspiration porn on the ships and beyond. At the time, it was a survival move made out of desperation and ignorance. It was before I was introduced to the wider FD community, before I became grounded in my disabled body. Now, I know it contributed to the myth: that individual personal accomplishment is the way to beat disability.

When stories like these are the only narratives to paint us in a positive light, it tells the world, "Look! Look, here! This one was able to overcome. Everyone else isn't trying hard enough." Highlighting one's personal accomplishments is not bad in and of itself, but we need more nuanced representation. Our community is made up of a sweeping diversity of experiences worldwide . . . not just inspirational and tragic, but the whole spectrum of complicated life that lies between. We can learn from other groups who have historically struggled with justice but are making progress in recent years due to a shift in how they are perceived. I know that the FD community can, too. But along with organizing within ourselves, we need the support of allies who are willing to amplify our voices and fight with us.

Let me be clear: We can't just fix ourselves through plastic surgery and personal achievement, nor should we have to. And this is not just an "us" problem. This is a humanitarian issue impacting every person on the planet, because at any time, *anyone* can acquire a facial difference. I imagine an idyllic world where looks are neutralized, where our appearance has no bearing on our worth. Even those who are not disfigured would feel these effects. So much prejudice is instigated by what we read into each other's appearance, when in reality, what we glean is as thin as vapor. So much time, money, and mental health are squandered trying to keep up with the status quo of appearance. The fear is that if we fall short, the repercussions will be swift and brutal. That fear is valid. The consequences are real. But we can change it.

* * *

A strong Facial Difference movement has already started within our community dating back to the work of activists from over at least the past 50 years. But this conversation has not yet reached common public discourse. The Body Positivity movement, originated by fat, queer Black women in the 1960s,[4] made great strides in changing the conversation, but unfortunately, that conversation mostly stops from the neck up. Within the movement, there is still a great deal of stigma against facial difference.

FEI, based in the UK, does significant work by mobilizing organizations from around the world who "support and represent people with facial difference and disfigurements." They have conducted research on the human rights violations of people living with FD in India, Nepal, and Mexico, and work tirelessly to push the media for better representation. Aside from FEI, however, there are very few organizations that serve the FD community in ways that amplify our voices and make political strides to dissolve the system that continues to shut us out. Most organizations in existence are medical non-profits, parent groups, or were created by plastic surgeons/surgery clinics to serve their patients. Aside from many providing travel/housing assistance related to medical procedures, most are focused on individual improvement and self-help. Not many have FD leadership in executive positions. We need our allies to listen to our wisdom to really understand what it takes to create access to the world.

* * *

Over years of becoming centered and connected to my various identities and the communities attached to them, I was led to the Adult Facial Difference Community[5] on Facebook, started and managed by Adele Capitella-Liu. This online space was life-changing as I connected with others like me around the world. It inspired me to imagine other gathering spaces online and in person, facilitated by facially different people internationally, where we could talk face to face and engage in activating progress for our movement. So I decided to create it.

It started with just a website featuring a few photos of my FD friends and me and a passionate open letter to society on a black background. Then it sat for almost a year as I toiled over what shape it should take until one day, I took a deep breath. When I let it out, *The FaceOut Project,* a grassroots endeavor with the goal of building community and empowerment for facially different people, was born. Every Monday night, we meet for the Activism Hub, a place to gather online, connect, and discuss how we can create change. The invitation is always the same: *Come as you are.*

Members join in from around the globe, ranging in age from young adult to mid-80s. Every meeting brings with it a sense of dynamic connection as we speak love and validation to each other's life stories and take steps to make change. Communing with others with similar lived experiences is incredibly powerful. There is a love that is generated in spaces that are built by us, for us . . . and that love radiates infinitely outward. As I allow that energy and life affirmation into my own retreated heart, I have begun to heal and find my power in the whole sum of who I am. It has made me consider that maybe I can feel strong on stage again. Maybe I'm not yet done as a performer. And I can see that same power growing within other members, as well. The energy from our meetings continues through the week in the form of new friendships, ideas shared, collaborations catalyzed into existence. This is how movements find their strength.

I didn't have the FD community growing up. Neither did most others like me. But as these networks of support grow, I can't help but be optimistic. As individuals and as a movement, we are finding our power and our voices. I know we are climbing an impossibly steep hill. Our work is endless.

But as we continue to integrate with other social movements, continue to work toward systemic change, continue to love and empower ourselves and each other, we will get there. As a community, we are creating our own metamorphosis story. But maybe this time, instead of "fixing" ourselves, it will be the world that's transformed.

Notes

1 Face Equality International. (2023, June 16). *Face equality international @ the United Nations convention on the rights of persons w disabilities* [Video]. YouTube. https://youtu.be/YXymhukCGIQ?si=-oi6siH3FrcFS7Zf
2 TEDx Talks. (2014, May 13). *Inspiration porn and the objectification of disability: Stella Young at TEDxSydney 2014* [Video]. YouTube. https://youtu.be/SxrS7-I_sMQ?si=P2vEnlEUrGbI8E2N
3 TED-Ed. (2021, December 2). *Can stereotypes ever be good? Sheila Marie Orfano and Densho* [Video]. YouTube. https://youtu.be/aFXmyNUaXFo?si=bBEmme6ykJcfgyV0
4 Martin, M. (2021, February 18). *The whitewashed, diluted reality of modern body positivity: The important black history of the body positivity movement.* The Ohio State University. https://u.osu.edu/studentwellnesscenter/2021/02/18/the-whitewashed-diluted-reality-of-modern-body-positivity-the-important-black-history-of-the-body-positivity-movement/
5 Adult Facial Difference Community. (n.d.) *Home* [Facebook page]. Retrieved November 20, 2024, from https://www.facebook.com/groups/facialdifferenceadults

Section 3

Representations of Disfigurement

7 Challenging Down Syndrome Prejudices in Today's Media Landscape

Charlene Pell

Early television portrayals of people with Down syndrome sought to inform the public about the condition, focusing on medical aspects. The depictions often followed a medical model that overlooked the environmental and social factors affecting an individual's ability to participate fully in society (Ellis & Goggin, 2015). Disabling stereotypes that "medicalize, patronize, criminalize, and dehumanize" people with disabilities perpetuate discrimination and exploitation experienced routinely by people with disabilities and contribute to their systemic exclusion from society (Barnes, 1992, p. 19).

Down syndrome is caused by an extra chromosome, resulting in intellectual and physical changes. Approximately 400,000 people in the U.S. have Down syndrome (Global Down Syndrome Foundation, 2024). The most recognizable physical characteristics are a flattened bridge of the nose, a round face, almond-shaped up-slanting eyes, and short stature (CDC, 2016). Individuals with Down syndrome are often susceptible to other health problems, including immune diseases and heart defects (Global Down Syndrome Foundation, 2024).

It is essential to cast individuals with disabilities authentically and proportionately in films and television to reduce the stigma associated with disability and to reduce prejudice toward this outgroup. Despite 26% of adults in the U. S. having a disability (CDC), during the 2019–2020 television season, only 27 characters with a disability appeared regularly on a network series (GLAAD, 2024). One of those individuals has Down syndrome. In the history of the Academy Awards, of the 27 winners nominated for their portrayal of a character with a disability, only two of the actors had an actual disability (Ruderman Foundation, 2017). Individuals without disabilities perform 95% of top show characters with disabilities (Ruderman Foundation, 2017). Actors pretending to be black and putting on "black face" sparks outrage, but actors pretending to be disabled are praised and rewarded with Oscars (Ruderman Family Foundation, 2017; Smith, 2015; Woodburn & Kopic, 2016).

There is minimal research about how the media has portrayed people with facial differences caused by Down syndrome, particularly since 1989, when ABC introduced the family entertainment series *Life Goes On*, featuring Chris Burke, an actor with Down syndrome (Stumbo, 2018). Burke portrayed the lead character, "Corky," a likable, capable middle son in a working-class family (Stumbo, 2018). Through his role, Burke challenged stereotypes of Down syndrome and

DOI: 10.4324/9781003535591-17

demonstrated his abilities, helping to educate the public about the stigma and psychosocial challenges of living with a disability, such as rejection, teasing, bullying, exclusion, misconceptions, and the underestimation of individuals with Down syndrome. However, little attention has been paid to the evolving, favorable, realistic media representation of people with Down syndrome in the time since *Life Goes On* premiered.

The chapter begins with the role of media in confronting prejudices and how using mediated intergroup contact has effectively reduced prejudice toward gay men and Black people. Mediated intergroup contact, or "mediated contact," involves exposing members from one social group to members from another through media (Park, 2012). People form judgments about different groups based on the media they consume. As such, the text explores the representation of individuals with Down syndrome in the media since 1989, showing how portrayals have evolved from stereotypical medical depictions to more diverse and authentic roles with depth and nuance. A critical cultural textual analysis of the recent film *The Peanut Butter Falcon* is included as a recent example of how individuals with Down syndrome are depicted in the media. Finally, though these portrayals can challenge prejudice, they must be promoted more broadly to reach audiences beyond those who already support people with Down syndrome. Mediated contact is crucial for Generation Z as most of their interactions are through media.

The Role of Media in Challenging Prejudices

Individuals form judgments about groups of people based on the fictional and factual media they consume and on what they read (Fujioka, 1999; Ortiz & Harwood, 2007; Schiappa et al., 2005; Tan et al., 1997). Most people "make the majority of their life acquaintances with disabled people only in film, television, and literature" (Snyder & Mitchell, 2006, p. 181). Globally, in free societies, mass media wields powerful influence in shaping opinions about individuals with disabilities. Non-disabled people learn about disabled people and issues through mass media and adopt symbolic themes and norms repeatedly maintained over time (Haller, 2010; Tuchman, 1978).

The role of the media as facilitators of intergroup contact emerged in the late 1990s. Schiappa et al. (2005) proposed that if people process mass-mediated para-social interaction like interpersonal interaction, the socially beneficial functions of intergroup contact may occur. Before 1990, the media research about different social and ethnic groups focused on negative stereotypes of minority groups and the effects those stereotypes had on audiences (Park, 2012).

Reducing uncertainty and anxiety is essential to enabling attraction (Kellerman & Reynolds, 1990). The media offers models for positive interaction with outgroup members in an anxiety-free environment (Ortiz & Harwood, 2007). In this "scripted environment it is possible for encounters high in group salience to retain a positive tone" (Ortiz & Harwood, 2007, p. 628).

Television imitates everyday situations and shares similar characteristics of real-life events (e.g., sound and sight); vicarious experience through television may become a part of our social experience (Shapiro & Lang, 1991) and provide a basis for social judgments such as racial attitudes (Armstrong et al., 1992) and ethnic stereotypes (Tan et al., 1997).

Other forms of mediated contact (e.g., computer-based interactions) are also beneficial. Reeves and Nass (1996) convincingly demonstrated that interactions with computers, television, film, and new technologies are identical to actual relationships. Parasocial interaction can increase (Schramm & Hartmann, 2008) if the television or film characters talk directly to the audience, as in documentaries and interviews. Schiappa et al. (2005) conducted three studies, two involving parasocial contact with gay men and one involving parasocial contact with a male cross-dresser. The results suggested that parasocial contact facilitates positive parasocial responses and changes in beliefs about the attributes of minority group categories. This finding supports the possibility that parasocial contact may work to reduce prejudice toward individuals and actors with Down syndrome.

Online social network platforms may offer individuals with facial differences caused by Down syndrome opportunities and provide the public with a richer understanding of all types of disabilities as individuals with disabilities share their stories and talents on their own terms. Madison Tevlin is proof of this: she posted a video of herself singing on YouTube and it went viral, leading to her acting career (Power, 2023). More than ever, mediated contact in reducing prejudice is essential because society continues to evolve deeper into the digital age, especially for Generation Z, since most of their contact is mediated. Digital online platforms such as Facebook, Instagram, X, Threads, and others offer an interactive contact experience of "participatory" (Ellis & Goggin, 2015) contact that may successfully reduce prejudice because individuals with disabilities can control their representation and speak directly to audiences. These new platforms may provide the means to transform disability representation and offer a "much broader notion of participation" for those with disabilities (Ellis & Goggin, 2015, p. 123).

Viewers typically choose media representing their ethnic group, avoiding outgroups, which can hinder exposure to outgroup-mediated contact (Schieferdecker & Wessler, 2017). Nondisabled people may intentionally or unintentionally not see online sites about Down syndrome and other disabilities because of echo chambers and self-selective viewing. Amy Ross Arguedas et al. (2022) described an echo chamber as a filter bubble situation some people experience because of media supply, distribution, or demand. Jamieson and Capella, authors of *Echo Chamber* (2008), defined it as "a bounded, enclosed media space that has the potential to both magnify the messages delivered within it and insulate them from rebuttal" (p. 76). Echo chambers and filter bubbles can hinder the effectiveness of mediated contact.

Filter bubbles are echo chambers created by "ranking algorithms engaged in passive personalization without any active choice on our part" (Arguedas et al., 2022, p. 11). These bubbles exclusively show us things we like while hiding things we do not like – based on data-driven display decisions dictated by platform companies' commercial interests rather than our active choices (Arguedas et al., 2022).

Authentic, under-representations or misrepresentations of people with disabilities have significant social, psychological, and economic implications. In her overview of disability media theorization, Ellis (2018) said, "the media plays a central role in both the social disablement and the inclusion of people with a disability" (p. 359). Nondisabled ingroup members experience outgroup individuals through their positive or negative portrayals in the media. "Attitudes toward, assumptions about and expectations of people with disabilities are based on their media depictions" (Ellis & Goggin, 2015, p. 26). Generally, nondisabled people avoid direct interactions with individuals with disabilities because of stereotypical misconceptions, fear of saying or doing the wrong thing, or fear of difference (Pell, 2019; Bauman, 2007).

Mediated Representation of Gay Men and Black People

The positive effect of intergroup contact has been most notably evident in the research related to reducing prejudice toward gay men and Black people. In a series of experiments, exposure to popular television shows featuring gay men or cross-dressers as the primary protagonists reduced heterosexuals' prejudice toward sexual minority groups (Schiappa et al., 2005).

Sink and Mastro (2018) found that viewing television programs between 2000 and 2015 that featured gay actors and recalling specific gay actors decreased the heterosexual participants' negative attitudes toward gay men in society. Other work in this domain has shown that exposing people to TV shows and films that feature positive portrayals of diverse characters can reduce prejudice (Joyce & Harwood, 2014).

Ortiz and Harwood (2007) used a social cognitive approach to examine whether "vicarious" contact in the media presents similar effects to real-world intergroup contact without the undesirable risk of accompanying anxiety. Limited support was found to support the hypothesis in examining two settings of mediated intergroup contact (*Will & Grace*, a sitcom about a straight-gay friendship, and *Real World: Austin*, a reality show about association between white and Black cast members). In both settings, exposure to the shows was associated with less social distance toward the respective outgroups among straight and white viewers. Causality cannot be inferred because of the cross-sectional nature of the research, although it is conceivable that viewing these shows may have affected attitudes toward the outgroup (Ortiz & Harwood, 2007).

Ortiz and Harwood (2007) suggested that fictional portrayals have more impact than others and that media portrayals of deep, long-lasting intergroup relationships that receive maximal screen time, such as *Will & Grace*, may be more effective than one-time exposures from movies. In the show *Will & Grace,* Will retains his sexuality as a salient element, while he and Grace share a caring friendship; Ortiz and Harwood (2007) described this scenario as the perfect recipe for positive attitude change, and it is not easy to achieve in face-to-face encounters.

Unscripted reality television has gained global popularity and has proven particularly effective in creating parasocial relationships. Individuals who perceive reality TV as more realistic are more likely to be influenced by the content (Busselle & Greenberg, 2000).

Schiappa et al. (2006) also used the sitcom *Will & Grace* to determine if the depiction of gay characters influenced viewers' attitudes and found that there was a significant relationship between the existence of parasocial interaction and how often the show was watched. They found that viewing the show was found to reduce prejudice between the viewer and gay men. However, people familiar with or friends with gay men might have been more prone to watch the show and experience parasocial interaction with the gay characters (Schiappa et al., 2006). Nevertheless, the study substantiated that favorable media depictions and parasocial contact can positively influence viewer beliefs about a minority group (Schiappa et al., 2006).

Mastro and Tropp (2000) found that media images may provide a catalyst for normalizing racial stereotypes and expressing prejudicial attitudes that consequently impact judgments and, possibly, behavior. They conducted a study to examine the influence of stereotypical TV portrayals, attitudes toward Black people, and interracial contact on appraisals of Black television sitcom characters. Their findings supported research identifying the media's ability to activate social stereotypes.

Misrepresentation can be harmful. Although mediated contact generally demonstrated a positive effect on evaluations of Black characters, the audience participants rated high in prejudice (as identified by their scores on the Katz and Hass (1988) Anti-Black Racial Attitudes Scale), consistently rating Black characters negatively when presented with stereotypical portrayals, despite the close contact they may have had with other Black Americans (Mastro & Tropp, 2000). These findings suggest that viewing stereotypical portrayals of Black people may reinforce one's prejudicial beliefs, and subsequently, one's beliefs may override the potentially positive effects of contact in evaluating outgroup targets (Mastro & Tropp, 2000).

Fujioka (1999) investigated the effect of television portrayals when direct contact is lacking in a study that examined the effects of mediated contact via television on stereotypes of Black people among white and Japanese international college students. The study found that the more television entertainment shows the respondents viewed with Black people as primary characters, the more positive their reported stereotypes of Black people. Additionally, positive portrayals of Black people on television were associated with more positive stereotypes, while negative portrayals were linked to more negative stereotypes of Black people (Fujioka, 1999). The study revealed that "respondents' positive or negative evaluations of television portrayals were significantly associated with their stereotypes of African Americans" (Fujioka, 1999, p. 66).

Media Representations of Down Syndrome

Beginning in the 1950s and 60s, children with disabilities appeared helpless and pitiful in fundraising ads (Hayes & Black, 2003), perpetuating the stigma and inaccurate stereotypes associated with disabilities. Ongoing media exposure to stigmatized stereotypes of disability reinforces the myth that people with disabilities are not as valuable as nondisabled people (Goffman, 1963). The media's representation of minority groups influences societal beliefs and cultural norms (Leavitt et al., 2015; Milkie, 1999).

Chris Burke's performance as "Corky" in *Life Goes On*, which aired from 1989–1993, disputed the prevailing stereotypes of individuals with Down syndrome by demonstrating Burke's ability to understand and process information, converse, perform activities of daily living, and defend himself and his sister. Burke portrayed an affable, fun-loving, multi-faceted teen entering Marshall High School, where he was often the target of bullies who taunted him and called him a "retard." At the moments when things almost got out of hand, someone stepped in to rescue Corky, a friend or his protective sister, but at other times, Corky managed challenging situations on his own. In one episode, two tough guys at school needle Corky into doing something he does not want to do to fit in with them. The guys tease him with expressions like, "What's the matter, you afraid," and "If you don't do what we say, you can't hang out with us anymore." Coerced, Corky walks over to a male student sitting beside his sister and rudely tells him to leave. His sister reprimands him, and one of the tough guys says something uncouth to her. Corky stands up to him and tells him to leave his sister alone. A fight ensues. In this pivotal scene, Corky becomes the rescuer instead of the one rescued. This favorable, authentic portrayal challenges the stereotypical depiction of someone with Down syndrome who is unable to understand, process, defend himself, or act on information. Corky's reaction and behavior mirrors that of a nondisabled person and "normalizes" Down syndrome.

In the 1990s, a research study examined the portrayal of individuals with Down syndrome in *Life Goes On*. It found that when participants saw active, socially engaged individuals with Down syndrome, it helped challenge negative beliefs about people with disabilities (Hall & Minnes, 1999). Additionally, nondisabled individuals began to perceive people with Down syndrome as more equal after viewing a documentary featuring a person with Down syndrome, and the character Corky from *Life Goes On* (Hall & Minnes, 1999).

Life Goes On laid the foundation for future actors with Down syndrome to be cast in other programs. Burke was nominated for a Golden Globe in 1990.

Diverse Contexts

Since 1989, individuals with Down syndrome have been portrayed with depth and nuance in various roles and contexts in TV series, films, documentaries, and reality shows. For example, Hollywood agent Gail Williamson's son, Blair, appeared in his first TV commercial, a Proctor & Gamble ad for the Special Olympics, in 1990 during the first episode of the second season of *Life Goes On* (Haller, 2010, p. 10). Blair is an accomplished actor and producer with notable credits to his name. Gail Williamson's experiences, her son's acting career, and her friendship with Perl Kingsley, mother of Jason Kingsley, the first child actor with Down syndrome to appear on a television show (*The Fall Guy*) led her to work as a contractor for the Media Access Office. The organization promoted access and employment opportunities in the entertainment industry for individuals with disabilities. Later, she worked for the Down Syndrome Society of Los Angeles (Haller, 2010, p. 10). In 2003, she established Down Syndrome in Arts & Media, a platform for performers with Down syndrome to enter the entertainment industry (Haller, 2010, p. 10).

Perl Kingsley wrote for *Sesame Street* from 1970 to 2015 (Haller, 2010, p. 10). Before Jason was born with Down syndrome, she introduced children with disabilities on television through *Sesame Street* (Esposito, 2018). Her son made numerous appearances on the show, and *she* was instrumental in showcasing actors with various disabilities on television. Author Malcolm Gladwell might have characterized the work and advocacy of Williamson and Kingsley as the vital "tipping point," the catalyst for inclusion of more disabled actors in television and film. Jason Kingsley continues to act and has been featured *in Touched by an Angel* in 1997, *Diffability Hollywood* in 2016, and *Far From the Tree* in 2017 (IMDb).

As noted by Schramm and Hartmann (2008), parasocial interaction can be enhanced when television or film characters talk directly to the audience, as in reality TV, documentaries, and interviews. It is essential for shows to present authentic narratives and avoid obscuring the harsh realities of some people with Down syndrome, and their mistreatment. (Thomas, 2021).

In 2015, a ground-breaking, Emmy-nominated reality show (docuseries) that follows the lives and everyday interactions of seven adults of different ethnicities and races with Down syndrome, entitled *Born This Way* (*BTW*), aired on network TV (Olson, 2018). Unlike other scripted shows, the actors told their stories their way. Media contact through programs like *BTW* is often the only contact nondisabled people have with individuals with Down syndrome (Leavitt et al., 2015), so it is critical that the messages audiences receive cultivate a positive influence because the audience will relate their impressions to the entire population of people with Down syndrome (Olson, 2018). Producer Jonathon Murray created the show to magnify the voices of minority and outcast groups (Grobar, 2017).

In addition to viewing the show, audience members could reach out to the actors on social media. Chung and Cho (2014) found that featuring individuals in reality TV shows motivate viewers to engage with the actors on social media, strengthening the parasocial relationship. Unlike the 1994 film *Forest Gump,* where Tom Hank's character is represented as childlike and innocent in an adult's body, the actors in *BTW* have age-appropriate desires that reflect adulthood (Olson, 2018). (Olson, 2018). They curse, watch R-rated movies, go to a bar, talk about baseball and celebrity crushes, and are involved in poetry, cooking, yoga, and dance lessons (Olson, 2018). The actors express various emotions, from crying and laughing to fear; they have relationships with their parents, siblings, and friends; many desire to date and one is engaged (Olson, 2018). All the actors share their goals and dreams (Olson, 2018). *BTW* provides a realistic representation of adults with Down syndrome; it does not hide their differences or limitations but focuses on their abilities, showing independence as a learned possibility (Olson, 2018).

Diverse Roles

Individuals with Down syndrome have been portrayed in various roles and contexts since 1989. For a while, Burke was the only actor with Down syndrome, but over time, more actors with Down syndrome began to appear in shows or movies. (Stumbo, 2018). Andrea Fay Friedman, an accomplished film and television actress, co-starred with Burke as Amanda in *Life Goes On.* She has starred in episodes of *Law & Order: Special Victims Unit*, *ER,* and *Saving Grace*, among many other TV shows and films (Stumbo, 2018). An accomplished actor, Tommy Jessop has starred in several TV shows, radio, film, and documentaries and played significant roles on stage (Stumbo, 2018). Lauren Potter is an actress and producer known for her role as Becky Jackson on the hit show *Glee* (Stumbo, 2018), another series that offered realistic portrayals of disability.

Visibility and Psychological Depth

In 2019, Gail Williamson secured a crucial role for Cole Sibus in the drama series *Stumptown* (Griffith, 2019). Sibus plays Ansel Parios, the younger brother with Down syndrome of the star of the show, Dex Parios, a former Marine veteran who served in Afghanistan and returned home with Post Traumatic Stress Disorder. Dex becomes a controversial private detective with questionable tactics and harmful habits such as gambling. In an episode titled "Forget it Dex," we see Dex returning home late after a night of losing more money playing roulette (Griffith, 2019). She greets Ansel, who is home alone. Concerned, Ansel asks Dex if they will be okay, and Dex reassures him and reminds him to brush and floss his teeth. This scene depicts Ansel as capable of being home alone, perceptive, and intelligent enough to be worried about his sister and their future, but possibly unable to remember to brush and floss his teeth (Griffith, 2019). In a dramatic scene, Dex is driving Ansel to the park to play soccer when she makes a quick stop to deliver something. Ansel gets out of the car and starts playing with a soccer ball; suddenly, he sees Dex's car speeding off without him. Instantly, he knows something is wrong and calls a co-worker at the bar to get help. Ansel's quick thinking and action helped the police find the kidnappers.

It is atypical for a character with Down syndrome to play a role like this or to be depicted as an intelligent, intuitive person able to take decisive actions in a time of crisis. This role makes Ansel more relatable to the public and demonstrates his abilities rather than his inabilities. Such portrayals may help to reduce prejudice and misconceptions about persons with Down syndrome. The fact that *Stumptown* was a series instead of a film may also increase the possibility of having a more positive impact on viewers because of increased exposure over some time.

Analysis of *The Peanut Butter Falcon*

Zack Gottsagen, a charming actor with Down syndrome, starred in a leading role in the 2019 film *The Peanut Butter Falcon.* Gottsagen's performance marks a significant departure from past representations of actors with Down syndrome. It lays the foundation for moving ahead and creating richer contact to foster meaningful engagement with this marginalized outgroup. Zack is a strong film co-star with an essential and equal role integral to the story.

Using critical cultural textual analysis, I reviewed *The Peanut Butter Falcon,* relying on Bainbridge's (2011) methodological steps of encountering the text, separating the text into component signs and signifieds, identifying and encoding themes, and analyzing the context of the text, including elements intentionally left out of the text, exnomination, and examining context from secondary texts. I reviewed the film twice, primarily from a speaker's perspective, transcribing the dialogue between the protagonists, Zak and Tyler, during the second viewing. I interpreted the signs and their meanings to identify themes and possible interpretations by audiences. Zach's character (also named Zak) portrays a good-natured, relatable, likable, intelligent, strong character eager to fulfill his dream of learning to wrestle at the Saltwater Redneck Wrestling School. Every day, Zak watches a VHS tape of the once-famous wrestler Saltwater Redneck, his hero. Zak lives in a retirement home with elderly residents because his parents abandoned him, and he became a ward of the state. In one scene, Zak says, "I am young; I am not old, I don't know why I am here." Zak's situation exemplifies the environmental and social limitations that restrict individuals with disabilities from participating equally in public life (Griffith, 2019).

In the film's opening scene, we see Zak retrieving his tray for a meal, thanking the server, and sitting across from an older woman named Eleanor. Zak shows Eleanor a clever drawing he created that instructs Eleanor to pretend to choke on her pudding so that he can escape while everyone attends to her. It works. Eleanor starts choking, and Zak runs out the door, but he gets caught and is returned to the home with the new designation as a "flight risk." As a result, iron bars are placed across the only window in his room to prevent him from escaping. Determined to see Zak pursue his dream, his roommate pries the bars open enough for Zak to escape and instructs him to rub ointment all over his body to help him squeeze through the iron bars. Wearing only underwear, Zak wiggles, forcing himself out the window and runs to the docks to hide under a tarp on a fishing boat.

Planning his escape from the rest home, Zak demonstrates that he is intelligent, creative, and strategic, characteristics rarely associated with depicting an individual with Down syndrome. Zak's behavior reflects what anyone would try to do if trapped in his situation.

Zak begins an adventure that changes his life when a grieving, guilt-ridden, beleaguered fisherman named Tyler jumps in the boat to escape the men who beat him up for stealing their crab cage traps and setting the empty traps on the dock on fire. Tyler has no idea that anyone is on the boat until he hides in the marshes to elude the men looking for him and hears Zak vomiting. Upon discovering Zak, he silences him and is unaffected by Zak's appearance. They escape the captors, speed into the Intracoastal waters, and then come ashore and leave the boat to sink.

In underpants and barefoot, Zak follows behind Tyler, who ignores him but allows him to tag along as he heads to Florida. Zak is relentless in his attempts to get Tyler to talk to him. "My feet hurt. Do you have a car? Can we walk on the road? Excuse me, can you answer me?" These questions are all reasonable and demonstrate Zak's intellect. Zak says, "I am a Down syndrome person." Tyler replies, "I don't give a shit." Gradually, Tyler opens up, and the two men become friends. Zak tells Tyler about his dream of becoming a wrestler and that he wants to go to the Saltwater Redneck's wrestling school. Tyler realizes they have a common bond; they are both men on the run. Tyler tells Zak, "You are going to have to carry your own weight," on the journey to the Saltwater Redneck school. This directive places Zak on an even playing field with Tyler as the two men encounter several dangerous incidents on their journey.

At one point, Tyler abandons Zak and hitchhikes to get a ride with a trucker. Tyler decides to go back and find Zak after learning from the truck driver about a roadblock set up to catch the person who started the dock fire. Tyler arrives at just the right moment to find some children taunting Zak, calling him a "retard" and daring him to jump off a high platform into the water. Zak cannot swim. One of the boys, taunting Zak, pushes him into the water. Tyler jumps into action and saves Zak; later in the film, Zak saves Tyler. This reciprocal action again places Zak on equal footing with Tyler.

Tyler treats Zak like any other guy. One evening, as they sit by the fireside, Zak says, "I wanna be a badass wrestler guy because my family left me." Tyler says, "That doesn't make you a bad guy; you're a good guy." Zak replies, "I can't be a hero because I am a Down syndrome," echoing the words of his teachers and coaches who labeled him a "retard" and underestimated his capabilities. Tyler tells Zak that his strength is unbelievable and that he nearly pulled his arm out of the socket to help him out of the water. Tyler starts helping Zak train the next day, and a genuine friendship takes root.

Gottsagen received a Special Jury Prize, "Outstanding Breakthrough Performance," from the Crested Butte Film Festival 2019 for his portrayal. The Global Down Syndrome Foundation praised *The Peanut Butter Falcon* and Zach Gottsagen's acting ability, as well as others involved in the production; however, Landmark (2022) argued that Gottsagen's role in *The Peanut Butter Falcon* maintained the subordination status of disability and should not be valorized.

Filmmakers Tyler Nilson and Michael Schwartz created *The Peanut Butter Falcon* to reflect Gottsagen's dream of becoming an actor, but Landmark (2022) contends the creators constructed the disabled character Zak as a patronized superpowered supercrip who upholds ableist ideologies. Landmark uses critical-cultural textual analysis to identify patterns of meaning that support hegemonic ideologies. Super-crip representations construct disability as something to be overcome or qualified for instead of accepted as ordinary (Ellis, 2018, p. 363).

Patronizing narratives occur when disabled people are represented as incompetent, inferior, as victims in need of rescue by nondisabled characters, objects of pity or sympathy, or dependent on nondisabled characters, submissive, unintelligent, and not vital in decision-making driving the plot forward (Tuchman, 1978, p. 156).

Potential for Expanded Media Representation

Over the years, more advocacy groups have called for the inclusion and authentic representation of disability in many countries, including America (GLAAD, 2024). Additionally, people with disabilities have taken to the internet to tell their stories through blogs, YouTube, Facebook, X, Threads, and other online platforms.

There are now studios such as Performing Arts Studio West and others developed exclusively to train actors with intellectual disabilities, and a few directors and producers with and without disabilities committed to creating authentic roles and opportunities for actors with disabilities (Esposito, 2018).

Research on the effectiveness of combining reality TV and social networking sites (SNS) offers new exciting opportunities to increase the effectiveness of parasocial contact and relationships. It is commonplace for viewers to reach out to stars on reality TV and celebrities on SNSs and to interact with them. This form of communication between actors and the audience has altered the role of "audiences from spectators and admirers to participants in media experience and friends of celebrities" (Chung & Cho, 2014, p. 47). The ever-evolving digital media landscape will offer new opportunities to improve engagement between actors with Down syndrome and nondisabled audiences and further the inclusion and authentic representation of actors with Down syndrome in film and television in the US.

* * *

The findings of this analysis indicate that media representations of individuals with Down syndrome have evolved since Burke's pivotal role as the main character of *Life Goes On.* His role "positively influenced future generations of actors with disabilities, as well as many US families that included a member with Down syndrome" (Haller, 2010, p. 9). Instead of portraying them in a negative or stereotypical way, recent film and television shows like *The Peanut Butter Falcon, Champions, Glee, BTW*, and *Stumptown* have depicted people with Down syndrome living intentional, happy, interesting lives. In the movie *The Peanut Butter Falcon,* Tyler teaches Zak how to shoot a rifle. Eventually, Zak uses the rifle to save Tyler's life when he is threatened by the men chasing him, illustrating what Ortiz and Harwood (2007) describe as the perfect recipe for positive attitude change. Zak retains his disability as prominent while he and Tyler share a friendship and Mark Twain-like adventure.

Such authentic representations can help change society's attitudes and perceptions toward individuals with Down syndrome, consistent with the previous research showing the efficacy of parasocial intergroup contact in reducing racial and sexual prejudice. Decreasing or eliminating societal prejudice opens social and economic opportunities for marginalized groups, leading to inclusion, employment, and equality.

This analysis extends our knowledge about how intergroup mediated contact initially intended to ease racial bias and discrimination and homonegativity extends to individuals with Down syndrome, and, most likely, to other outgroups of disability.

It is not enough that mediated contact changes attitudes and makes people feel better and more empathetic toward individuals with Down syndrome; spectators of media need to become active participants and change their behaviors toward this marginalized outgroup.

Negative, stereotypical depictions of people with Down syndrome as dependent upon others to perform typical activities of daily living reinforce harmful and prejudicial societal beliefs and behavior toward this group. Favorable portrayals demonstrating decisive thinking, action, spontaneity, and relationships and engagement with family and friends are the most effective at improving attitudes toward people with Down syndrome. Nondisabled people relate to actors with Down syndrome who exhibit agency, action, humor, and social engagement, actors like Zach Gottsagen, Chris Burke, Blair Williamson, Andrea Fay, Tommy Jessup, and Lauren Potter.

Through more exposure over time, a television series may offer increased potential for changing negative attitudes toward gay men, Black people, and people with Down syndrome, as demonstrated in the studies of *Will & Grace* by Ortiz and Harwood (2007), Schiappa et al. (2006). According to Sink and Mastro (2018), scholars agree that broader, frequent exposure of an outgroup in mass media creates more opportunities for positive mediated contact. The studies on parasocial contact with gay men and Black people demonstrated that viewers form judgments about people based on the media they consume, and negative portrayals perpetuate harmful stereotypes. Nondisabled viewers relate to the actors in real-life situations in the stress-free environment of their home or through contact on social media sites where they can engage directly with the actor.

Future research should identify specific characteristics of actors with Down syndrome that shape public opinion and greater acceptance and the specific conditions that enhance success with mediated contact. Social psychologists should study the negative factors that deter intergroup contact from reducing prejudice (Pettigrew & Tropp, 2006). Portrayals of disabled people should avoid patronizing narratives and representations that depict them as incompetent, inferior, victims in need of rescue by nondisabled characters, objects of pity or sympathy, or dependent, submissive, unintelligent, and not vital in decision-making when driving the plot forward (Tuchman, 1978, p. 156). As society evolves deeper into the digital age, the effectiveness of mediated contact in reducing prejudice is vitally crucial, especially for Generation Z, since most of their contact is mediated. The use of ongoing, favorable, authentic mediated contact to craft messages about people with Down syndrome and other disabilities may help them become less stigmatized and considered equal members of society.

References

Arguedas, A. R., Robertson, C. T., Fletcher, R., & Nielson, K. (2022, January 19). Echo chambers, filter bubbles, and polarization: A literature review. *Digital News Report. Reuters*. https://reutersinstitute.politics.ox.ac.uk/echo-chambers-filter-bubbles-and-polarisation-literature-review

Armstrong, G. B., & Neuerdorf, K. A., & Brentar, J. E. (1992). TV entertainment, news, and racial perceptions of college students. *Journal of Communication*, *42*, 153–176.

Bainbridge, J. (2011). Textual analysis and media research. In J. Bainbridge, N. Goc, & E. Tynan (Eds.), *Media & journalism: New approaches to theory and practice* (2nd ed., pp. 224–237). Oxford University Press.

Barnes, C. (1992). *Disabling imagery and the media: An exploration of the principles for media representations of disabled people.* The British Council of Organizations of Disabled People. Ryburn Publishing.

Baumann, A. E. (2007). Stigmatization, social distance and exclusion because of mental illness: The individual with mental illness as a "stranger". *International Review of Psychiatry, 19*, 131–135.

Busselle, R. W., & Greenberg, B. S. (2000). The nature of television realism judgments: A reevaluation of their conceptualization and measurement. *Mass Communication & Society, 3*(2–3), 249–268.

CDC. (2016, March 3). *Facts about Down Syndrome.* Center for Disease Control and Prevention. https://archive.cdc.gov/#/details?q=facts%20about%20down%20syndrome&start=0&rows=10&url=https://www.cdc.gov/ncbddd/birthdefects/surveillancemanual/quick-reference-handbook/trisomy-21-down-syndrome.html

Chung, S., & Cho, H. (2014). *Parasocial relationship via reality tv and social media: It's implications for celebrity endorsement* (pp. 47–54). Research Collection Lee Kong Chian School of Business.

Ellis, K. (2018). Media and disability. In P. M. Napoli (Ed.), *Mediated communication* (Vol. 7, pp. 359–378). De Gruyter Mouton.

Ellis, K., & Goggin, G. (2015). *Disability and the media.* Palgrave.

Esposito, A. (Director). (2018). *Diffability Hollywood* [Film]. Indie Rights.

Fujioka, Y. (1999). Television portrayals and African-American stereotypes: Examination of television effects when direct contact is lacking. *Journalism and Mass Communication Quarterly, 76*(1), 52.

GLAAD. (2024). *Where we are on TV report 2023–2024.* https://www.glaad.org

Global Down Syndrome Foundation. (2024). *Facts and FAQ about Down Syndrome.* https://www.globaldownsyndrome.org/about-down-syndrome/facts-about-down-syndrome/#freq

Goffman, E. (1963). Stigma and social identity. In *Stigma: Notes on the management of spoiled identity* (pp. 1–40). Prentice-Hall, Inc.

Griffith, J. (Writer). (2019, September 25). Forget it, Dex (Season 1, Episode 1) [TV series episode]. In G. Rucka, M. Southworth, J. Greenwood, & K. Newman (Directors), *Stumptown* [TV series]. ABC Studios.

Grobar, M. (2017). *BTW EP Jonathan Murray discusses reality TV journey & focus on "the ability within the disability".* Deadline Hollywood. https://deadline.com/2017/08/born-this-way-jonathan-murray-emmys-reality-interview-1202146289/

Hall, H., & Minnes, P. (1999). Attitudes towards persons with Down Syndrome: The impact of television. *Journal of Developmental and Physical Disabilities, 11*(1), 61–76. https://www.academia.edu/7419803/Attitudes_Toward_Persons_with_Down_Syndrome_The_Impact_of_Television

Haller, B. (2010). *Representing disability in an ableist world: Essays on mass media.* The Avocado Press.

Hayes, M. T., & Black, R. S. (2003). Troubling signs: Disability, Hollywood movies and the construction of a discourse of pity. *Disabilities Quarterly, 23*(2), 114–132.

IMDb. (2025, January 9). *Jason Kingsley.* https://www.imdb.com/name/nm1094369/?ref_=fn_all_nme_1

Jamieson, K. H., & Cappella, J. N. (2008). *Echo chamber: Rush Limbaugh and the conservative media establishment.* Oxford University Press.

Joyce, N., & Harwood, J. (2014). Improving intergroup attitudes through televised vicarious intergroup contact: Social cognitive processing of ingroup and outgroup information. *Communication Research, 41*, 627–643. https://doi.org/10.1177/0093650212447944

Katz, I, & Hass, R. (1988). Racial ambivalence and American value conflict: Correlation and priming studies of dual cognitive structures. *Journal of Personality and Social Psychology, 55*, 893–905.

Kellerman, K., & Reynolds, R. (1990). When ignorance is bliss: The role of motivation to reduce uncertainty in uncertainty reduction theory. *Human Communication Research, 1*(5), 75.

Landmark, S. (2022). The patronized supercrip: A textual analysis of *The Peanut Butter Falcon*. In M. S. Jeffress (Ed.), *Disability representation in film, TV, and print media*. Routledge.

Leavitt, P. A., Covarrubias, R., Perez, Y. A., & Fryberg, S. A. (2015). "Frozen in time": The impact of Native American media representations on identity and self-understanding. *Journal of Social Issues, 71*(1), 39–53.

Mastro, D., & Tropp, L. (2000). The effects of interracial contact, attitudes, and stereotypical portrayals on evaluations of black television sitcom characters. *Communication Research Reports, 21*(2), 119–129.

Milkie, M. A. (1999). Social comparisons, reflected appraisals, and mass media: The impact of pervasive beauty images on black and white girls' self-concepts. *Social Psychology Quarterly, 62*(2), 190–210.

Nilson, T., & Schwartz, M. (Directors & Writers). (2019). *The peanut butter falcon*. Lions-Gate Canada. https://www.lionsgate.com/movies/the-peanut-butter-falcon

Olson, B. (2018). *Down side up: Representations of Down syndrome in born this way* [Master's thesis, University of Alaska]. https://scholarworks.alaska.edu/bitstream/handle/11122/8737/Olson_B_2018.pdf?sequence=1&isAllowed=y

Ortiz, M., & Harwood, J. (2007). A social cognitive theory approach to the effects of mediated intergroup contact on intergroup attitudes. *Journal of Broadcasting & Electronic Media, 51*(4), 615–631.

Park, S. Y. (2012). Mediated intergroup contact: Concept explication, synthesis, and application. *Mass Communication and Society, 15*, 136–159. https://doi.org/10.1080/15205436.2011.558804

Pell, C. (2019, October 16). What to do when people stare: A workshop to teach individuals with dis-figuring conditions to contend with staring and improve control of social interactions. *Journal of Burn Care & Research, 6*, 743–751.

Pettigrew, T. F., & Tropp, L. R. (2006). A meta-analytic test of intergroup contact theory. *Journal of Personality and Social Psychology, 90*(5), 751–783. https://doi.org/10.1037/0022-3514.90.5.751

Power, T. (2023, April 14). Madison Tevlin on *Champions* and getting advice from Woody Harrelson. *CBC Arts, Q with Tom Power*. https://www.cbc.ca/arts/q/madison-tevlin-q-tom-power-interview-1.6809136

Reeves, B., & Nass, C. (1996). *The media equation: How people treat computers, television, and new media like real people and places*. CSLI Publications.

Ruderman Family Foundation. (2017, August 23). *Ruderman family foundation condemns "blind" film for casting Alec Baldwin in disability role*. https://rudermanfoundation.org/ruderman-family-foundation-condemns-blind-film-for-casting-alec-baldwin-in-disability-role/

Schiappa, E., Gregg, P. B., & Hewes, D. E. (2005). The para-social contact hypothesis. *Communication Monographs, 72*(1), 92–115.

Schiappa, E., Gregg, P. B., & Hewes, D. E. (2006). Can one show make a difference? Will and Grace and the parasocial contact hypothesis. *Journal of Homosexuality, 51*(4), 15–37.

Schieferdecker, D., & Wessler, H. (2017). Bridging segregation via media exposure? Ingroup identification, outgroup distance, and low direct contact reduce outgroup appearance in media repertoires. *Journal of Communication, 67*, 993–1014.

Schramm, H., & Hartmann, T. (2008). The PSI-process scales: A new measure to assess the intensity and breadth of parasocial process. *Communication, 33*, 385–401.

Shapiro, M., & Lang, A. (1991). Making television reality: Unconscious processes in the construction of social reality. *Communication Research, 18*(5), 685–705.

Sink, A., & Mastro, D. (2018). Mediated contact with gay men as a predictor of modern homonegativity: An analysis of exposure to characters appearing on television between 2000 and 2015. *Communication Reports, 32*(2), 78–90.

Smith, S. E. (2015). How to win an Oscar-cripface. *Global Comment.* http://globalcomment.com/how-to-win-an-oscar-cripface/

Snyder, S., & Mitchell, D. (2006). Body genres: An anatomy of disability in films. In *Cultural locations of disability*. University of Chicago Press.

Stumbo, E. (2018, February 23). 25 actors with Down Syndrome. *The Mighty*. https://www.yahoo.com/lifestyle/25-actors-down-syndrome-191306491.html

Tan, A., & Fujioka, Y., & Lucht, N. (1997). Native American stereotypes, TV portrayals, and personal contact. *Journalism & Mass Communication Quarterly, 74*, 265–284.

Thomas, G. M. (2021). "The media love the artificial versions of what's going on": Media (mis)representations of Down's Syndrome. *The British Journal of Sociology, 72*(3), 693–706. https://doi.org/10.1111/1468-4446.12807

Tuchman, G. (1978). Introduction: The symbolic annihilation of women by the mass media. In G. Tuchman, A. K. Daniels, & J. Benét (Eds.), *Hearth and home: Images of women in the mass media* (pp. 3–38). Oxford University Press.

Woodburn, D., & Kopic, K. (2016). *The Ruderman white paper: On employment of actors with disabilities in television* [White paper]. http://www.rudermanfoundation.org/wp-content/uploads/2016/07/TV-White-Paper_7-1-003.pdf

8 Facing Up to *IT* is Worth It; James Partridge Revisited

J. Michael Murphy

'How is it possible for a man with a face like that to have children? Have a job? Appear to have such high self-esteem . . .?'

(Partridge, *Face IT*, 2020a, p. 146)

James Partridge passed away suddenly but peacefully on Sunday August 16th, 2020 at the age of 67 from complications related to a long struggle with lymphoma. Although at the time of writing four years have passed since his death, his legacy of life-changing work continues to inspire and lead others. James was the architect of the global face equality movement, a social entrepreneur, founder of multiple nonprofit organizations, and author, as well as a loving husband, father, and grandfather.

As someone who had met and collaborated with James over a decade and whose research overlapped with his work, I have been inspired by James both during his lifetime and even after his death. As a clinical and research psychologist at Shriners Hospital for Burned Children in Boston on and off for more than 30 years, I have worked with many patients with disfiguring conditions and am always looking for more effective ways to help them. When he was alive, James had been the source of many powerful ideas and programs that were relevant to people with disfiguring conditions. Since he died, I found myself thinking of him and his work and wishing I knew more about his life. So I welcomed the opportunity to check in with his colleagues, friends, and family members, and to write this chapter about James' life and one-of-a-kind journey.

Looking at the pictures of James Partridge from before and after his disfiguring burn injuries, the questions he asked in the chapter-opening quote seem like the right ones. How could someone who looked like James marry, have children and a career, and live not just a normal life, but a remarkably full and wonderful life? According to his wife, Caroline:

> James found a way of using his disfigurement as a positive attribute to challenge and overturn the norms. He saw and did things differently – metaphorically captured in those glass-half full, Rubin's vase perceptions which intrigued him. His changed face shaped his life, from ordinary to

DOI: 10.4324/9781003535591-18

Figure 8.1 Partridge before the accident

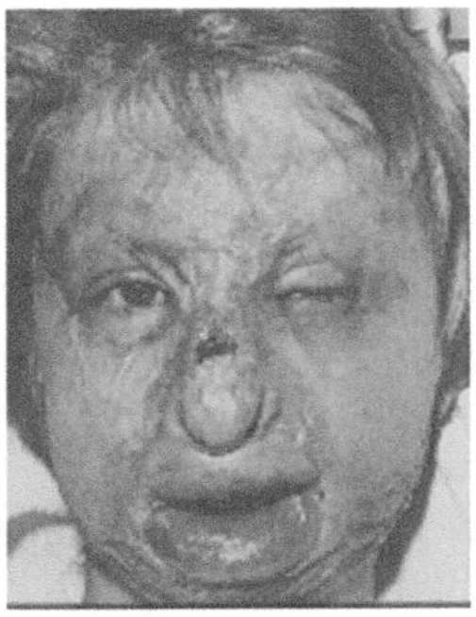

Figure 8.2 Partridge after the accident

Figure 8.3 Partridge speaking at the 2020 Guernsey Literary Festival

> distinguished. [. . .] I am proud that he was able to use the platforms of his upbringing, personality, happy family life and cumulative career experiences [. . .] as a springboard to make people's lives better and give voice to the issue of face equality. He abhorred injustice and discrimination.
>
> (Caroline)

In Carrie's view, James's ability to use his disfigurement as a positive attribute allowed him to build on his upbringing, personality, happy family life, and career experiences to help others. According to James, another factor that contributed to his success was his decision soon after his accident to face his changed appearance head on.

In answer to the question of how to face *IT* – the term he used to describe his burn-disfigured face – James wrote that his approach began to take shape when he saw his face for the first time after the accident:

> I very deliberately and slowly drew the mirror across *IT*. . . from the left side ("The better side?" "Yes") across the bridge of my ruined nose . . . Oh God . . . to my right eye, three-quarters closed, jagged with scars and skin grafts . . . and then, oh dear God, to my gaping mouth and jaw . . . I gasped but had no breath . . . and finally to my right ear (totally unrecognisable as an ear). And then the whole thing. *IT*. My stomach churned and I felt faint. [. . .]
>
> (Partridge, *Face IT*, 2020a, p. 40)

Despite the shocking first encounter with his changed face, he instinctively knew that he . . .

> had to take ownership of *IT* for one simple, immediate reason: so as to manage the reactions that I saw in the shocked faces and minds of the people around the bed. People who cared so much for me. If I disowned *IT*, they – the people I'd come to rely upon for so much – would be even more devastated than I was. [. . .] Now, as darkness set in . . . I wept inwardly, sobbed silently, trying not to draw attention or give away anything of how I was feeling to those I didn't want to be open towards. Stiff upper lip seemed a difficult reaction given a complete absence of a top lip, but that, I knew, would have to be my public stance. [. . .] And so began my long, long struggle to face up to *IT*.
>
> (Partridge, *Face IT*, 2020a, pp. 41–42).

In December 1970, at the age of 18, James had been just months away from beginning his first year at Oxford University when he was severely burned in the car accident and fire that changed his face, and his life, forever.

> In a few microseconds, everything changed. The Land Rover, still going too fast, careered and crashed onto the driver's side, my side, and skidded across the dual carriageway – and, seconds later, during which I had time to think we'd need to get a crane to set it upright again, IT EXPLODED IN FLAMES. [. . .] I had a millisecond to think about all that I loved about my life – so much – and then I felt an immense surging desire to LIVE. Struggling to undo my seat belt . . . so little air . . . desperate . . . I had to use my left hand to push myself up from the flames that were all around me . . . HURRY . . . and then I was free and crawling out of the back of the vehicle. OUT. "Thank God, I'm out – a bit singed, I think." My face felt battered, puffy, painful.
>
> (Partridge, *Face IT*, 2020a, p. 25)

It turned out that he had burns over much of his body, and that those on his face were especially serious. Despite more than 50 operations over the next five years, his face remained noticeably disfigured for the rest of his life. Moreover, in their own way, the psychological wounds and scars were probably just as deep and disfiguring. In just a matter of minutes, James had gone from a handsome young man with a feeling of almost unlimited potential to someone who would never be free of *IT*. For nearly a half year James was hospitalized, hidden, reluctant to interact with the world, almost defeated, close to despair. And yet, somehow, James was able to keep an ember of hope alive.

In his eulogy for James, Reverend Matthew Barrett pointed out how James ". . . somehow found an inkling of hope" and managed to "rebuild his life so that it became so hope-filled, and so blessed." Talking about a passage James had written about the accident, Barrett marveled at how just one year later, at the end of his first term at Oxford, James had told his parents that he thought he had actually gained from the accident, a "glimmer of hope":

> In true James style, he liked to use metaphors of fire – I think probably to break the ice a little and to help others not to feel too awkward – such was his immense kindness. [. . .] James wrote; "My pre-accident optimism had been radiant, like a camp fire sparking with life. The accident in the heavy drizzle . . . had drenched the fire, just like a huge rainstorm would, rendering it cold, lifeless and dark. But a skilled firelighter (and I became one of those later on) knows that even after a major storm, there may still be life in a doused fire. If you can very carefully unearth that tiny ember, it may hold just enough heat to spark a little bit of paper, and then some dry kindling wood, and if carefully nurtured with enough oxygen – but not too much – the whole fire can be reignited into a new blaze."
>
> (Barrett, 2020)

As his son recounted during his eulogy, James had found the strength to go on thanks to his family – especially his parents and three siblings, David, Clare, and Alison.

> Alison's early childhood memories include their endless games at their home in Flax Bourton and their family holidays: laughter, chilly wet picnics and lots of heartiness whether climbing mountains, surfing in freezing seas or beach cricketing. So perhaps these seeds of early childhood experience came in handy as he faced the enormity of the hill he had to climb after his accident – and later the determination to fight against the restrictions others with facial differences faced too. [. . .] Clare [James's sister] mentions in her tributes that "he had so many good qualities. He liked to get on with it, and procrastinating was not his thing. I think he had his mother's cheerful spirit, along with that huge sense of humour. He was so strong, so hopeful and positive." Behind everything it was clear he had a deep attachment to his mother and father, their support being the root of his strength after his accident.
>
> **S. Partridge**

On October 1971, ten months after the accident, with his face still raw from recent surgeries and dark glasses and a hat covering as much of *IT* as possible, James started his college career at Oxford University. He later described what he went through and a crucial decision that he made at that time:

> I was learning how to live with the certainty that a high percentage of the people I met in my everyday student life and most of the strangers I walked past or stood next to or was observed by looked at *IT* with sympathy. They might applaud my bravery, but more than likely also labelled me as damaged goods and imagined my sadness and shame. These are instinctive public reactions over which I had little control. And although I was fearful of those reactions and completely unskilled in how to handle them, I lived less and less in a survival, lonely mode, beginning a trial and error existence instead. Although it was only in the privacy behind my student room door that I could ease up my daily struggle, I didn't stay there. Instead I [went out although I still] chose to hide my scars and conceal my shame. I became an expert in disguise. Big flat-brimmed hats in the Clint Eastwood Spaghetti Western styles of the era were a favourite. And high-neck shirts and sweaters, long trousers, never shorts, gloves, hands in pockets to hide my distorted fingers, long overcoats and, above all, dark glasses; big ones. I became a bit of a celebrity in Oxford – "There goes that man with the scarred face" or words to that effect. My hat and dark glasses increased the mystery but also told of my vulnerability.
>
> (Partridge, *Face IT*, 2020a, pp. 84–85)

During an interview with journalist Harriet Griffey in 2020, he described how, on his own during his first year at Oxford, he began to get an inkling of how to deal with the stigma of disfigurement:

> I chanced on *Stigma: Notes on the Management of Spoiled Identity* by Erving Goffman in the sociology section of a bookshop as a first year student and it resonated with so much of what I recognised about myself except it offered no solutions. What it did give me, however, was a what-if moment. What if I could discover self-respect (which seemed highly unlikely), could I gain the respect of those around me which seemed denied to me because of my disfigurement? At that point I had no idea what the solutions might be, but I had a sense that finding my self-respect might enable me to deflect others' stigmatising of me.

In the first years after his accident, apart from a support group run by the plastic surgery department's medical social worker, he was unable to find useful professional help, which in turn led him to feel "very alone, trying to deal with the trauma, shame, guilt and grief for my old self." It was only after five long years of work on his own that, "surprisingly and by trial and error I had come to respect my new self and like my face's features – scars, skin grafts, asymmetry and all. The stigmas of disfigurement could no longer touch me" (Griffey, 2020).

James found that although the stigma was still there, it now had no power over him, because he had developed "very proactive communication skills and a potent mental armour-plating to manage other people's reactions in hundreds of different settings." As he reflected on his experience over the first five years after the accident, he attributed his success to ten key "transformations":

1. Discovering that concealing my face, although it allowed me some anonymity, did not gain me the acceptance I craved.
2. Becoming proactive in my approach and my communication skills in every single social encounter . . . a massive effort at the beginning but with huge dividends later.
3. Building on my talents and capabilities to the utmost yielded the best results possible, because I was then judged on them and not by people's views of my face.
4. Finding one or two people with a face like mine who could inspire me meaningfully (not superficially) was a big bonus, probably a prerequisite.
5. Reigniting the tiny ember of hope inside me took years, but the critical thing was never letting it die, despite my despair.
6. Finding out about reconstructive surgery options and taking a calculated risk to improve my facial appearance – but realising that there was no magic bullet.
7. Creating and purposefully cultivating an intellectual and philosophical identity that was congruent with my face and the insights I was gaining through it.
8. Taking the plunge into the job market well prepared to show my ability in answering technical questions and unafraid to be firm if asked personal ones.
9. Not allowing myself to get too depressed by failed relationships and eventually opening myself to love and loving.
10. Dealing with my loss not by denying it but by confronting it and revisiting "the corner" – definitely critical in enabling me not to heap all the blame for the accident on myself.

(Partridge, *Face IT*, 2020a, pp. 145–147)

In an obituary that ran in *The Guardian*, Andrew Jarvis, a family friend, provided a thumbnail sketch of James's early career: from his graduation from Oxford in 1975 with a degree in philosophy, politics, and economics, to "an MSc in medical demography, relating disease and mortality to the structures of populations, at the London School of Hygiene and Tropical Medicine. In parallel came his first job, as a research assistant in health economics at St Thomas' hospital in London." Jarvis highlighted the importance of James' friends' support in the aftermath of the accident. He also wrote that James had gradually rediscovered hope and the strength to move forward by learning techniques for coping with intrusive attention.

After his graduate work, James met Carrie (Caroline) Schofield in 1977. They got married in 1978 and welcomed three children over the next few years. According to Claire Julian, a colleague and friend: "I really think she [Carrie] saved his life, certainly giving him so much that he had thought was not destined to be his. Her love enabled him to live the life he did, bursting with vitality, achievement and, yes, inspiration". (Julian, 2020).

Without Carrie, Julian believes, the charity Changing Faces could not have happened. Love of his family was a part of everything he did. For example, James "often reminisced with misty eyes about the time all the 'kids' refused to take the Sainsbury's shopping out of the trolley when the cashier rudely asked him: 'What on earth happened to you!' – talk about bursting with pride". (Julian, 2020).

During her eulogy, James's daughter Charlotte Venter summarized other major steps in his career, paying special attention to the years the family spent farming on the island of Guernsey. "Together they [James and Carrie] decided to just make the move, embrace 'the good life', and 'go for it'! – crazy as it was . . . Those farming days were so formative and defining for all of us with many shared happy memories visiting us there--never a dull moment!" (Venter, 2020).

While still farming, James began to feel that the insights he had gained during his prolonged adjustment to facial disfigurement should be put to positive use, and so when an editor encouraged him to write his first book (*Changing Faces: The Challenge of Facial Disfigurement* [1990]), he accepted the challenge. One of James' insights was to view disfigurement as a process:

> If disfigurement happens to you for any reason, here are some ideas that might help you deal with it, adapt to it, live fully with it . . . even come to embrace it. The journey of "changing faces" is one that you and your family need to travel . . . learning to live life to the full with your unusual looks . . . and that applies just as much if you have been born with a congenital condition or a birthmark . . . and "changing faces" is also a process that many people you meet need to go through, a process that you can encourage and facilitate.
>
> (Partridge, *Face IT*, 2020a, p. 123)

Shortly after the book was published, James met Dr. Nichola Rumsey, a professor of psychology and co-author of *The Social Psychology of Facial Appearance,* who went on to establish the Centre for Appearance Research (CAR) . Diana Harcourt, on the staff at CAR and Professor of Appearance Psychology at the University of the West of England, describes this as "a meeting of minds," in which they both came to the same conclusion – that there was a lack of support for people with visible differences that needed to be addressed – albeit from their different perspectives. While James brought his lived experience, Nichola brought her academic research. Through conversation, James established Changing Faces and Nichola established what would ultimately become CAR. James was a very valued member of the Centre's Steering Committee (Harcourt, 2024).

In the early years of Changing Faces, James and his colleagues created a number of types of interventions that adapted evidence-based psychological techniques like Cognitive Behavior Therapy (CBT) and social interaction skills training (SIST) to the specific needs of people with disfiguring conditions. Changing Faces has refined these interventions as needed and even now, more than 30 years later, continues to use them to provide one-to-one counselling and wellbeing sessions, peer group support, and workshops for parents and young people, as well as an online forum, self-help guidance and other types of information.

James knew that his idea of inventing a charity was crazily ambitious. The aim was to innovate and promote new forms of psychosocial help for people with disfigurement and their families. He believed:

> Working in partnership with people with disfigurements and condition-specific support groups, researchers, clinicians and many fellow travelers, it might just succeed. The first step I specified for Changing Faces was to pioneer and provide a new package of psychosocial help – and its effectiveness would be evaluated objectively by an independent research project managed by Nichola Rumsey. If that first step proved possible, we would then start to advocate for the widespread adoption of the new help. And, eventually, I hoped we would try to start a movement to raise public awareness and challenge attitudes to people with disfigurements.
>
> Partridge, *Face IT*, 2020a, p. 134

As Andrew Jarvis remembers, Changing Faces went on to become "the UK's leading charity for anyone with a scar, mark or condition that affects their appearance . . . Its approach depends on providing specialist psychosocial support and to lead the way in campaigning for face equality – the fair and equal treatment of all, irrespective of appearance. James's campaigns led to ensuring that facial disfigurement was included in the Disability Discrimination Act of 1995 and more recently in the 2010 Equality Act. (Jarvis, 2020).

In summarizing James's legacy in the field of burns, burns awareness, and global facial equality, Johnathan Reinarz, Professor of the History of Medicine at the University of Birmingham wrote:

> What he felt people like him required was not more surgery, but confidence and support. Those who read his book, blog or attended Changing Faces workshops, learned how to deal with the "SCARED" responses to disfigured people – Staring, Curiosity, Anguish, Recoil, Embarrassment and Dread – gaining the necessary skills to rebuild self-esteem and lives. . . . What was needed was a group that would help people with facial disfigurements deal with "stigma". . . and "facial prejudice". This of course is what Changing Faces, the organisation he established in 1992, would do so effectively under his leadership.
>
> (Reinarz, 2020)

With the implementation and evaluation of individualized approaches to appearance-related problems well under way, James was able to devote increasing amounts of time and imagination to creating larger scale structural interventions.

As summarized by Jonathan Cole, a neurologist who served as an adviser to Changing Faces for many years:

> Changing Faces had two main aims: 1) to offer psychosocial support for those with a disfigurement and show them they could and should manage others' reactions to them, and 2) to change society, perhaps beginning with those amazing posters [see Figure 8.4] in train stations which encouraged people to interact with rather than avoid people with visible differences and which avoided soliciting pity at all. Changing societies' attitudes was behind not only the posters, but through all James's appearances and importantly, legislation he helped to create, through the UN as well as nationally. So, Changing Faces was not really about changing faces but about accepting diversity, challenging prejudice and above all changing minds.
>
> (Cole, 2024)

Along the same lines, Andrew Jarvis mentioned another of James's creations, a unique awareness course called "Dining With a Difference" that introduced corporate chief executives and their boards to disability opinion formers: "James believed that professionals played a key role in helping people adjust to their changed appearance; whether it was surgeons, doctors, teachers or HR departments, they all needed to become skilled in creating a society where face equality was at its heart." And his effort made it possible for many people who wanted to hide to find confidence instead. Not only did James advocate for these ideas, but he also put them into practice: "In 2009, James read the lunchtime television news bulletin on Channel 5 for a week as part of the charity's campaign work. 'I live with my very distinctive face with pride;' he said. His ambition was for all those with some sort of facial difference to feel the same". (Jarvis, 2020).

James was creative and persuasive in asking for what was needed for the cause of face equality and, as with everything he did, he did so with great charm. A chance meeting with the wife of the creator of the immensely popular television series *Downton Abbey* led to a collaboration in which the cast of the show attended and promoted fundraising galas for Changing Faces. Not only were these events successful in raising money, they also demonstrated the ways in which visual media could be used to fight stigma. Even today, a simple Google search turns up dozens of pictures of a beaming James and many of the internationally famous actors and actresses from the cast. James and his colleagues at Changing Faces were similarly effective in using visual media to challenge unconscious bias when they produced a highly acclaimed short film titled *Leo* starring burn survivor Leo Gormley and *Downton Abbey*'s "Lady Mary" (Michelle Dockery), who became a patron of the charity. *Leo* was shown in British theaters and is thought to have been viewed by close to a million people. These outside-the-box efforts to increase the awareness of stigma and to fight against it eventually coalesced into what came to be called a campaign for face equality.

In the years since then there have been, as shown in Figure 8.4, poster campaigns in the London subway system, large-scale research projects that documented and

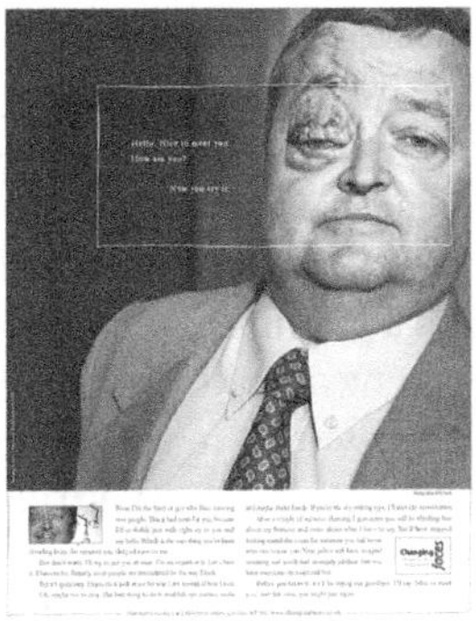

Figure 8.4 Poster from campaign run in the London Underground.

quantified the prevalence of bias against people with visible differences, a book of photographs titled *Faces of Equality* that showcased 22 champions of face equality in all their glory, organizational pledges to challenge appearance bias, and annual Face Equality Days (or Weeks) each spring to generate media interest and discussion, to name just a few of the projects. One of the most important spinoffs of these campaigns was the creation of a whole new charity called Face Equality International.

In 2017 James stepped down from Changing Faces to start Face Equality International (FEI), an alliance of NGOs and charities from around the world working together to campaign for "face equality" and to challenge disfigurement prejudice and discrimination. As James described his vision for FEI in 2018, its purpose was

> to bring attention to the fact that disfigurement is a neglected global human rights issue. I argued that millions of people with disfigurements, wherever they live in the world, face many challenges in living confident, successful lives in the twenty-first century. Many report (and academic studies bear this out) feeling very self-conscious, isolated and friendless, facing teasing, ridicule and staring in public, low expectations in school, problems getting work, discrimination in the workplace, abuse on social media and stereotyping in the media just because of the way they look. In many countries, disfigurement goes hand in hand with poverty, prejudice and exclusion.
>
> (Partridge, *Face IT*, 2020a, p. 350)

He then describes how the project developed in the following years:

> At the beginning of 2020, Face Equality International had already become an alliance of thirty NGOs/charities around the world that are supporting and representing people with many different disfigurements. [. . .] Working together on these common problems will create the critical mass and solidarity needed to gain global attention to tackle these injustices. The alliance

> will be a powerful mouthpiece to enable the voice of many excluded people to challenge the cultural forces that are increasingly global concerns. It will raise the profile of disfigurement and put the issues people with disfigurements experience on the agenda of the UN Convention on the Rights of Persons with Disabilities (CRPD), international bodies, companies and social media outlets. [. . .] It will be a learning exchange and set global standards on how to challenge disfigurement discrimination (e.g. on social media and at work) and promote face equality (e.g. in schools).
>
> (Partridge, *Face IT*, 2020a, p. 352)

James's fight for face equality has continued after his death, at least in part due to the efforts of Face Equality International and its member groups. One example is the proclamation of a statewide Face Equality Week in May 2024 by Roy Cooper, the former governor of North Carolina. Like similar efforts in Massachusetts and Michigan, this proclamation was made possible by persistent advocacy over several years by FEI members and face equality advocates, in this case by Charlene Pell, founder of Facing Forward, Inc., one of FEI's first members.

The fight for face equality was also advanced by the publication of James's second book, *FACE IT; Facial disfigurement and my fight for face equality,* which was published just a few months before he died.

As summarized by James in a 2020 blog post: "*FACE IT* is an honest **memoir** of my battle after severe facial burns; it's a practical **self-help guide** for anyone with a facial difference and a **manual** for health professionals trying to help them. And, finally, it's a **manifesto** for face equality, rooting out the stigmas of face-ism that oppress us all . . . and urging new face values in our 21st century world". (Partridge, *Blog*, 2020b).

FACE IT is available through the FEI website where all payments are donated to Face Equality International. According to Professor Rumsey the book is:

> Fizzing from start to finish with candour, humour and passion [. . .] James Partridge charts his journey along the path to self-acceptance, self-esteem

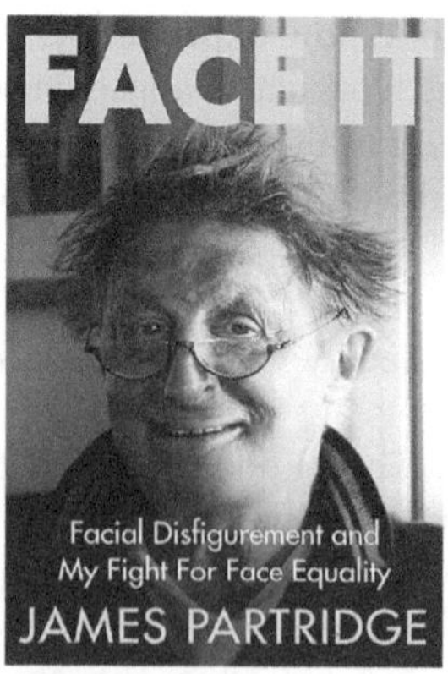

Figure 8.5 Cover of *FACE IT* (Pebble Press, 2020).

> and confident living [. . .] There is much in this book to help those longing to thrive with a distinctive appearance, as well as food for thought for health care professionals and policy makers [. . .] and the monumental effort needed to remove the stigma and discrimination currently experienced by people living with not-perfect faces.
>
> (Partridge, *Face IT*, 2020a, p. 8)

In her interview with James about *FACE IT*, Harriet Griffey describes him as "Engaging, interested, intellectually savvy, attractive, amusing and, not least because of what he's achieved, inspirational." Griffey sees the book as "the introduction to a much bigger story about the stigma of facial difference, the extraordinary work he has done campaigning for face equality and how he worked to help create evidence-based models of psychosocial support which are now something of an industry standard". (Griffey, 2020).

James received many honors for his work including: an OBE from Her Majesty the Queen in 2002, an honorary fellowship from the Royal College of Surgeons of Edinburgh, and honorary doctorates from the University of Bristol and the University of the West of England, as well as a number of national awards, including the Third Sector award for Most Admired Charity Chief Executive and the Beacon Prize for Leadership, both in 2010.

As impressive as his accomplishments are, his impact on people is probably even more important. The quotes that follow give some sense of the importance that James had both for his friends and colleagues, like Claire Julian and Alex Clarke, as well as family members like his daughters, Charlotte Venter and Harriet Saddington.

> It's still hard to believe that someone like James who was so vital isn't with us any more . . . But, what a life he had lived! I believe what he did with the cards he was dealt was truly great. To have turned such a devastating event into a kind of triumph, and to have had the capacity to gain, and then share, such penetrating insights – life-changing for many – was a monumental achievement. [. . .] His legacy really can't be overstated. [. . .] By his own example, his unique insights and the sheer force of his personality, James changed lives and attitudes forever, raised hundreds of thousands of pounds to support charitable causes, and made a lasting contribution to the struggle for disability rights and face equality. I will miss him very much. As will all those with "not-perfect" faces who are so much in his debt.
>
> (Julian, 2020)

> I was struck forcibly by how much worse off people with distinctive faces would have been if James had not had that life-changing accident back in 1970. Disfigurement would have remained a "neglected global human rights issue" – James's own words. But his mother was right when she said – and according to James made him believe – "that all the pain would not be in vain and would have meaning someday. [. . .] Many children, young people and adults would not have benefited from the Changing Faces social skills

> training, gaining confidence to face the world in their own way. Who else could have understood so absolutely? [. . .] There would have been no social skills workshops, individual counselling and confidence-building, no Changing Faces Practitioners, no legal protection for people with severe disfigurements under the Disability Discrimination Act (1995 and 2020), fewer role models with distinctive faces, no OFSTED-supported teaching resources for use in schools, no guidelines for employers on recruitment and customer service, no guidelines for the media, the list goes on . . . The next target for Face Equality International is recognition within the UN Convention on the Rights of Persons with Disabilities (130 countries).
>
> (Julian, 2024)

> When I think "who are the great people I've met in my life" there are remarkably few. And of the one or two people who stand out, I put James Partridge in that category, somebody who would have been successful no matter what he'd done. He turned [the accident that left him permanently disfigured] into something fantastic. So, now for other people in that situation, they know they are not on their own, and because of James they now have a few strategies that they can try out for themselves that worked for him.
>
> (Clarke, 2024)

According to his daughters:

> He gave a voice to so many. Accepting all humans, no matter their difference. He turned personal misfortune into an amazing legacy of helping others to 'Face It' – his face and their faces with charisma, a 'disarming' smile and great humour. So many have said that their life would not have been the same had they not met him. He held a commanding presence when public speaking, often to hundreds and thousands at a time, but also an incredible ability for private, meaningful conversation – he always sought deep empathy. [. . .] During his chemotherapy and illness, and much to the medical staff's amazement when he arrived at hospital, he would set up his 'station' – laptop, strong coffee, newspapers, a pile of books and of course his notepad with pencil brainstorms. We have a pile of these brainstorms just from the week before he died – on it things to do, people to reach out to, causes to set up, "on, on" he would say! [. . .] We have been flooded by memories and thoughts from so many people – Dad would have loved it! Descriptions of him have come in as "a human colossus", "8ft tall and grinning", "a man for whom the word 'character' was invented", "quite simply the most remarkable and extraordinary man I have ever met", "a true saint", "a gentle giant". [. . .] In my head he has his hands in the air waving, grinning, gesticulating wildly and a booming voice saying, "Yo!". He was larger than life. So alive right until the end. He will live on in everything we do and I hope in so much that you all do too.
>
> (Saddington, 2020)

> I want to say one final thing. Dad may have been all these things to all these people but he saw his most important job as being here with us. He was more than anything a really present family person. He was an amazing grandfather and father to us and husband. He was so committed to us, he'd have a quick snooze on the beach, and then he'd be up playing cricket with everybody, and then taking us off for a swim. And yet at the same time that sort of ticking over of ideas was going on, and it wasn't hiding himself away, needing to have all this time and thought and strategy and process for his work removed from family life. He was really in the thick of everything that we were doing, as well as quantifying on how on earth to try and change the world, and to improve legislation, and lives of others too. He was able to do all that multi-tasking and be super present for us.
>
> (Venter, 2024)

Why James Partridge Is *Still* So Important

I wanted to close by reflecting on what I learned while writing this chapter. First of all, it was a true pleasure to spend time interviewing James's wife, Carrie, his daughters Charlotte and Harriet, his son Simon, his colleagues Claire Julian, Jonathan Cole, Sam Cheadle, Alex Clarke, and Diana Harcourt, and to read what they and others have written about James. After talking with his family for an hour, I told them I wished I could become a part of their family and that in some ways I felt like I already had. Second of all, I wanted to review the questions raised at the beginning of this chapter.

How Did He Do It?

The message of a lovely family movie called *Angels in the Outfield* suggests some simple but easy-to-overlook resources for understanding how James did it. In the movie, spectators at a baseball game keep asking, "How did he do it?" when they see players from a last-place team make impossible catches or hit homeruns way out of the ballpark. The answer, that only a little boy with faith born of necessity can see, is that there are invisible angels in the outfield who are helping the players. And when, by the end of the season, the team has gotten to the World Series, the angels inform the players that from now on they will have to rely on their own, unaided skills. The players soon learn that they can still do great things because they now use their own heretofore untapped talents.

There can be little doubt that James had an angelic start. He was blessed with most of the commonly cited facilitators of resilience. He came from a loving and supportive family and had good friends before and after his accident. He himself was warm and engaging with an upbeat approach to life that most people responded to (according to a member of the Changing Faces board, "James was absurdly sociable and appealing; he could charm a room like few others"). Fierce drive and determination were always a part of his nature, but so was an immense sense of humor. He was tall and athletic and excelled at many sports. He came from an economically advantaged family of origin and was further graced in adulthood with a supportive spouse and children. He had received an excellent education. If faith is a gift, he was gifted in this area as well. He credited a number of religious leaders and books and the Christian school he had attended with providing him with resources that helped him to get through some of the most difficult times in his recovery. So, although his many advantages provided a springboard to start, he soared past them on his own.

According to James, one of the most important things he learned and that I learned from him in writing this chapter is the importance of a proactive approach to interpersonal communication in dealing with disfigurement. James taught himself and others how important it was to take charge of each encounter by proactively engaging and making eye contact with each person he met to put them at ease.

Given that our faces are the first thing that we project to others, someone with a disfigurement might seem to be at a disadvantage. But as James has shown in his life and work, social skills can be learned and, with a proactive approach, we can all find ways to project a positive image of ourselves and so in this way the person with a disfigurement has an added advantage of being able to generate a memorable impact. As quoted earlier, second on James's list of the essential transformations that he made was: "Becoming proactive in my approach and my communication skills *in every single social encounter*" (emphasis added). Furthermore, as James said in his interview with Harriet Griffey, "When someone with a facial difference meets a stranger, they are the ones having to make 80–90% of the effort, whereas when there's face equality it's a 50/50 ratio. It may not seem fair that I have to make that effort, but by harnessing my self-respect and skills to do so, I found I could deflect their stereotypes." If a big part of how James did all that he did was by being proactive "in every single social encounter," that can be good news for those of us who start off without as many gifts. James's successes demonstrate the impact that a proactive approach to managing social encounters can have.

At the end of my interview with his family, Charlotte mentioned that even now, four years after his death, she and her mother and siblings still talked to James often when they came across something interesting or important. Although it is probably not that unusual for people to talk to loved ones after they die, what I did find unusual was that, for me at least, James talked back. What I heard him say, in a booming voice was, "Yo! Facing *IT* is possible and being proactive is a key to success." Based on what I have learned from James's life, I have come to the conclusion that it is worth a try.

References

Barrett, M. (2020). *Eulogy for James Partridge August 27, 2020, at the Town Church in Guernsey*. https://www.familynotices.gg/moreinfo/69663/partridge

Changing Faces UK. (2012). *Leo*. https://www.youtube.com/watch?v=6va7WsWyWTM

Clarke, A. (2024). Interview with the author.

Cole, J. (2024, September). Email to author.

Cooper, R. (2024). A proclamation by the Governor of the State of North Carolina. *International Face Equality Week*. https://governor.nc.gov/governor-proclaims-international-face-equality-week-2024/open

Griffey, H. (2020, July 7). *Face IT: An interview with James Partridge*. https://welldoing.org/article/face-it-interview-james-patridge
Harcourt, D. (2024, October). Email to the author.
Jarvis, A. (2020, August 27). James Partridge obituary. *The Guardian.*
Julian, C. (2020). Letter to James's family after his death.
Julian, C. (2024). Email to the author.
Partridge, C. (2024). Email to author.
Partridge, J. (1990). *Changing Faces: The Challenge of Facial Disfigurement*. United Kingdom: Penguin.
Partridge, J. (2020a). *Face IT: Facial disfigurement and my fight for face equality*. Pebble Press.
Partridge, J. (2020b). *Blog*. https://jamespartridge.wordpress.com
Partridge, S. (2020). *Eulogy for James Partridge August 27, 2020, at the Town Church, Guernsey*. https://www.familynotices.gg/moreinfo/69663/partridge
Reinarz, J. (2020, October 12). *James Partridge (1952–2020); forged by fire, changing faces and minds*. https://forgedbyfiresite.wordpress.com/2020/10/12/james-partridge-1952-2020-forged-by-fire-changing-faces-and-minds/
Saddington, H. (2020). *Eulogy for James Partridge, August 27, 2020, at the Town Church, Guernsey*. https://www.familynotices.gg/moreinfo/69663/partridge
Venter, C. (2020). *Eulogy for James Partridge August 27, 2020, at the Town Church, Guernsey*. https://www.familynotices.gg/moreinfo/69663/partridge
Venter, C. (2024, August 1). Interview with author.

9 The Stories That Need to be Told

Phyllida Swift

As I sat down to write this, with every intention of trying to ignore my phone and focus for as long as possible, dozens of WhatsApp notifications kept catching the corner of my eye as more and more came through. Glancing, I spotted the name of a good friend and fellow activist, Tina Raj. As the leader of what was previously grassroots online support, now a newly established charity, Tina supports others living with Ichthyosis through advice, well-being support, and help to access vital creams and treatments across South Asia, Africa, and beyond. This is a multi-disabling 'rare disease', often presumed to be purely 'cosmetic' despite causing difficulty with sight, mobility, chronic pain, difficulty regulating body temperature often leading to internal organ failure, and so much more. All are reliant on access to healthcare, and yet this condition often falls short of being considered a disability by governments. Particularly when it comes to legal status in India, where Tina lives. Until perhaps this very moment in time.

A moment hand-delivered from the universe, where Tina has shared the news that the Supreme Court of India explicitly mentioned 'Ichthyosis' – alongside other underrepresented and often overlooked disabilities such as autism – in a statement to frame mandatory rules for accessibility of public spaces in India (LiveLaw). She writes, "5 decades and finally Ichthyosis is included. The first half of the battle is won. Now, the final step, where I file a PIL in the Delhi High Court for Ichthyosis to be included in the disability category. We owe this to you. Thanks so much for coming into our life. You are a beacon for us."

My response? A selfie of me in tears.

These moments of tangible progress, especially those relating to policy, are rare, even rarer are the compliments. Not least the ones that I truly feel like I can truly own. And so this feels like a perfect moment in time to reflect, to squash the imposter syndrome, and to remind myself of the constant fight, the knock-backs, the ignorance, the outright hate, the constant shouting into what so often feels like a void. It's all for moments like this – when we get to see when we get to see the real-life impact of our work at Face Equality International.

I was able to introduce Tina to an academic, Amita Dahnda, who was instrumental in crafting the United Nations Convention on the Rights of Persons with Disabilities. With thanks also to Face Equality International ambassador Carly Findlay, who also has Ichthyosis and was the one who introduced us to Tina. And

DOI: 10.4324/9781003535591-19

so, together, Tina and I met multiple times during my time in India whilst conducting our Stigma & Human Rights in Lower and Middle Income Countries (LIMCs) project.

Face Equality International (FEI) is a UK-based non-profit, previously set up by Dr James Partridge OBE in Guernsey in 2018. We became a a UK charity in April 2022. Our current vision is to build a world free of barriers, where people with facial differences are thriving and proud to be themselves. Our mission is to work together to ensure the facial difference community is seen, protected and respected. What this looks like in practice is working with an Alliance of nonprofits, all of whom provide services to the facial difference community, and providing tools, sharing knowledge, and ensuring they have the resources to build a movement that addresses the societal, social, and attitudinal issues impacting our collective communities. Shifting the all too often 'medical-model' focus to systems, policies, and practices outside of the community itself is also the way that we work with the community at large. We work with individual activists to amplify their stories, steer community-led campaigns, or through consulting on the real-life issues impacting the worldwide facial difference (FD) community. This consultation piece is fundamental, because only by working as a dedicated and unique community can we prevent silos or the sense of isolation so many experience and we can also present a unified, representative voice at the highest level. By doing so, we can ensure this issue remains on the agendas of decision makers. Our plans for next year are to expand this work with individuals much more, and so this is an exciting time to be documenting our work.

Had this moment with Tina not aligned beautifully with sitting down to write this piece, I probably would have started with James. Where it all began for me, and for so many others. A moment where despair turned into hope, when I took to Google to grasp for information and support, to find others who might be able to understand what I was going through in the following months after I got my facial scars. Within a few clicks I found the charity founded by James Partridge, Changing Faces, an immense privilege I would only later come to really appreciate. And from that point on I had a source of validation, a source of community, and without me knowing it yet, I had found the source of purpose I needed and continue to need to this day.

That first interaction was less about me seeking emotional support and more so me being a complete and utter control freak and wanting to 'get involved' and somehow turn the absolute nightmare I was living in into some sort of positive outcome. There were two pathways when first reaching out to Changing Faces – supportive services or becoming a media champion. I was insistent when going through a phone call for psychological evaluation that, given the two options, I wanted the latter and that I 'was fine' and I was emotionally ready to talk about what had happened to me. Which, to summarise, was me getting into a major car accident whilst travelling in Ghana and thankfully coming out alive, but with a lot of broken bones and essentially a broken face. One big, long laceration from forehead to nose and narrowly missing my eye.

That resistance to seeking counseling was a common theme for me, having had many people suggest it to me in the past off the back of other traumatic life events like losing my brother when we were teenagers. That resistance, incidentally, remained right up until the moment James died. It was only then that I finally reached out and sought to speak to someone. Not least because he had become such a wonderful and supportive influence in my life. But, as though a part of me knew I was going to need to prepare myself for something big, and to finally take a look back on all life had thrown at me. More on this later.

And so within months of the accident, I was selling my story, and what would later feel like selling my soul to the *Daily Mail*. And for what? What I sought was a moment to control the narrative, at a time when so much felt out of control and I could feel the prying eyes of others' judgement, and worse still, pitying eyes, every time I left the house or met back up with friends and family.

Seeing one of the most pivotal and traumatic experiences of my life laid out like that, littered with embellishments for the sake of shock factor before the reader inevitably scrolls onto the next clickbait piece. All this made me think: what narrative was someone being sold about those of us who are 'scarred for life' in a 'horrifying crash'? With surgeons 'working tirelessly' to fix my face. Does reading my story help? Is it making a difference? My gut-wrenching feeling was the opposite. That, essentially, people would temporarily think, "Oh poor girl, shame she's never going to feel beautiful or confident again. Glad that's not me." And then onto the next story.

And so it was seeing my life reduced to a headline that gave me an insight into the extent of this damaging, warped, sensationalised, othering of people with disfigurements. It was witnessing this that led me to delve deeper into how the stories of others were being told, and this experience ultimately flipped the switch for me. I had come into this space pretty much to serve my own control freak self, which then turned into a fire in me, that still burns now to address the collective issue, the collective narrative, and to serve others.

These narratives, whether mistold or simply untold, are sadly just one example of the inequities that make up the shared experience for anyone with a facial difference, irrespective of where they are in the world or what their background is. I would later come to discover just how deep these inequities run. And just how privileged I was, and am, with experiences that are relatively innocuous in the context of the human rights abuses experienced by the community at large. Something I would later become exposed to on a daily basis.

Another FEI ambassador, and dear friend, Jono Lancaster helped me to understand the importance of how I could now see things from both sides, and how this prepared me for my job, having lived a previous life where I hadn't given a thought to what it must be like to look different in this world, where beauty is prized above all else. But now, my eyes were open to how the way in which our stories are told is just one of the many, many injustices that are keeping this marginalized community, of which I'm proud to be a part of, in the shadows.

So, in the months following the *Daily Mail* debacle I continued to volunteer for Changing Faces, even signing up to do the London Marathon less than 2 years after breaking my hip, which once again was likely a way to prove to myself and others that I was not broken. I continued to put myself out there in the media for a multitude of reasons, but definitely not all of them desperately healthy or oriented to proper healing. But I can say that I was evolving the way in which I wanted to tell my story, realizing that I could say no to questions I didn't want to answer. At a time when I was coming to the end of university, with no intention of pursuing a career in what I'd studied for, this part of my life was grounding me with some much-needed purpose.

In the months that followed, whilst working casual jobs and feeling rather adrift, a twist of fate meant that one day, when idly scrolling through Instagram, I stumbled across an ad for a Campaigns Officer Job at Changing Faces. Thank goodness for whatever faith, or ignorance, it was that compelled me to think, "I could do that!"

And so, despite having zero Comms experience, and a rather irrelevant art degree, I managed to convince two major mentor figures in my life that I could actually do it. This was in 2017, right before the first-ever Face Equality Day in the UK, and I've now proudly worked on every annual campaign since, leading the first International Face Equality Week in 2019 with James at FEI.

At the time, the former Comms Manager, Steve Taylor, who brought expertise from a career in both political Comms and running Pride in London, I got to see first-hand how exciting things were behind the scenes of running a big campaign. But I was 100% completely and utterly out of my depth and I had to learn absolutely everything on the job. Every task was outlined in detail. Many a mishap. From having to ask how I could tell whether an email had been opened, to being told off for the foul language I'd carried over from university and had somehow thought was appropriate in an office environment. I will forever be grateful for the grace given to me back then. The occasional swear word still comes into conversation in our 'virtual office' at FEI, but not in polite company, of course.

Thankfully, I had the support of an incredible manager, the then-Head of Advocacy, Henrietta Spalding. One of the best teachers I've ever had. Henrietta's calm wisdom, empathy, diplomacy, and commitment to arming yourself with as much knowledge as possible in dedication to the cause and the community has been a guiding light. But above all else, what I have cherished is the friendship this wonderful woman has shown me throughout my career, with the never-ending chatting, philosophising, and giggling, having led a department in advocacy spanning healthcare, business, government, education, and beyond. The progress we've seen in the UK in the way in which the FD community navigates these spaces is a testament to her leadership.

All in close collaboration with James of course, whom I actually didn't cross paths with much during my two years at Changing Faces, during which James was going through cancer treatment, before handing over the CEO role. But when we did meet, the time we got to spend together was for dreaming big dreams, scribbling sprawled notes, and thinking up ways to solve complex problems. Wracking his brains for who out of his not-so-little black book he could call on for support – this will forever be a standout memory. One of my first big tasks at Changing Faces was to take all of the recommendations from 'Disfigurement in the UK' (Changing Faces) and to consult with all staff on how we could make them happen. I don't remember any of the other meetings, just the one with James.

After two hectic years at Changing Faces, riding out the waves of a change in leadership and the associated restructure, and strategy overhaul, all whilst working multiple face equality weeks, a hate crime campaign, 'pledge to be seen,' 'portrait positive,' a Christmas appeal or two, and starting the campaigner's program, I was feeling a little burnt out already, which serves as another reason to respect and admire all those mentioned earlier. I essentially planned to take a step away from the facial difference space and figure out who I was and what I wanted to do with my life outside of making my facial difference my entire identity.

Working over eight hours a day on an issue so close to your heart, and reliving your traumas, hearing them mirrored back to you in the stories of the incredible campaigners you're working with, when I evidently didn't take much time out to actually deal with my own, all became rather a lot. Especially working in the centre of London, which was never for me. In a bigger organisation like that, which was also delivering services, albeit vital ones, but this was never really the stuff that really made me tick, and truth be told, I didn't get to have a huge amount of influence on the way in which people's stories were told, which as I hope is now clear, I have rather a specific opinion on.

And so I quit, without much lined up other than a freelance events gig. But that damned universe, or in this case, James, pulled me back in with an offer I couldn't refuse. And I am so unbelievably glad I took it.

Just five hours a week, in my own time, running the social media/comms channels of this tiny new charity, which at this point I hadn't even heard of – Face Equality International. And here I am, five years later having written and spoken those words endless times, clocked more hours than I'm willing to count, learning as much about the global FD community as I possibly can. All whilst quite literally learning on the job how to run a non-profit, something I couldn't have done without leaning on those far wiser than I, doing my best to keep the endless relationships James built with experts across every aspect of this space. It's been a constant learning curve, stretching my non-academic brain beyond belief.

I guess some part of me knew in the aftermath of James's death back in August 2020 that I needed to get my shit together and go to counseling. Not only because losing him so unexpectedly (thanks to me being fooled by his unwavering energy throughout cancer treatment) had been so awful, after having spent 18 months learning from him and finally getting to know this incredible human a little better. Losing him brought up a lot of unprocessed stuff, but mostly because a part of me knew I was going to need to take on some more responsibility. Little did I know quite how much.

With FEI being in its infancy, with just us two and the trustees running it, It was too important to me, too important to the world in fact, to let his death be the death of the charity too. So at some point during the process of the trustees consulting far and wide on the best course for the future of FEI, I threw my name into the hat and essentially said to the chair that I'd be up for being considered to run it.

And now here I am. I couldn't imagine myself doing anything else. Continuing to do my best to bring the stories of the facial difference community to the forefront of public consciousness. The stories that for too long have remained hidden.

I can't see myself doing anything else. At least until I know the organisation needs a brain better equipped than mine, to do what it needs to do, which is my intention. To grow the charity to a point where it can be sustainable long into the future, because the deep-rooted inequities in our systems, in our mindsets, our policies, aren't going anywhere any time soon. There's endless work to do. It's overwhelming even if you look at things on an individual basis, on a specific country basis, let alone worldwide. But thankfully, there is so much passion, so much skill out there, and I want to make it my mission to ensure the world starts to truly value it. What's exciting is that we've barely scratched the surface in reaching people that care about making change.

And so to bring it back to FEI's storyline, here are some of the key chapters to highlight in my time as CEO, since January 2021.

Some of the most extreme examples of violence and ill-treatment of the community happen in low-income environments. Yet these were the stories least visible to the wider world, so exposing these truths quickly becomes a strategic priority in seeking funding. Thanks to Smile Train, together with social workers and charity teams throughout 2023, we consulted with over 100 people, documenting stories of parents, adults with facial differences from India, Nepal, and Mexico, and from people experiencing human rights violations such as those told by Tina Raj earlier in this chapter. We visited orphanages, hospitals, schools, homes, some of which barely consisted of much more than a tin roof and a smoke-filled room. All to gain an insight into the extent of the challenges of living with a disfigurement, to find those stories that weren't being told other than a nameless statistic in a medical journal (if even that).

Before this, it was only the anecdotal insights I would hear from FEI member non-profits that alluded to what life with a disfigurement in an LMIC looks like. From babies being abandoned at birth, left in bins, caged, hidden away, mothers and girls shunned, women and men subject to acid and burn violence, honour violence, and infanticide, the list goes on. And yet nowhere are these atrocities being recorded, let alone addressed by governments. This is now changing, with a strategic priority to continue to reach the most underrepresented and underserved within the FD community and a growing network of devoted non-profits committed to going beyond their duty of service delivery to also approach this issue with a rights-based approach.

So what of the legal and political story surrounding Facial Difference? Policymakers have either never thought about disfigurement, or if they have, they often deliberately overlook it, to put it bluntly. It's right at the bottom of their priority list thanks to being shrouded in stigma, overt bias, and buried in murky legislation that offers little to no concrete recognition or protection. Without a concrete answer as to where this issue sits legally, whether within disability law, wider equality laws or simply as appearance-based discrimination, it's no wonder FDs have been avoided. For example, every 5 years, 193 UN Member States go through a peer review process that assesses human rights records. *It's our understanding that none to date have mentioned the experiences of people with facial disfigurements.*

It's important to frame at this point that the relationship between facial difference/disfigurement and disability is contentious and fundamentally flawed. Some laws, such as those in the UK and US, do recognise facial difference in some cases as a disability, but not universally. Yet the experiences of discrimination, and the social and attitudinal barriers (the social model of disability) experienced by these two intersecting groups, is very much universal. When it comes to the way in which people personally identify, this too is complex and deeply personal. Whether someone identifies as disabled or not in day to day life, under any model this shouldn't prevent a person from being afforded rights, protection, access to equitable healthcare, education, and all of the other fundamentals of human rights which have been recognised under disability policy. When it comes to the UN Convention on the Rights of Persons with Disabilities, which does not rely upon a medical model or proof of 'impairment,' this model is very much inclusive of appearance affecting disfigurements and differences.

This ambiguity in policy quickly became a strategic storyline to home in on, with thanks also to the playbook James had passed on, with UN recognition as a priority for FEI. As yet another fluke and/or gift from the universe, a golden opportunity presented itself within just over a year when we were invited to feed into a thematic report on AI and disability via the UN Special Rapporteur on Disability, Gerard Quinn, via yet another instrumental mentor and previous friend and ally of James's, Susan Scott-Parker.

Hopefully she doesn't read this, but I came off the first call we ever had and cried. Very early on in the role, whilst doing my best to maintain James's network of trusted advisers, I sought to learn from Susan's impressive wisdom from a career in disability rights and inclusion, having pioneered the Business Disability Forum. She could clearly sense my uncertainty. And rightfully so, she didn't shy away from probing as to where I intended to take this mission that she was so personally invested in. But that discerning nature is no longer something I fear, or take personally as a sign of my ineptitude. Learning to lean into the fear of judgement and placing the success of the mission above personal pride was needed from the outset. And I can say that our semi-regular calls are now filled with far more support and praise, after having seemingly earned her respect – which, let me say, is a real personal achievement for me. Maintained at least for the time being anyway!

Back to the policy stuff. One of the first new trustees I brought in was Paul Wilden, who quickly landed us a pro bono law firm to help us conduct a piece of what would later become a series of 'pioneering' (as coined by Susan) research to expose the extent of the failure to adequately, explicitly recognise and thereby protect and advance equity for people with disfigurements or appearance-affecting conditions in current law. We now have a huge piece of research and accompanying factsheets for the UK Equality Act, the US Americans with Disabilities Act, the European Charter of Fundamental Rights, and the UN Convention on the Rights of Persons with Disabilities (CRPD). As I write this, we're about to launch a series of factsheets covering 13 other countries, with a focus on where FEI has representative non-profits.

As the only non-profit representing the global FD community with consultative status into the CRPD, we have big plans to use this research to influence policy and hold governments to account for extending rights and inclusion efforts to the community. Having just hired a new Head of Policy and Education, Dr Hannah Saunders, yet another close ally and adviser as an expert in UK law and visible difference, one of my proudest moments has been sourcing the funding to bring her into the team officially this year. Or at least for a day and a half for a year.

In her first few months, she's already been working on major projects such as a disability position paper, an AI community survey and associated pitches to major corporations, educational content to serve our members. She is also building a workplace inclusion programme which aims to create safer and more supportive environments for the FD community to thrive at work and a priority space where people face countless challenges from recruitment through to bullying at work. This programme will provide paid opportunities for those with lived experience to deliver the training and will support FEI to generate sustainable income. There is so much opportunity out there for change. Our challenge will always be capacity and funding. I can only hope to read this back one day when this role is full-time, permanent, and we're of course continuing to do incredible work.

This is the stuff that keeps me awake at night, all too often having dreams about work. Fundraising to grow the mission, to cover the costs of delivering our campaigns, to serve our members, and to ensure we have the expertise to deliver the programmes we know the world desperately needs whilst paying people for their energy and expertise and sustaining a business at the end of the day. Fundraising was one of the many entirely new skill sets I needed to learn, and quickly! I've learnt that balancing reactive, opportunistic, often UK-centric funding mechanisms will often come at the cost of larger, global efforts. Made clear by our recent, and frankly iconic, partnership with Sephora UK.

The ability to partner with businesses, in particular corporate businesses, is a great way to generate income for UK non-profits. Especially since COVID, trusts and foundations have become at least two to three times more competitive in recent years. But that means the activity often has to be UK-centric, and so our current partnership with Sephora, a global cosmetics brand, so far has been limited to campaigns primarily with UK FD community members and UK audiences. We're of course pushing for more global projects, but as a very separate UK business, Sephora have already done so much for us and they only have so much space to push. In partnership with Zebedee, a diverse talent agency, we pitched out to several businesses to support our *My Face is a Masterpiece* campaign for Face Equality Week 2024. Sephora was top of my list, as a globally renowned, inclusive brand, they were on my 2024 vision board as a dream brand to work with.

And so here we are, having delivered two incredible campaigns, one for Face Equality week, a dream come true Halloween campaign that challenged the use of makeup prosthetics and 'costume' mimicking facial difference as something to be feared. It was a prime example of 'if you don't ask, you don't get' when we pitched this second campaign as a highly confronting, perhaps controversial, concept, that could be seen as calling out, or worse still 'cancelling' Sephora's loyal following of makeup artists. They welcomed the idea with open arms, as a much-needed conversation starter, which has since gathered widespread, global praise. And so another special note of appreciation goes to Sephora UK's head of brand, Jen Cox, for championing FEI time and time again.

Looking ahead, we're going through a consultation process to figure out how we can better reach and serve grassroots/informal groups, individual activists, and professionals working in key industries who have lived experience of facial difference. With an already stretched team of the equivalent of 2.5 members of staff, taking this on will likely require us to grow again, so here's hoping we can make that happen. This comes off the back of yet another proud moment to see more and more people coming to us and saying that they want to be a part of what we're doing, they needed support to campaign, and they liked our approach – hoorah! And so we recognised our model wasn't reaching the most underrepresented groups and voices, and this needs to change if we're to generate that truly global, much-needed critical mass devoted to face equality that has been written into our language from the outset.

So how are we going to get there? Well, keeping myself and the team well, as a disabled and disfigurement-led organisation is paramount. Making sure I don't go back to that headspace where I wanted to pack it all in, has been a top priority. And so this is also well timed in that I also happen to be writing this from Bali, where I'm both working remotely and taking some time out for forced rest and recuperation for the final months of 2024. I'm not so good at switching off. A quality I clearly share with my predecessor.

Granted, I do have good boundaries around my working hours, with a quality-over-quantity approach, but that energy then goes into all of the other areas of my life. I could feel myself getting closer and closer to burning myself out. I feel like my mind can keep going and going, exposing myself to more and more demands, more stress, and more second-hand trauma. But my body, that always keeps the score. Whether it's the year-long eczema flare-up that coincided with becoming CEO, or the current acne that I'm experiencing for the first time in my life at the ripe old age of 31. That plus the fact my hip is now playing up, 9 years after I injured it in the crash, which may or may not be self-inflicted given I've been pushing it pretty hard with CrossFit too . . .

What I failed to anticipate as a 27-year-old stepping into a leadership role was just how difficult it is to do 'the work' when you're also doing the work. What I mean to say is that keeping a board, a staff team, and a community engaged, and on the whole happy with what we're doing, and keeping the lights on, is all challenging enough. But throw in life behind the scenes: multiple losses, multiple house moves, multiple world crises, and multiple major life events. I might present as having it all together (especially if you judge the highlight reel that is my Instagram feed), but as those closest to me have witnessed through being my lifeline, behind the scenes, I've quietly crumbled, consistently.

And so a big part of this current trip has been a yoga teacher training course. Half of which I've now completed, but the other half I need to find the time to complete online. Having taken up yoga during COVID times to calm an anxious mind, I wanted to study it further as a tool to keep in my arsenal to keep my body, my mind, and my spirit all on track so that the work can continue to be the joyful rollercoaster ride that it is. The open nature of the way in which this religion and philosophy has been shared with the wider world is fascinating. From the virtues, the values, and the disciplines of living a life of devotion to one's self and others through selfless action, sustaining our life force (prana in Sanskrit), surrendering to the divine, be it God, spirituality, or simply a belief in powers such as nature. This is a culture to appreciate, not appropriate. And I'm so excited to continue to learn and apply these disciplines across my life and my work, to nurture my own practice, and do all I can to sustain my life force in this movement that's become my temporary home, until such a time that I get to pass the torch.

There is much work to be done, there is much to learn, there are endless stories to be told. It is a privilege to hear them, to help people tell their stories, and to ensure that powerful and influential people truly listen to our beloved community.

References

Changing Faces. https://www.changingfaces.org.uk/wp-content/uploads/2021/05/disfigurement-in-the-uk-report-2017.pdf

LiveLaw. https://www.livelaw.in/top-stories/supreme-court-directs-union-to-frame-mandatory-rules-under-rights-of-persons-with-disabilities-act-for-accessibility-of-public-spaces-274704

Index

For Product Safety Concerns and Information please contact our
EU representative GPSR@taylorandfrancis.com Taylor & Francis
Verlag GmbH, Kaufingerstraße 24, 80331 München, Germany